IMAGES
of America

CENTERVILLE FREMONT

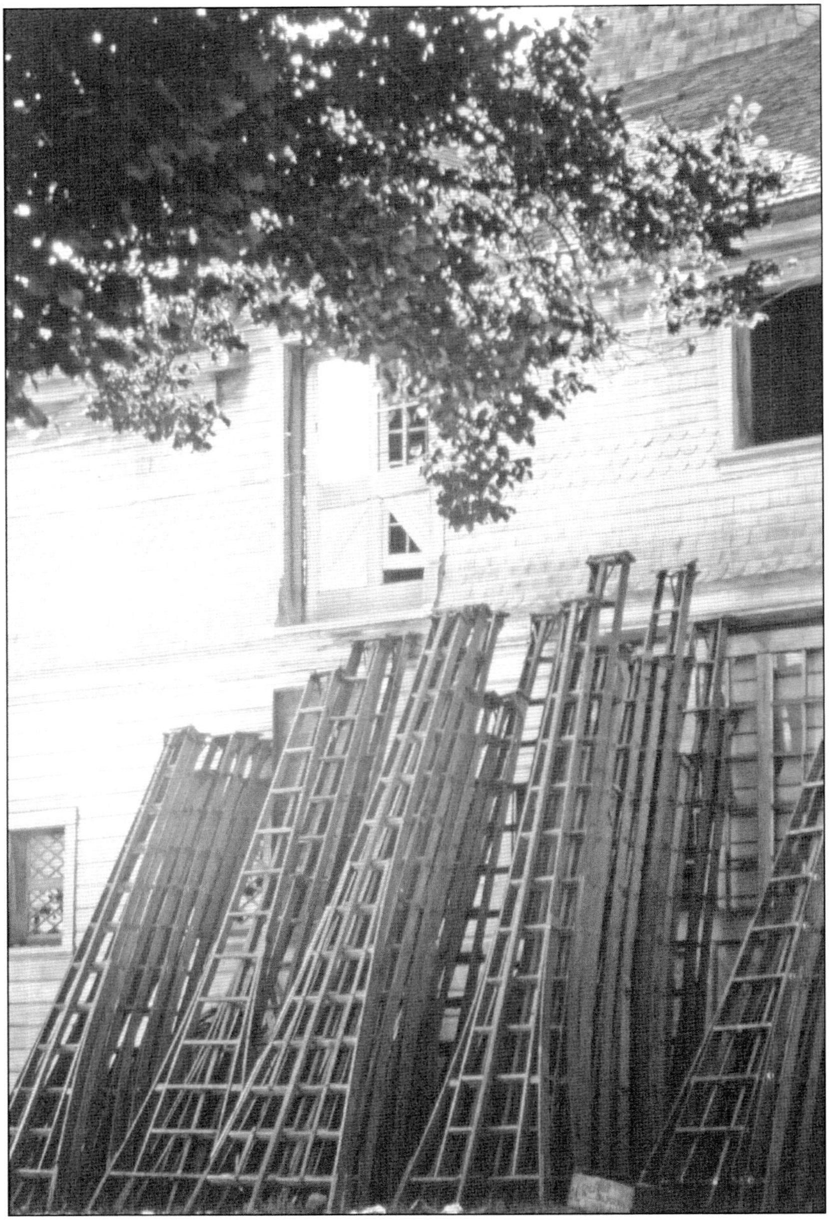

Pictured in 1967, orchard ladders rest against the vacant Bunting mansion. Booth Cannery had burned in 1959, the Bunting mansion and Sycamore Farm would burn in 1968, and the ladders were lost history. (Photograph by Julianne McDonald Howe.)

On the Cover: The Freitas family is pictured at the apricot drying yard on Sycamore Farm, north of Thornton and Alder Avenues. The truck shows both boxes of fresh fruit ready to go to the Booth Cannery and flats of dried fruit for shipping. This photograph was taken around the time that Centerville combined with four other towns to create the City of Fremont in 1956. (Courtesy SB.)

IMAGES
of America

CENTERVILLE FREMONT

Philip Holmes
and Jill M. Singleton

ARCADIA
PUBLISHING

ISBN 978-0-7385-8177-4

Published by Arcadia Publishing
Charleston, South Carolina

Printed in the United States of America

Library of Congress Control Number: 2010932071

For all general information, please contact Arcadia Publishing:
Telephone 843-853-2070
Fax 843-853-0044
E-mail sales@arcadiapublishing.com
For customer service and orders:
Toll-Free 1-888-313-2665

Visit us on the Internet at www.arcadiapublishing.com

This book is dedicated to Philip Brazil, Wallace and Bernice Eckersley, William "Bill" Walsh, Doris Machado Van Scoy, and all other teachers, parents, and coaches who inspire the best in their kids and their students.

Contents

Acknowledgments

We would like to thank everyone who persevered with us while we put this book together, especially Regina Dennie and Pat Schaffarzyk at the Museum of Local History in Fremont. Thanks to Don Driggs, Woody Minor, Rosemary Ramsell, Dolores Rose, and Larry and Vermilda Sylva. Thanks to Sharon and Bill Marshak at the *Tri-City Voice* newspaper and all the former journalists and photographers at the Centerville-based *Washington News/Township Register*, the *Hatchet*, and the *Washingtonian* at Washington High School. Long overdue thanks to the writing of Charles Shinn and all the work by the Country Club of Washington Township in compiling and publishing editions of the *History of Washington Township* in 1904, 1950, and 1965.

All photographs are part of the Museum of Local History, including the collections of Dr. Robert B. Fisher, George Oakes, Dino Vournas, and others, unless otherwise noted. We would like to thank all those who contributed their photographs and the stories that go with them. Other photograph credits go to the Asakawa family (AF), Shirley Banda (SB), the Bauhofer family (BF), Billy Leah Berchtold (BLB), Alex Bernard (AB), Phil Brazil Jr. (PB), B. J. Bunting (BJB), the Fudenna family (FF), Chuck Grimmer (CG), Susan Vargas Murphy (SVM), Mary Nunes (MN), Rosemary Ramsell (RR), Jim Reeder (JR), the Manuel Simas family (MS), Vermilda Sylva (VS), and Jill M. Singleton (JMS). The Museum of Local History is located at 190 Anza Street, Fremont, California, 94539. More information is available on the museum's Web site, www.museumoflocalhistory.org.

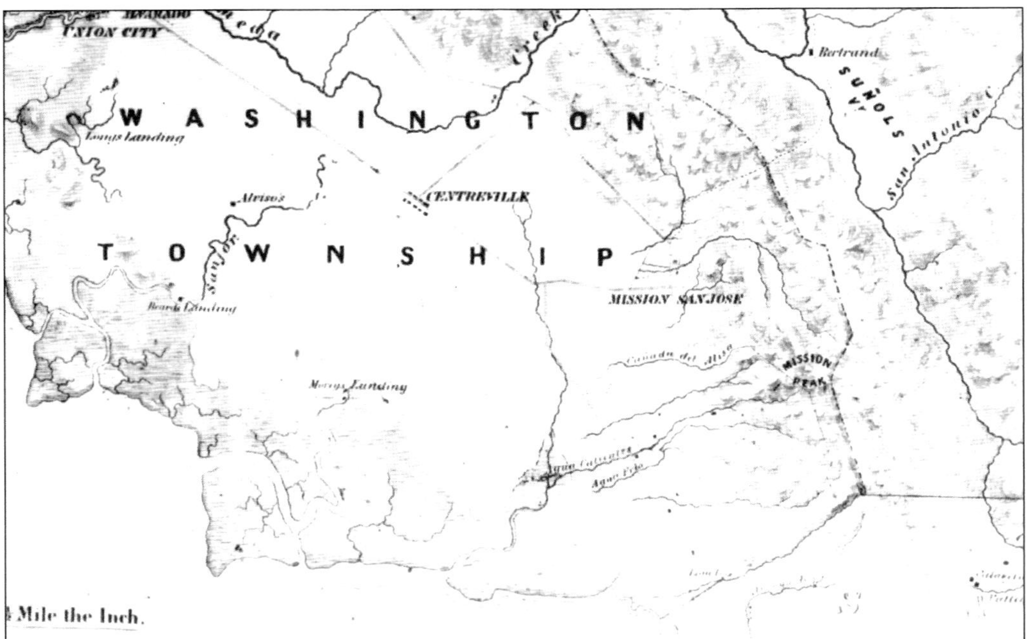

Centerville is shown in its central location in Washington Township, not long after Alameda County was formed in 1853 from parts of Contra Costa County and Santa Clara County.

Introduction

Lt. Col. John Charles Frémont and his California Battalion never visited Centerville or its immediate vicinity. On January 25, 1846, the soldiers traversed along the base of the foothills near Mission San Jose, commandeering horses, cattle, and saddles from Don Jose de Jesus Vallejo, the majordomo at Mission San Jose and grantee of Rancho Arroyo de la Alameda (translated as the "ranch of the creek with the cottonwoods").

If Frémont's soldiers had come farther west through the tall grasses and wheat fields, they would have visited the Rancho Potrero de los Cerritos (the "ranch of the pasture of the little hills"), which was granted to Spanish soldiers Augustín Alviso and Tomás Pacheco in 1844 by Gov. Manuel Micheltorena.

This book describes, from 1850 onward, both the town site of Centerville and its surrounding school districts of Centerville and Alviso. These two country schools served all the ranches (as farms were referred to) from Alameda Creek to the north to Walnut Avenue to the south.

Centerville, or Centreville as it was first known, has always been in the center of activity in Washington Township except briefly at its very beginning. In 1850, when Alameda Creek was the northernmost part of Santa Clara County, the first cluster of dwellings that was soon to be Centerville was briefly referred to as Hardscrabble. In 1853, Alameda County was formed, and Centerville took up its place at the center of an agricultural gold rush.

Centerville's first business was a classic bit of western entrepreneurship: a toll to cross the ford at Alameda Creek (or Arroyo de la Alameda as it was then known) just a mile or so west of the mouth of Niles Cañon. It was here in 1850 that squatter Capt. George Bond set up shop and started charging a toll for would-be miners to cross the ford, since it was part of the overland route to Mission Pass and the gold fields. To the south, county assessor Charles Breyfogle built an adobe house in 1852 on what would be known as the Chadbourne ranch from 1866 to 1941.

The first plantings of fruit trees took place at the small ranches that flourished along Alameda Creek to feed the ranchers' families and their hired help. The plantings originated from seed stock that came from the orchards at Mission San Jose or from pear and walnut cuttings that survived the trip overland and around Cape Horn. However, it was the apricot that became the queen of Centerville orchards.

Augustín Alviso grew wheat in the deep soils of Rancho Potrero de los Cerritos, north of the Alameda Creek, for the Russian settlers at Fort Ross in the 1840s, before American settlement. Alviso shipped the wheat from his landing on Coyote Slough. Settlers such as Elias Beard of Indiana proceeded to also grow wheat on the rich land they bought from Alviso, exceeding all production records and selling into the Gold Rush mining boom. One could grow rich with enough land, easy access to water, the right crops to sell to San Francisco, and the means to transport the crops to market.

In the 1850s, settlers came from all over the world looking for gold, but the soil and productive crops of the Alameda Creek delta proved to be the real treasure, certainly for George Patterson. In 1857, his bachelor farmhouse was built; it was expanded to a Queen Anne–style mansion in 1889. By the time of his death in 1895, Patterson owned 6,000 acres, 46 of which are retained today as Ardenwood Historic Farm.

In 1868, Centerville was like any small Western town: a collection of wooden false-front facades facing a street that was mud in winter and dust in summer. The town was unique because its community leaders met in a miniature Greek temple–style town hall that was financed by the women of the town in 1868. By 1878, Centerville was a town of substance and an agricultural supply center for the region. Many of its estates and ranches were profiled in the Thompson and West Historical Atlas that year.

By 1898, Centerville was the main source of dried apricots in Alameda County. The narrow-gauge South Pacific Coast Railroad carried 5,000 tons of freight per year, mostly of dried apricots, from Centerville to Newark in its unique horse-drawn freight cars. This was also the year that Centerville became famous in the San Francisco sports pages because its new Centerville Athletic Club sponsored long-distance cycling events and regional baseball matches for the Bay Area.

The Bunting estate at Sycamore farm became a showplace model farm in 1900, surrounded by apricot orchards. In 1908, plans developed for a railroad that would connect Centerville to Niles Canyon in 1909, and Centerville had a full railroad by 1910. Dried apricots were a rations staple for American soldiers in both world wars. The Bunting estate was sold to silent film actors Clarence Kolb and May Cloy in 1918, and the orchards continued to thrive under the Asakawa family and later with the Freitas family.

Booth Cannery began operating in Centerville in 1922, replacing the Alden Fruit Drying and Packing Company. The Williams brothers' vegetable packing began in 1924, and warehouses were added to the business in 1927. The first automobile bridge across the San Francisco Bay opened in 1927 at Dumbarton Point, crossing over the Beard Slough. Washington High School relocated to a larger parcel between the town site and the Chadbourne ranch, which at the time was leased to Innes-Cloverdale Sanitary Dairy of Alameda. Also in this decade, the football team at Washington High School began to be known as the Centerville Huskies. Main Street was paved in 1930 and became part of the state highway system as Route 17. By then, Centerville was mainly a farm community of Azores-Portuguese immigrant heritage and was surrounded by truck-farming acreage, dairies, and extensive apricot orchards. Burdette Williams purchased the Chadbourne ranch in 1941 to expand his vegetable growing business.

After World War II, changes came quickly, one after the other. Center Theater opened in 1946 as the largest movie theater in the township. Glenmoor Gardens began transforming Centerville into subdivisions in 1951. Public meetings dedicated to creating an official local self-government began in 1955 and were held in the auditorium of Washington High School. The City of Fremont became a reality in 1956, and Centerville became home to Fremont Fire Station No. 1. Federal policies during the cold war era had impacts on Centerville. The Oakland Aviation Center for the Federal Aviation Administration relocated to Central Avenue in 1956. The Nike missile base at Coyote Hills operated from 1955 to 1963, then became home to the Stanford Research Institute.

Bill Walsh, Super Bowl–winning head coach of the San Francisco 49ers and head coach of Stanford University's football team, came to Washington High School for his first full-time coaching job from 1957 to 1959. Negotiations were underway in 1956 to sell the Chadbourne/Williams ranch to the local developers Hapsmith Company. Booth Cannery closed in 1959 after a massive fire. The Hapsmith Company opened the Fremont Hub Shopping Center as a landmark mall in 1961, complete with Sputnik-style signage. With the agricultural era of Centerville coming to an end, Burdette Williams moved his operation to Ardenwood, and Centerville had become a key part of the new city. Main Street, also known as Old Highway 17, was renamed Fremont Boulevard. The Centerville Farmers Market opened around 2000 near the city's restored train station, bringing apricot days to Main Street Centerville once again.

One

Go West, Young Man 1840–1879

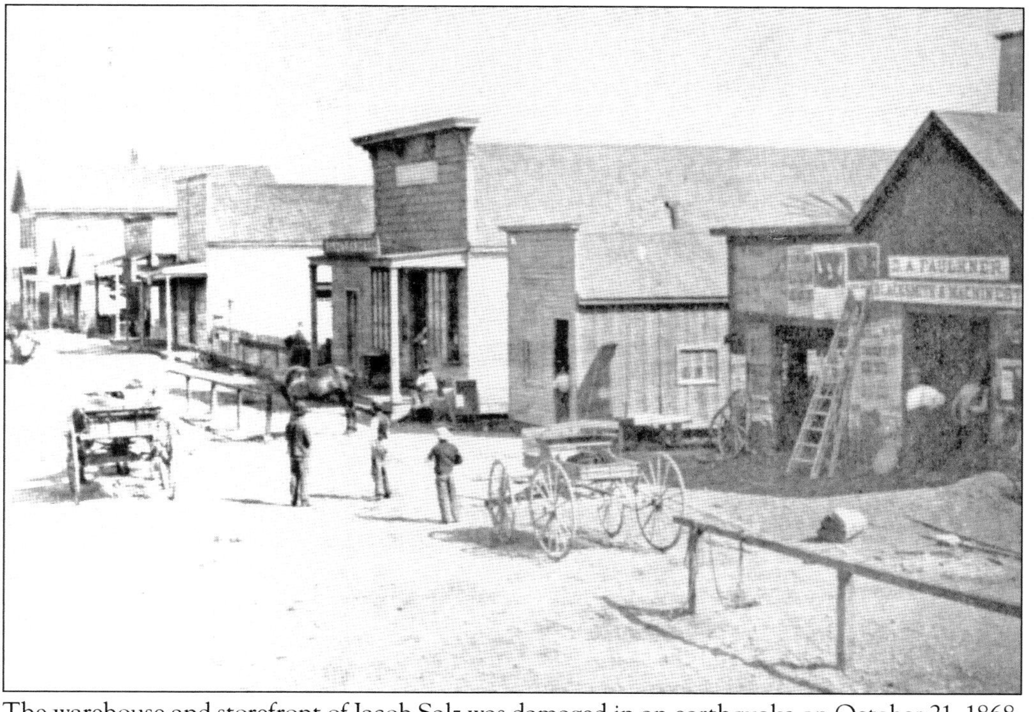

The warehouse and storefront of Jacob Salz was damaged in an earthquake on October 21, 1868, that became known as the Hayward Earthquake. The structure was still standing in the center of this 1868 stereoscope photograph of Centerville taken earlier that year. The names of early enterprises such as Bond and Randall (the town's first store), Faulkner Blacksmith and Machines, and Salz and Company grain wholesalers can be read on the false front signage.

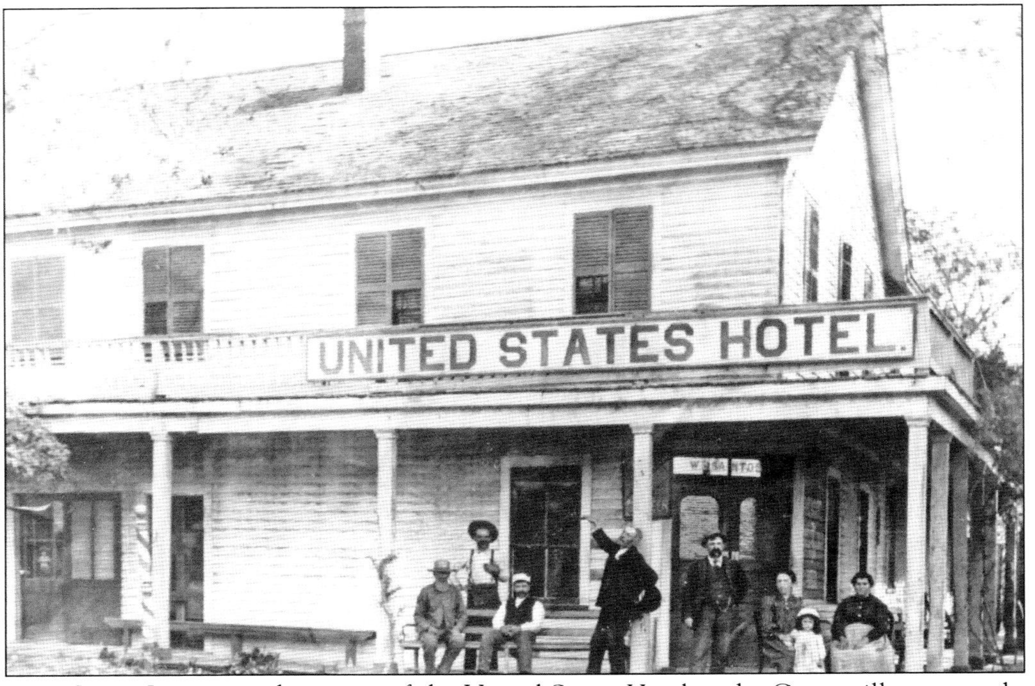

Capt. James Lewis was the owner of the United States Hotel at the Centerville crossroads. According to an excerpt from the *History of Washington Township*, written in 1904, Lewis "was a rebel sympathizer, hoisted on his flag-pole a Confederate flag; he was waited upon by a committee of Union men and given the alternative of hauling down the flag or having the pole cut. The flag came down." Lewis served as a naval captain until 1842, in the mercantile marine from 1842 to 1850, and with the Pacific Mail Steamship Company in the 1850s. The hotel was built in 1858.

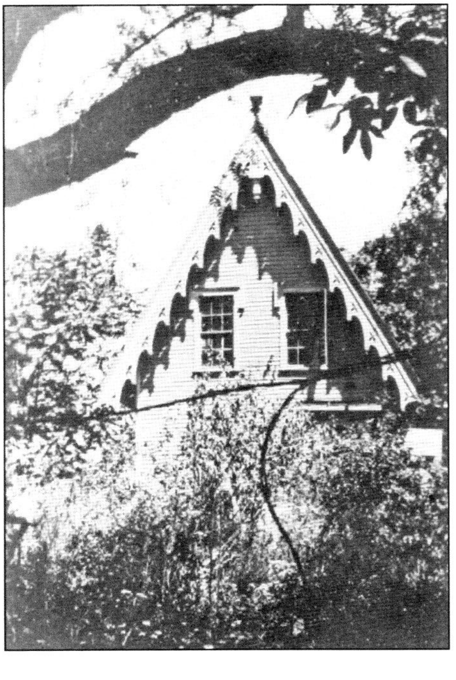

The Charles Kelsey home, pictured here, was built in the Carpenter Gothic style in the early 1850s. It was located at the main ford of Alameda Creek and was one of the prefabricated houses of the day that was brought around Cape Horn from New England. It is similar to Gen. Mariano Vallejo's 1852 home, named Lachryma Montis, which is still standing on 500 wine-producing acres in Sonoma. The rear portion of the John Cabral Bettencourt house, which moved to Ardenwood in the 1970s, may have been the Kelsey house.

In 1852, Rev. William Wallace Brier came to Centerville from Indiana, where he studied under such uncompromising ministers as Dr. Lyman Beecher. Brier founded the Presbyterian church in Centerville, preaching there until 1860, when he left to establish more church "plants" throughout pioneer California. He and wife, Elizabeth, raised five children at their large farm at Oakland and Decoto Roads. His 1887 obituary noted, "the Brier mansion has long been known for its pleasant and generous hospitality."

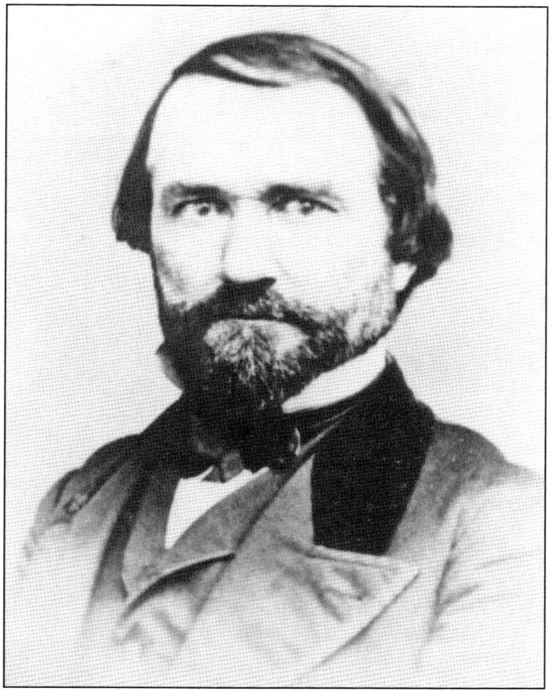

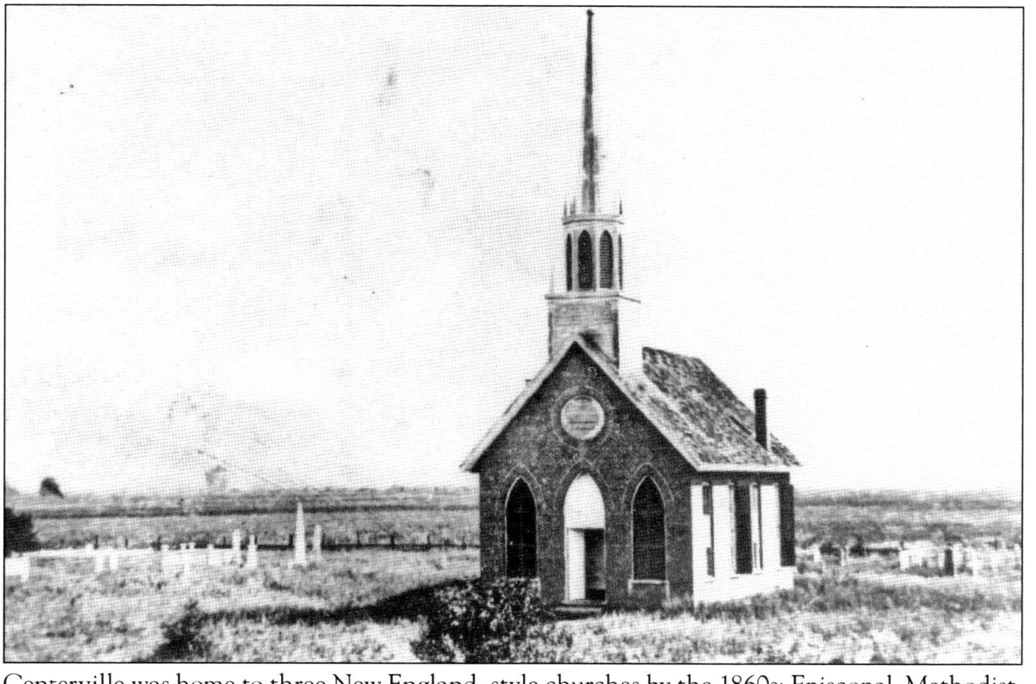

Centerville was home to three New England–style churches by the 1860s: Episcopal, Methodist, and Presbyterian. The Alameda Presbyterian Church organized in 1853 and three years later built its first edifice in brick on a lot donated by George Lloyd. The distinctive New England steeple was added in 1859. The brick edifice was replaced with wooden balloon framing and siding after the 1868 Hayward earthquake destabilized the brick walls.

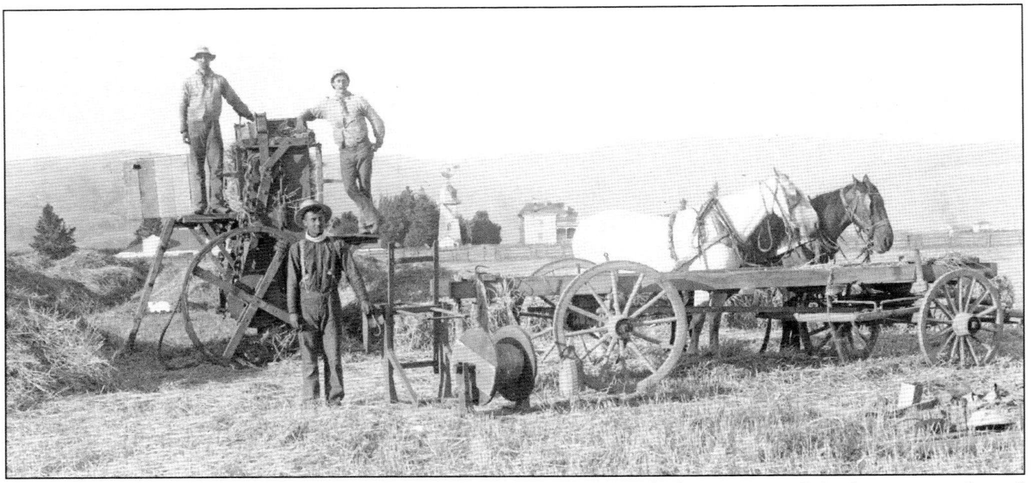

First-generation farm families in the Centerville vicinity settled on some of the best agricultural soils in California. Dryland farming was typically done on parcels of land 200 acres and smaller, and grains such as potatoes, onions, wheat, and barley were farmed as cash crops. Growing high-nutrient hay crops such as timothy and oats was essential for fine livestock, as was the maintenance of excellent grazing pastures. In the early 1840s, Augustín Alviso and Tomás Pacheco cultivated the extensive rancho acreage in grains, selling substantial quantities of it to the Russians at Port Rumyantsev, part of Port Ross, at Bodega Bay.

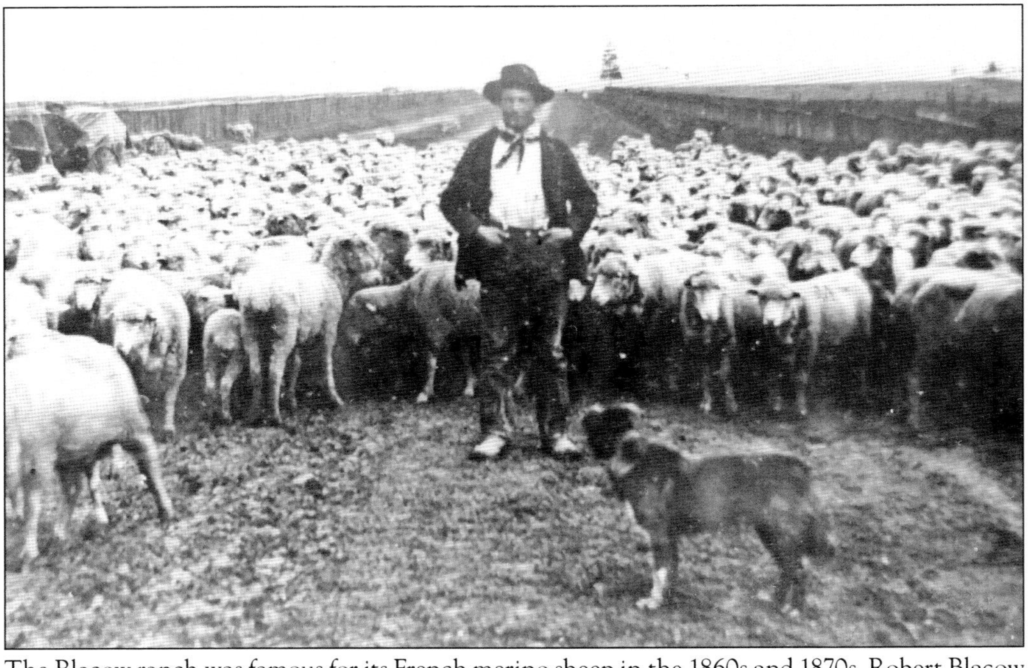

The Blacow ranch was famous for its French merino sheep in the 1860s and 1870s. Robert Blacow emigrated from England when he was 25, engaging in dairying in St. Louis from 1839 to 1849 before leaving for California via the Isthmus of Panama. He mined in the gold country until 1851, then relocated to Centerville on 358 acres. In 1853, he brought his wife and family to the ranch. He died in 1873 age 59.

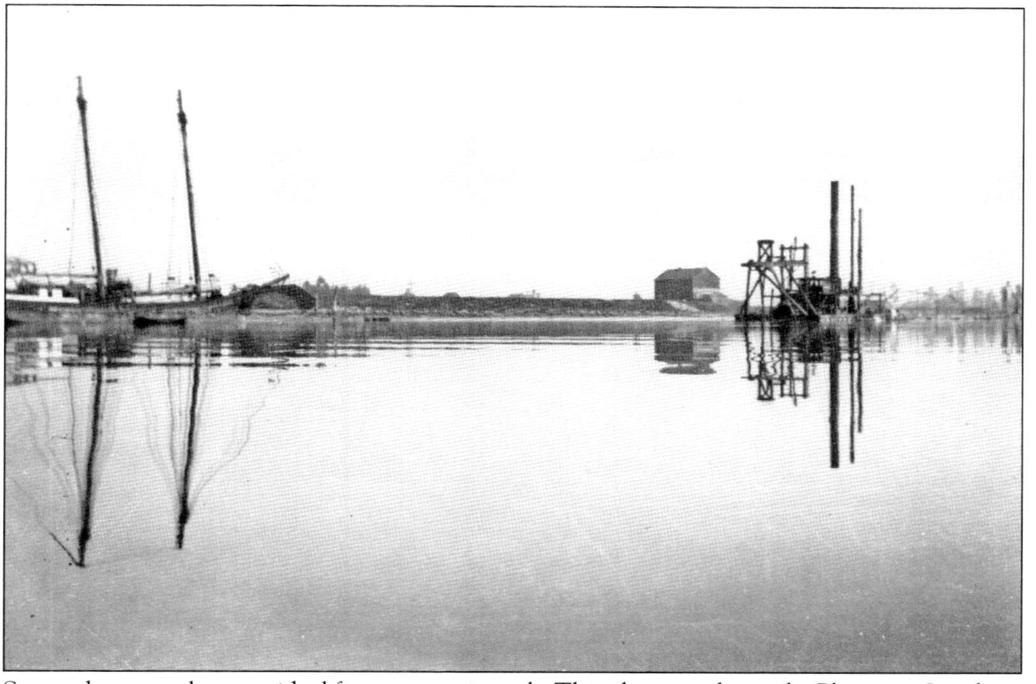

Scow schooners also were ideal for transporting salt. This photograph may be Plummers Landing, located just north of Patterson's Landing on Alameda Creek. Regular shipping of sun-dried salt from Turk's Island began within a few years of the property purchase by John Plummer in 1864. The tall swing beams could hoist pallets of sacked goods such as salt, coal, or potatoes as easily as they could larger items such as house parts, lumber, or hay bales.

John Horner laid out the land between the present communities of Irvington and Centerville and established the town that became Centerville. He built a schoolhouse there in 1850 that also served as a church and the first English-language school in what became Alameda County. The school building (pictured in 1891) was moved from Centerville to Irvington in 1862.

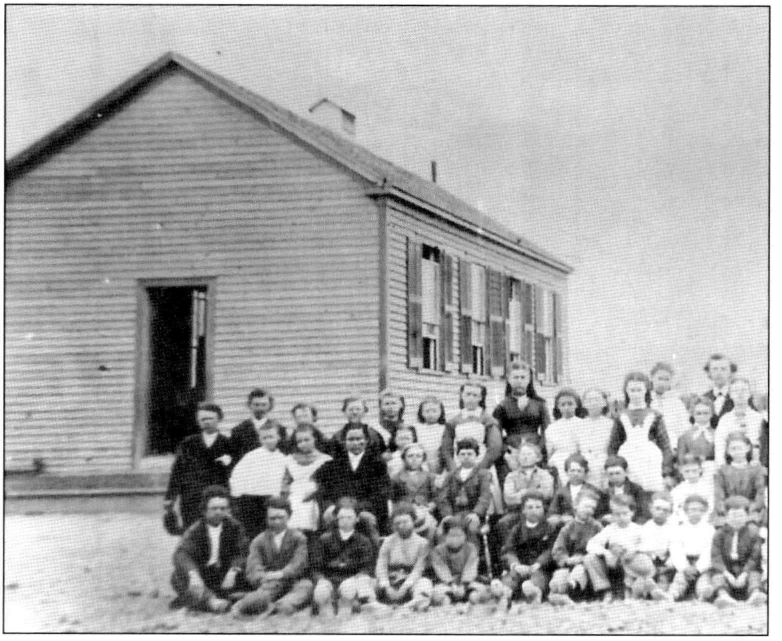

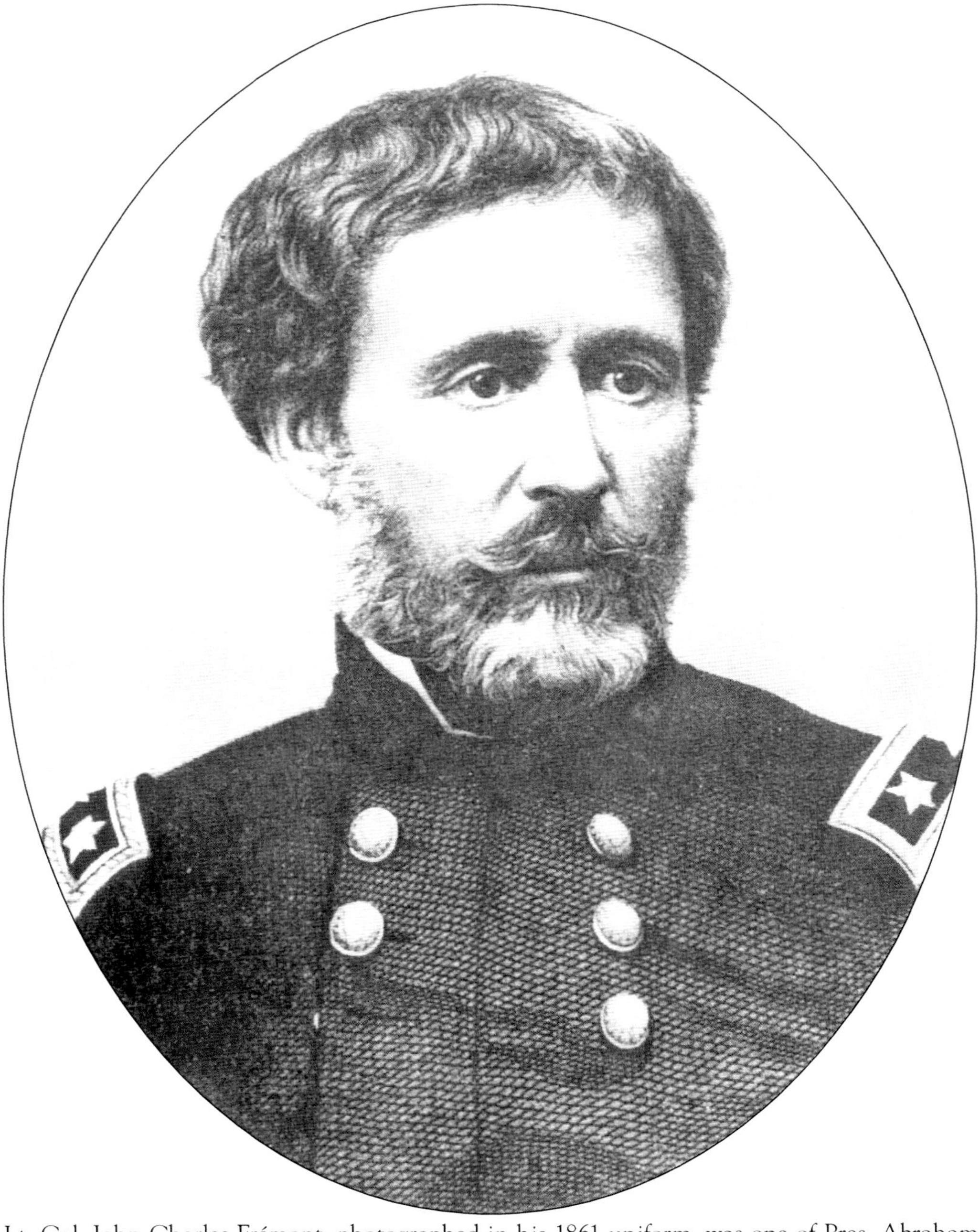

Lt. Col. John Charles Frémont, photographed in his 1861 uniform, was one of Pres. Abraham Lincoln's first major generals in the Civil War. In 1863, under a new state law, Maj. DeWitt Clinton Thompson of Oakland was commissioned to raise a battalion for active service in the Civil War, so a company of dragoons was organized at Centerville known as the California 100. Frémont's wife, Jessie Benton Frémont, wrote, "great cities will rise from the ashes of his (John C. Frémont) campfires." The Oakland–San Jose Road was called Main Street in Centerville proper by 1900, Route 17 in the mid-1900s, and Fremont Boulevard after the City of Fremont incorporated in 1956.

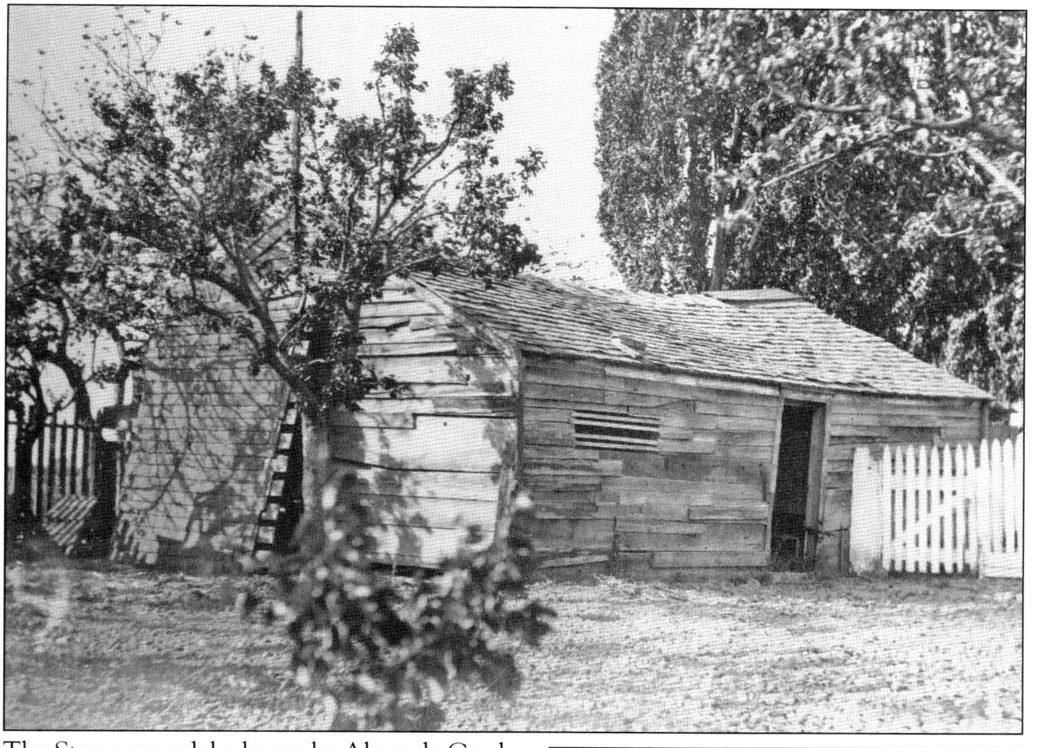

The Stevenson adobe house by Alameda Creek may have been similar to the adobe structure described by Charles Shinn in 1889: "The old adobe of John Naile's, on the Michael Overacker place, built in 1849 or 1850, was the scene of 'The First Ball in the Bottom' . . . this must have been in the autumn of 1851. . . . The ball was a regular 'fandango' with the 'coyote dance' and all the other dances of the era. Among the belles of the occasion were the Vallejos, the Pachecos, and four or five American ladies. Valentine Alviso, Poncho Pacheco, Simeon Stivers, George Moore, Jake Longfellow, the blacksmith on the Horner Ranch and Black Hawk Coombs were among the gentlemen present . . . and [the ball] deserves record in the annals of 'hospitable old Washington Township.' "

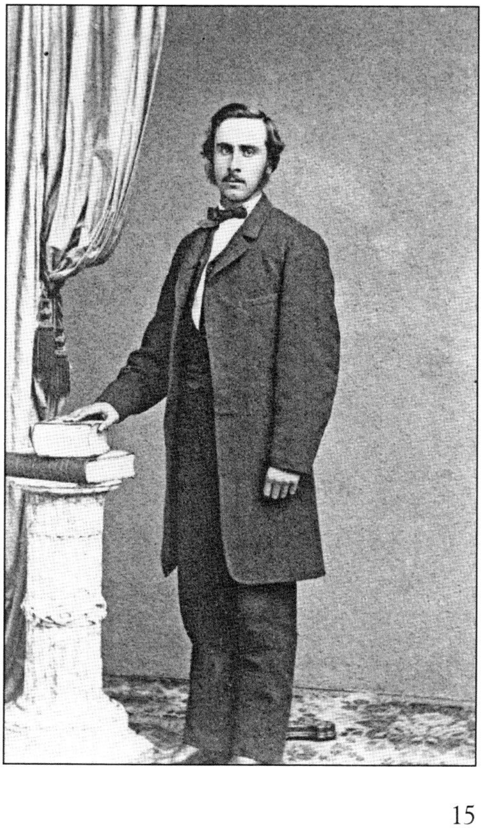

Valentine Alviso represented the 14th District (Livermore) in the California State Assembly from 1881 to 1883.

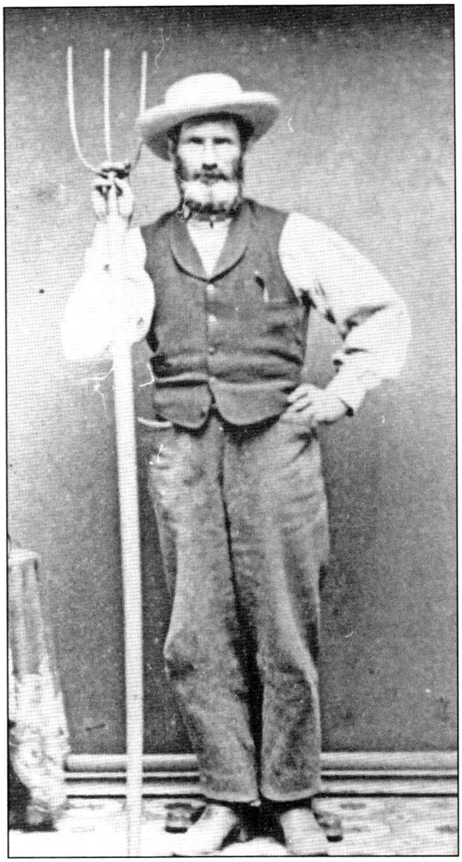

Garrett Schuyler Norris (pictured at left) came to California via the Isthmus of Panama in 1851 and worked on the Blacow sheep ranch. He applied for a land grant and purchased Dr. Bacon's cabin, located nearby, on a large parcel of farmland approximately opposite the present-day Washington High School. Pictured below is the farm and the second Norris home built in 1879 located on the Centerville-Irvington Road (Fremont Boulevard) near Central Avenue.

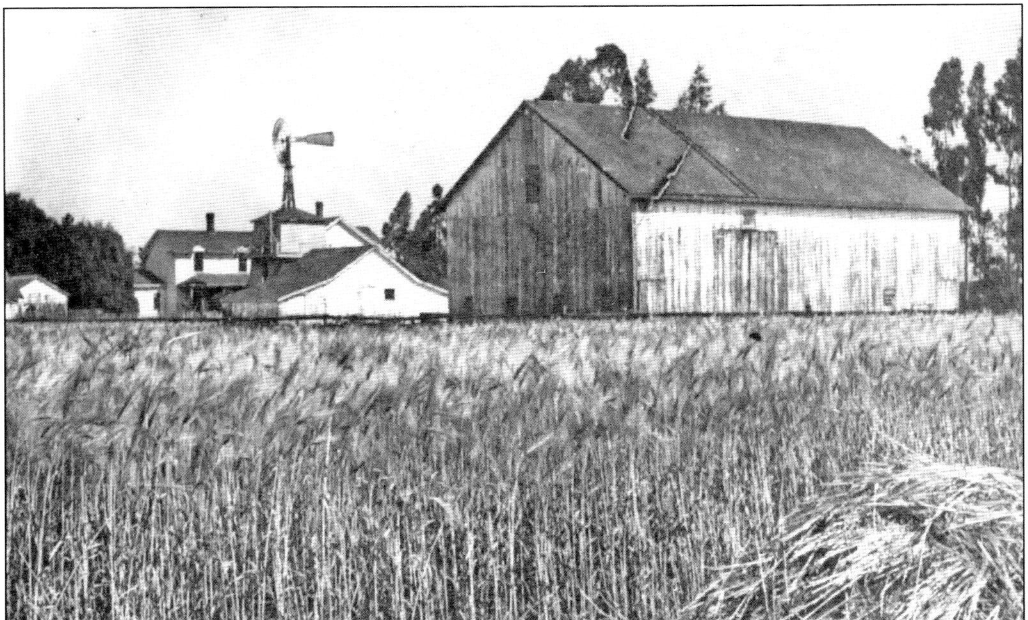

Two

Salt of the Earth
1880–1899

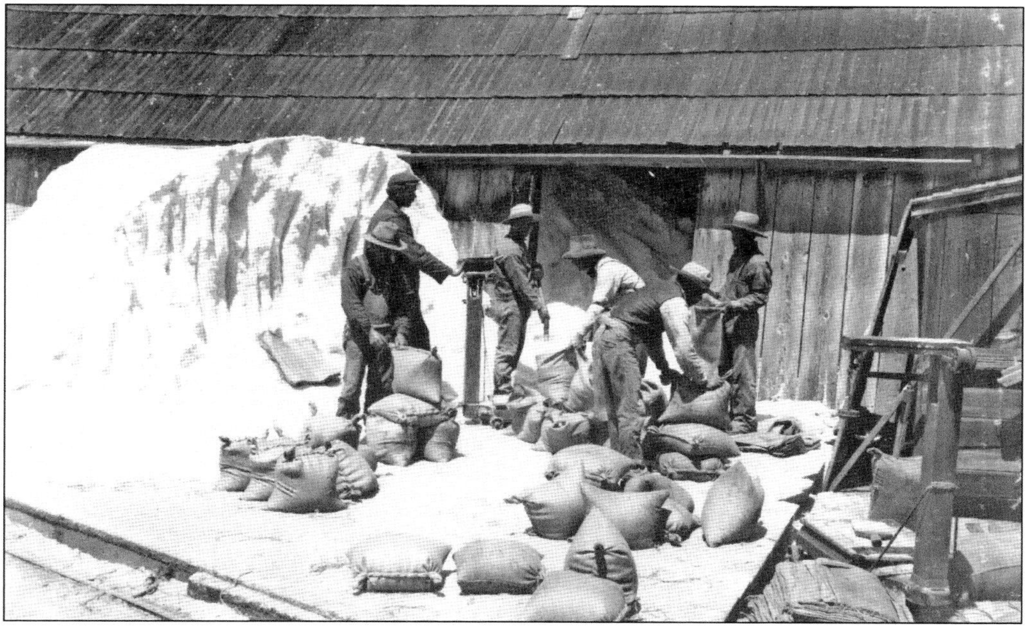

Solar salt drying dates back to 1682 on Grand Turk Island in the Caribbean, and the name may be the inspiration for the Turk Island Salt Works on Salt Works Creek, at the mouth of Alameda Creek. Isaac Long began the salt drying operation in 1852. Forty-niner John A. Plummer, from Massachusetts, purchased the adjacent landing in 1855, then he bought the entire operation in 1864. It was not long before the slough was called Plummer Slough.

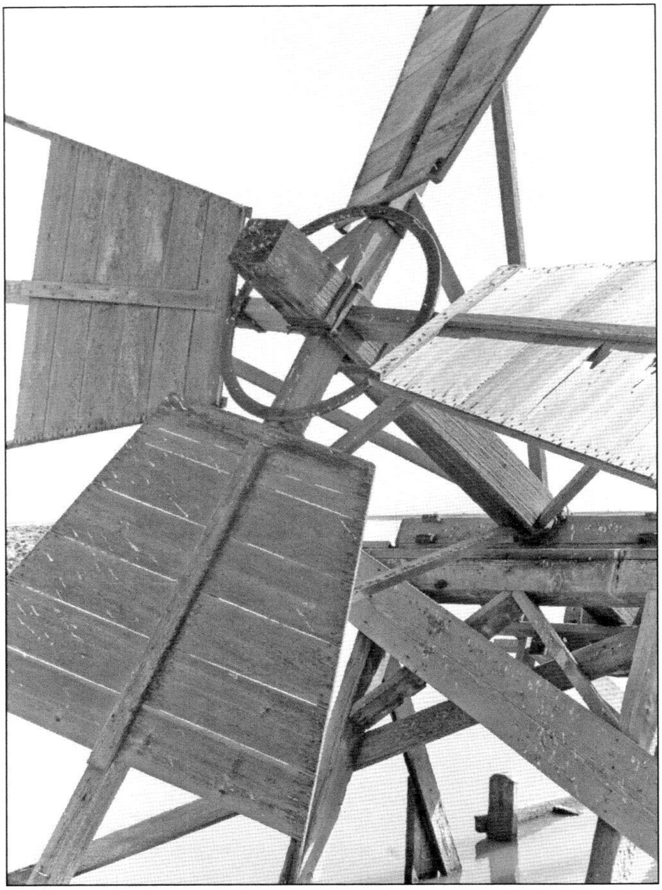

Windmills were used at the Turk Island Salt Works to pump brine into flat-bottom pans created by dikes, an approach that led to a higher-quality product. The discovery of the Comstock Lode in 1858 and the demand for salt for silver refining was a major incentive for salt entrepreneurs taking up opportunities around the shores of the San Francisco Bay. In 1878, the Plummer operation was the second largest salt operation in Washington Township. Plummer's two sons, John and Charles, became partners with their father in 1869 and eventually expanded by purchasing the Crystal Salt Works at Newark. By the 1890s, the Plummer brothers shipped more than 2,000 tons of salt annually from their own operations. The business also served as a shipping middleman for other operations. The brothers' offices were located at 14 Spear Street in San Francisco.

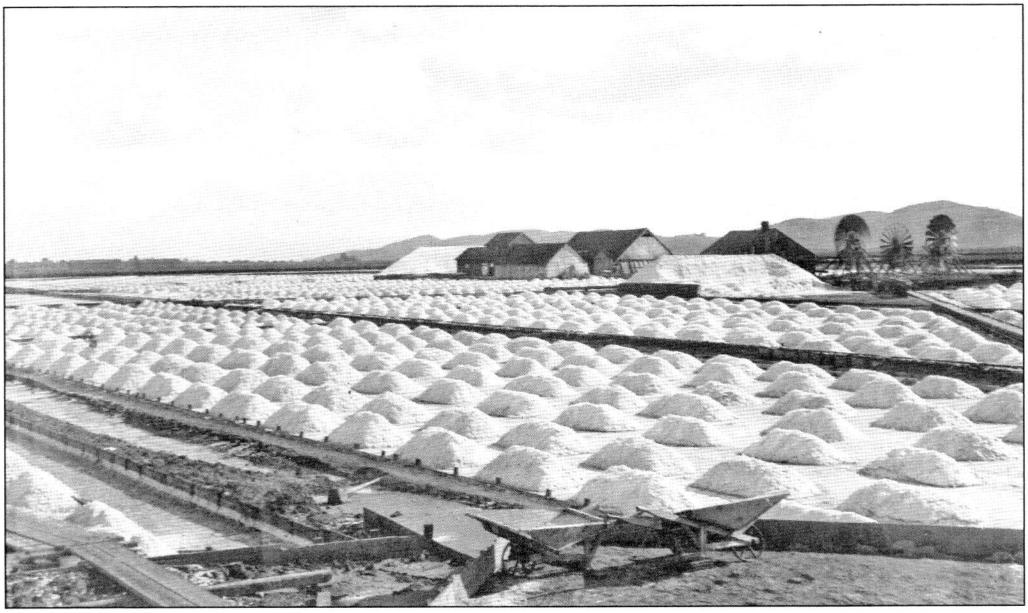

In 1896, twelve men worked at the Plummer brothers' Turks Island Salt Works near Alvarado, and eight worked at their Crystal Salt Works near Newark. Not until 1919 was there nearby competition, when San Francisco spice importer A. Schilling and Company located a salt works at the tip of Dumbarton Point and incorporated as the Arden Salt Works. Centerville endorsed the privately owned Dumbarton Bridge franchise in 1916. Arden Salt Works moved to the present toll plaza in 1923. The state acquired the bridge in 1951 and rebuilt it in 1982.

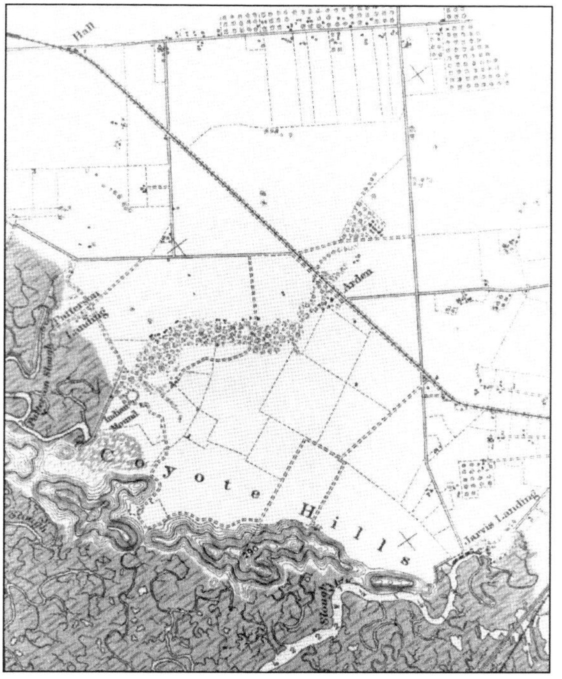

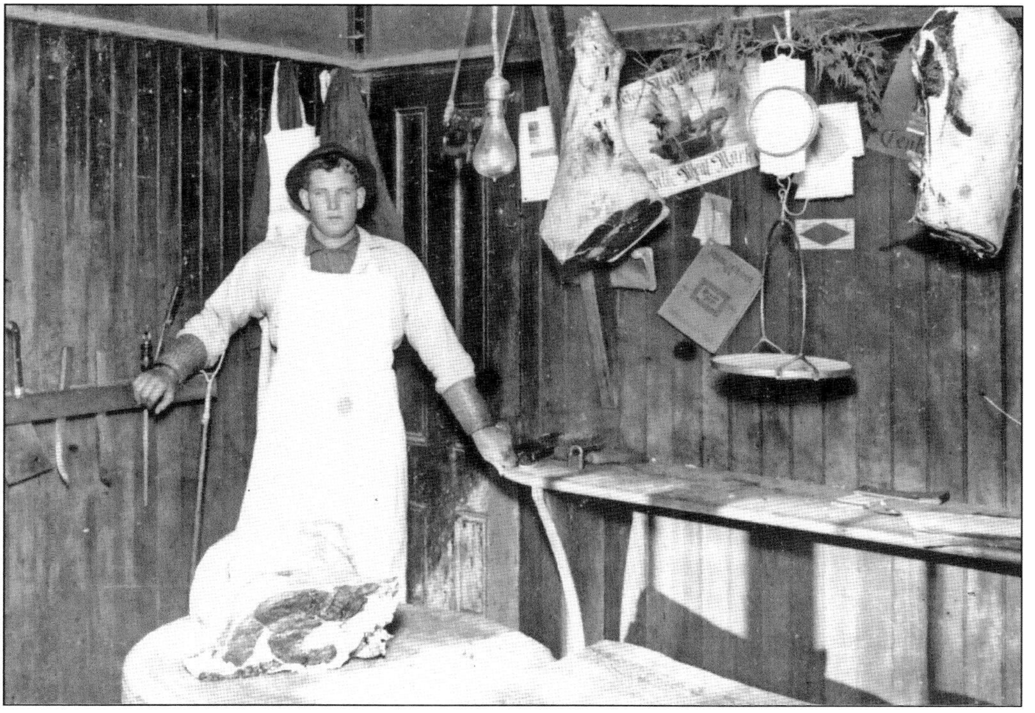

Peter Mathiesen was the butcher in Centerville. His shop was lit by a carbon filament lightbulb; Centerville had electricity by the 1890s. Mathiesen did not have far to go for his butcher salt since he was only five doors south of the Charles Plummer family residence and steps away from the horsecar ride down to the Crystal Salt Works.

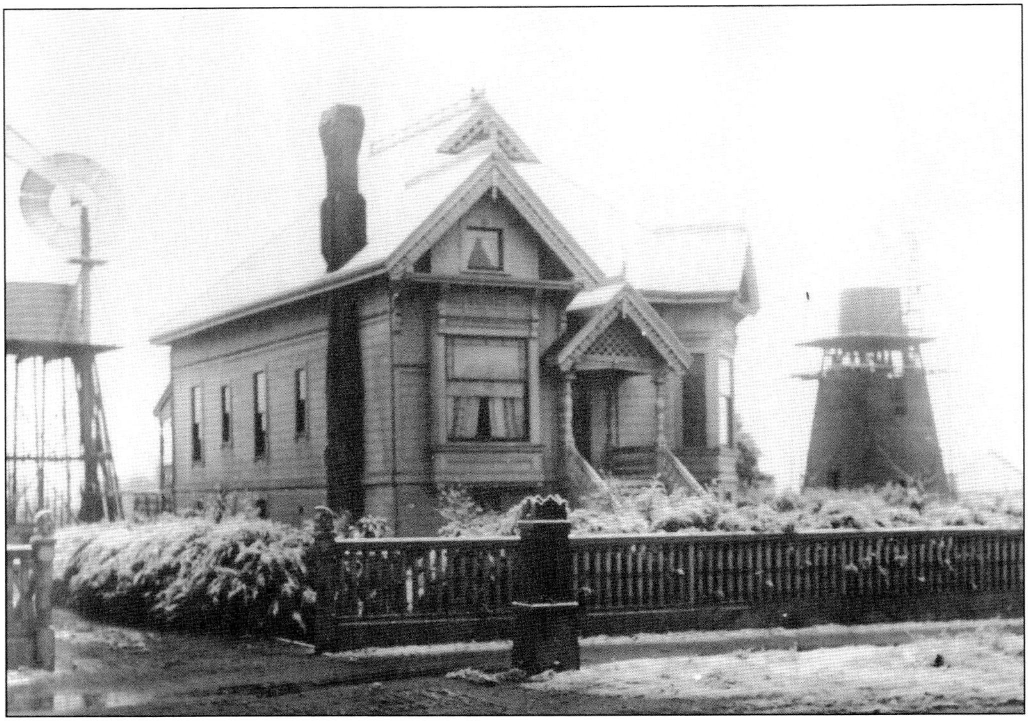

Charles Plummer commissioned the Newsom brothers of San Francisco in 1874 to build an elegant small residence across from the Presbyterian church (above). In September of that year, Plummer married Annie Miller of New York. In February 1887, Centerville received an overnight blanket of snow (below). The Plummer family had excellent camera equipment, before the days of the Kodak, perhaps to record the work at the salt works.

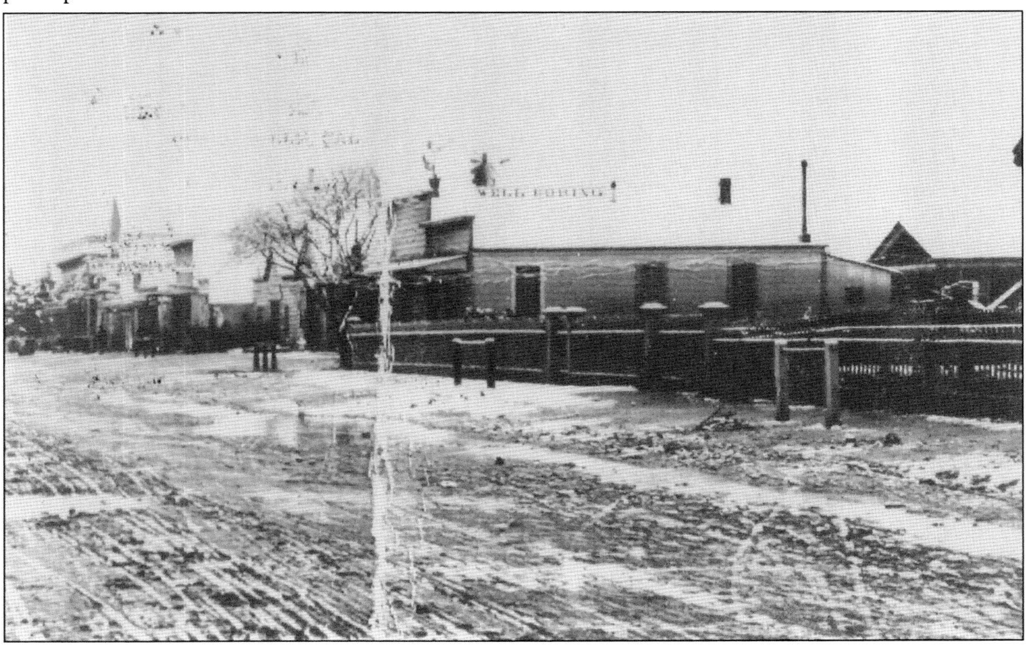

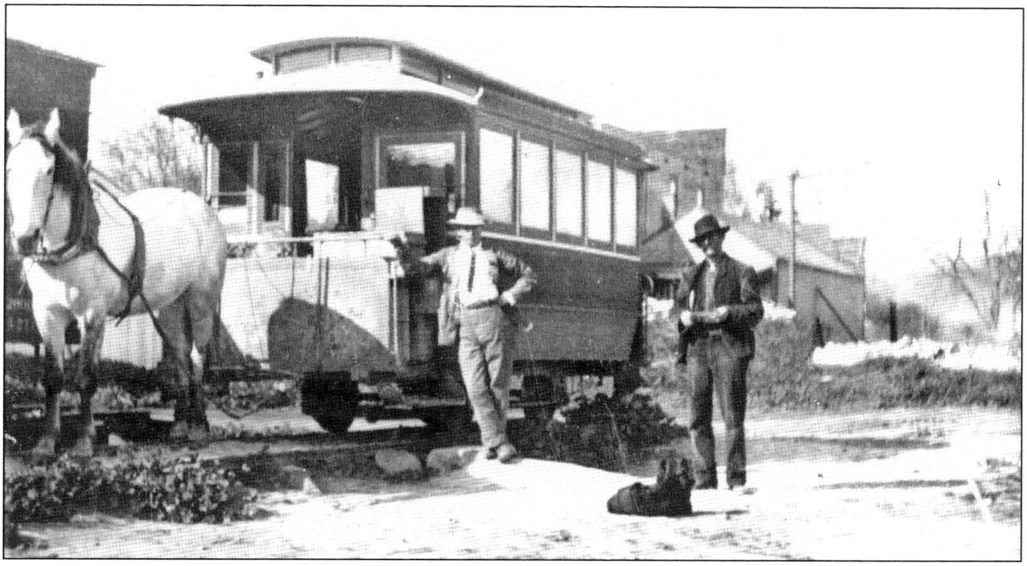

The South Pacific Coast Railroad (SPCRR) was established in 1882 and connected Newark and Centerville, running horsecars for passengers and freight several times a day. The operator was Henry "Bones" Burdick for many decades. The line was a useful commute to catch the train to Oakland from Newark or for students to commute in the other direction to get to Washington High School, a short distance from the horsecar terminus. May Burdick was the first Washington High School graduate in 1893.

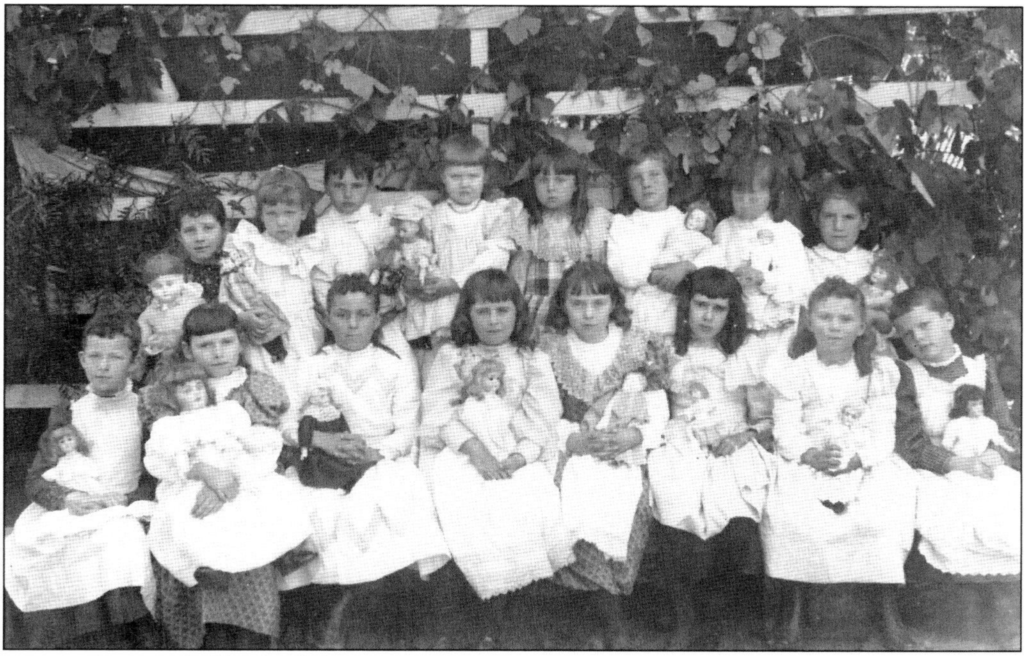

Annie Plummer held a birthday party for her daughter Muriel about 1887. More than a dozen little girls were dressed in long, frilly white dresses and held similarly attired dolls. About the same time, a doll tea party was held for the Plummers' other daughter, Dorothy, with girls seated at a long table with the best linen and teacups set out for both them and their dolls.

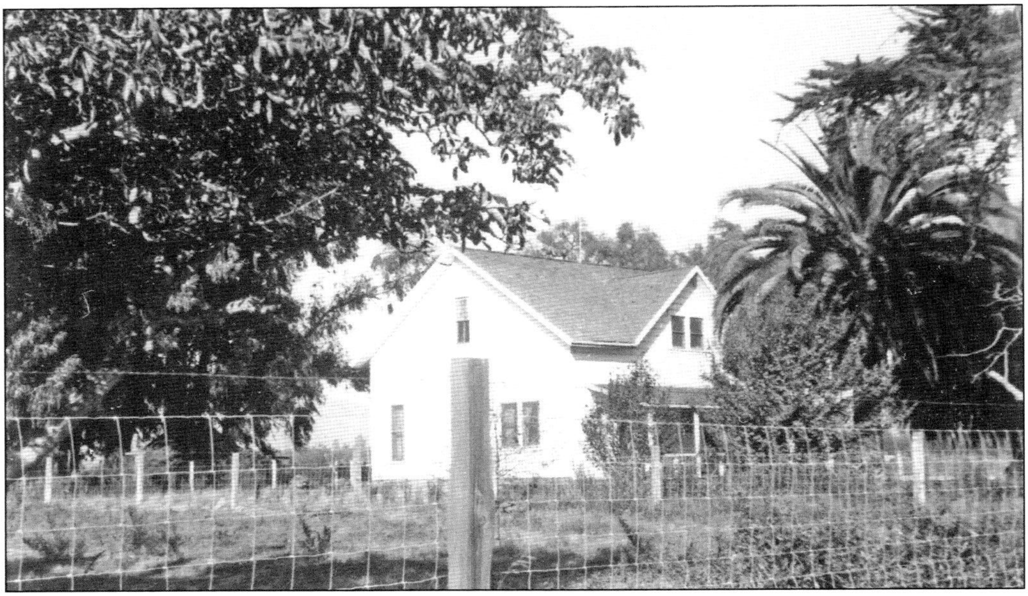

The Ashley Cameron home on Blacow Road is pictured before the Glenmoor subdivision was developed. The Cameron brothers, Duncan and Ashley, were famous competitive stagecoach drivers between San Antonio, Oakland, and San Jose in the 1850s and 1860s. They competed fiercely with the McLaughlins around 1856 for the mail and express contract, cutting prices as low as 25¢ from the usual passenger fare of a $1 a head. The Cameron Brothers Stagecoach Line was eventually absorbed into the Wells Fargo Express. In 1867, Ashley Cameron settled on this 160 acres.

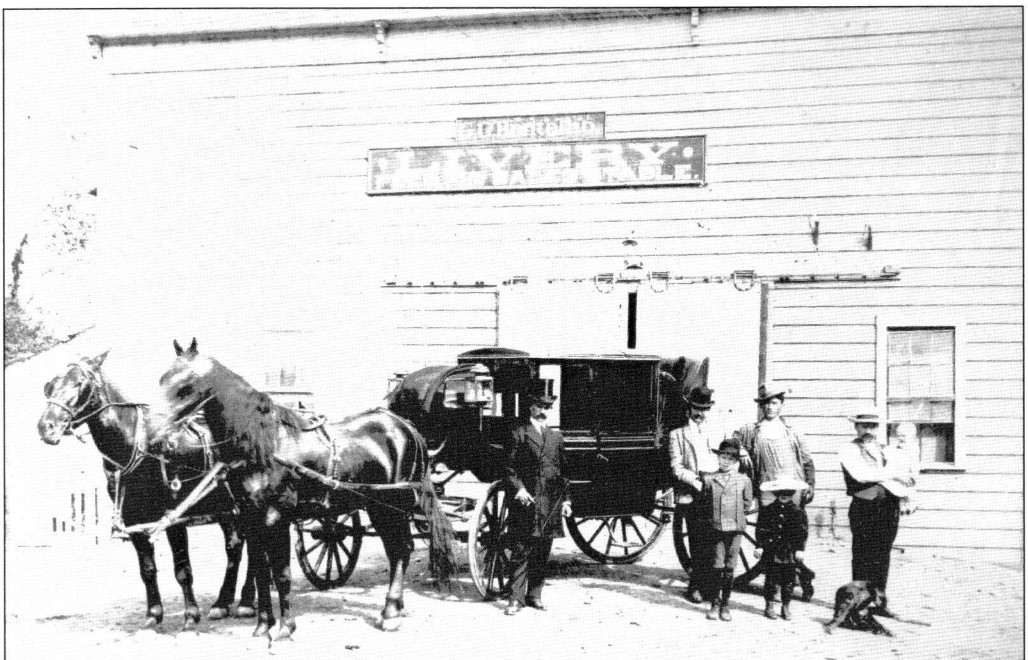

The Botelho Livery Stable was located near the United States Hotel.

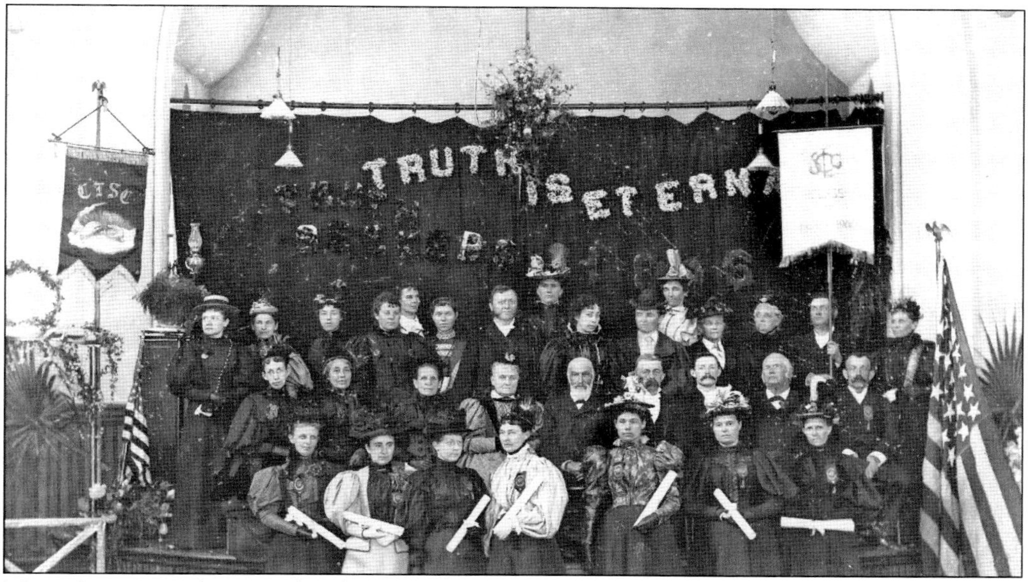

Miranda Norris's photograph of her "Truth Seekers" group indicates a special event with a banner reading "Truth is Eternity." This may have been a chautauqua-type society that met weekly to discuss lectures on free thought, education, feminism, and other liberal topics. In 1886, the Truth Seeker Company published *The Truth Seeker Annual and Freethinkers Almanac*.

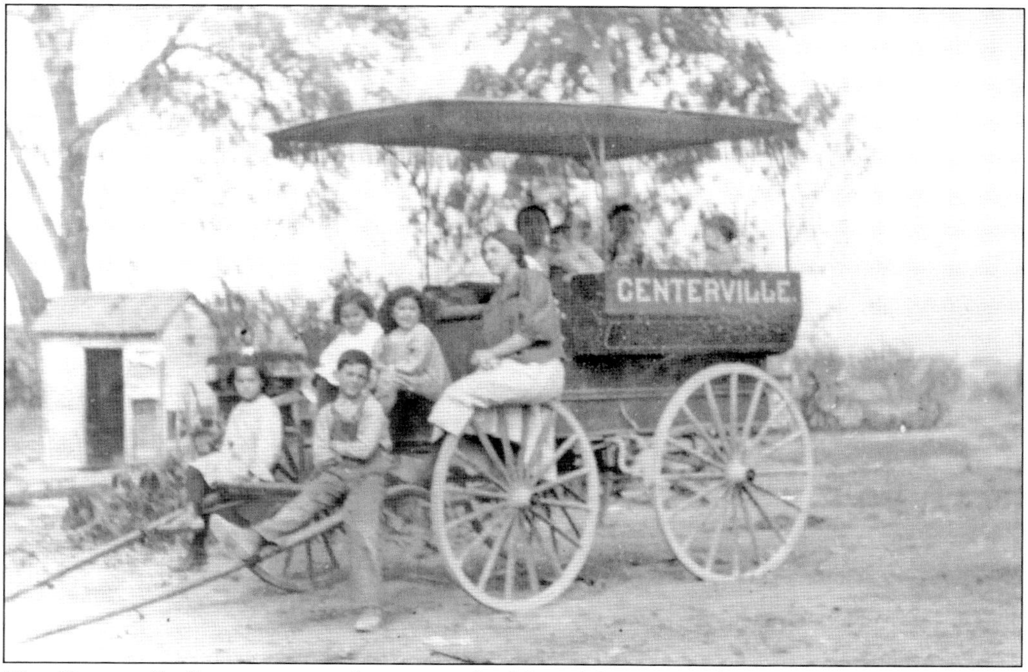

The Centerville Stage stagecoach waits at the United States Hotel grounds in 1900. It met all passenger trains in Niles, according to the hotel advertisements, making it easy to plan a visit to Centerville. In 1909, the hotel was torn down to make way for the Southern Pacific Railroad train station, which was constructed in the standard design known as "Type 23." Train passengers could then travel directly to Centerville, making the Centerville Stage obsolete.

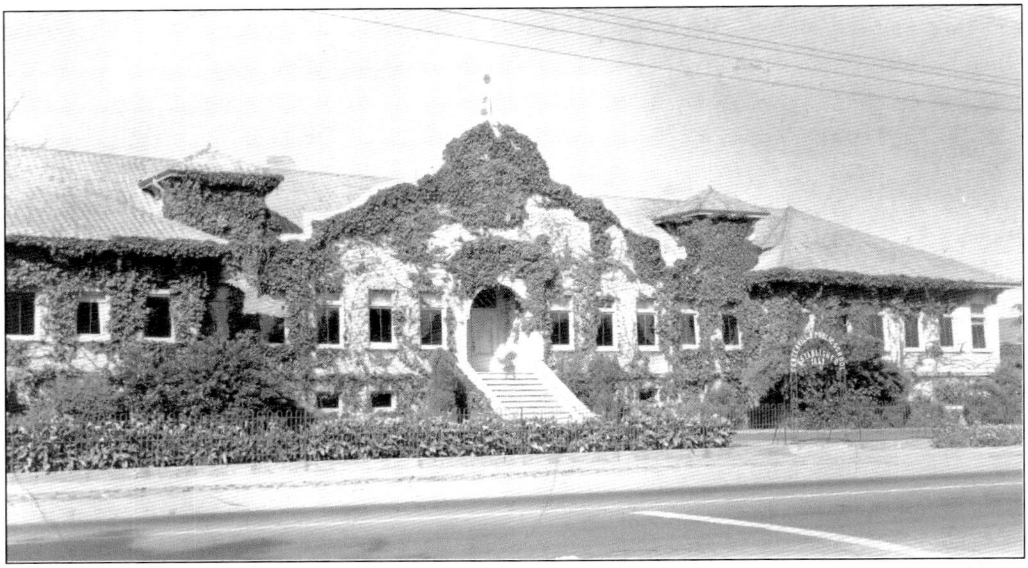

The first Centerville Grammar School on the present site was built in 1881 with the address of 267 South Main Street. In 1904, the school had four teachers and the largest attendance in Washington Township for grades one through eight. This wrought iron sign was installed in front of the second building, constructed in 1913, though the sign is not quite accurate; the Centerville School District was formed in 1855. The 1913 building was replaced in 1940, and a bell tower was added to call children to school.

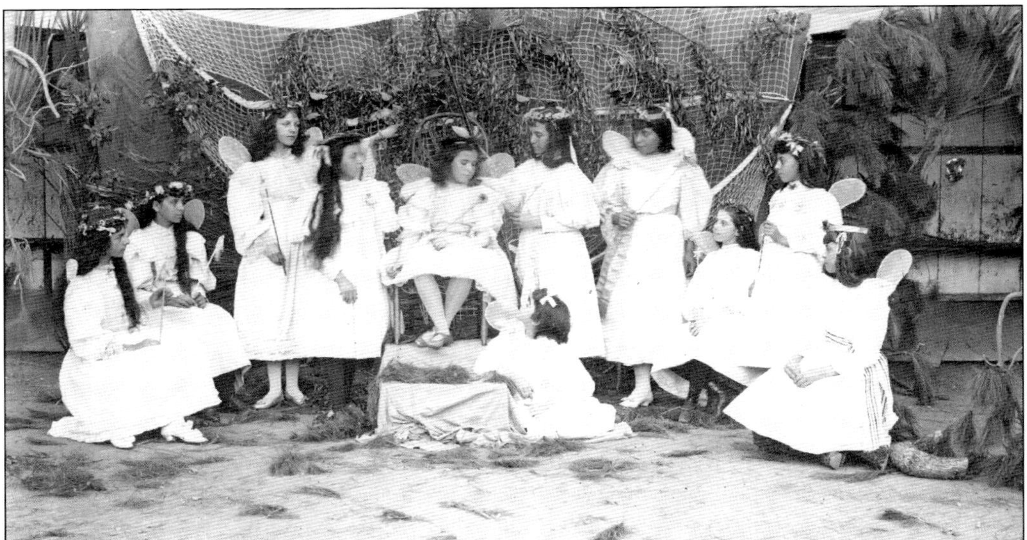

Elma Salz is the "fairy godmother" seated in the middle. Birthday parties were definitely as popular in the late 1800s as they are more than a century later. Clarence F. Salz owned Salz and Company, the main dry goods and general store in Centerville, located opposite of the United States Hotel.

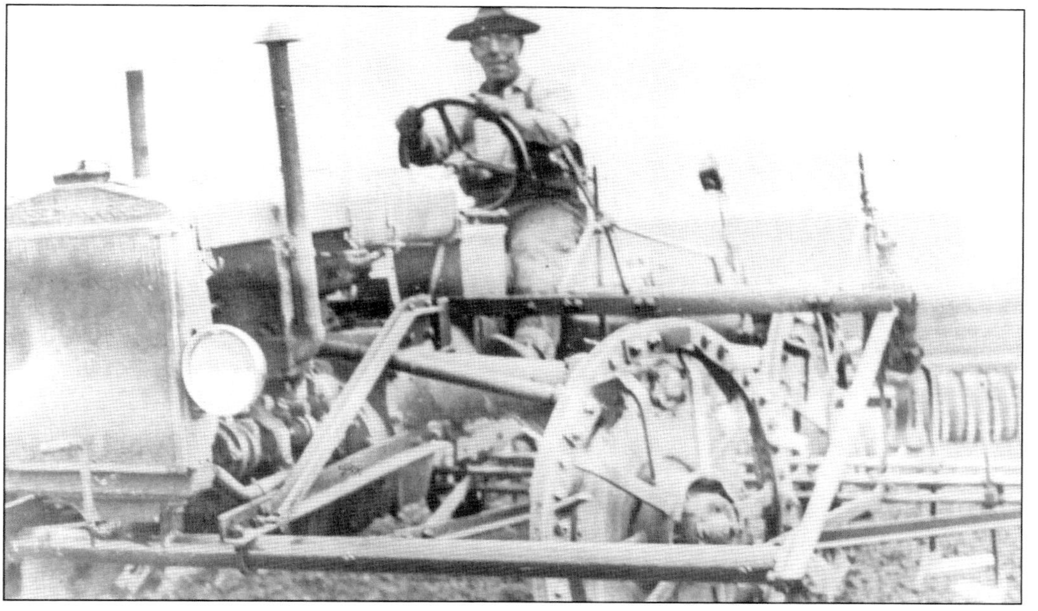

Early mechanized farm machinery was used at the Patterson ranch, photographed here with John Amaral at work. Below, an earlier-era wheat combine is at work on the 6,000-acre Patterson ranch. The ranch maintained its own blacksmith shop as the farm operation expanded for shoeing horses and repairing farm machinery.

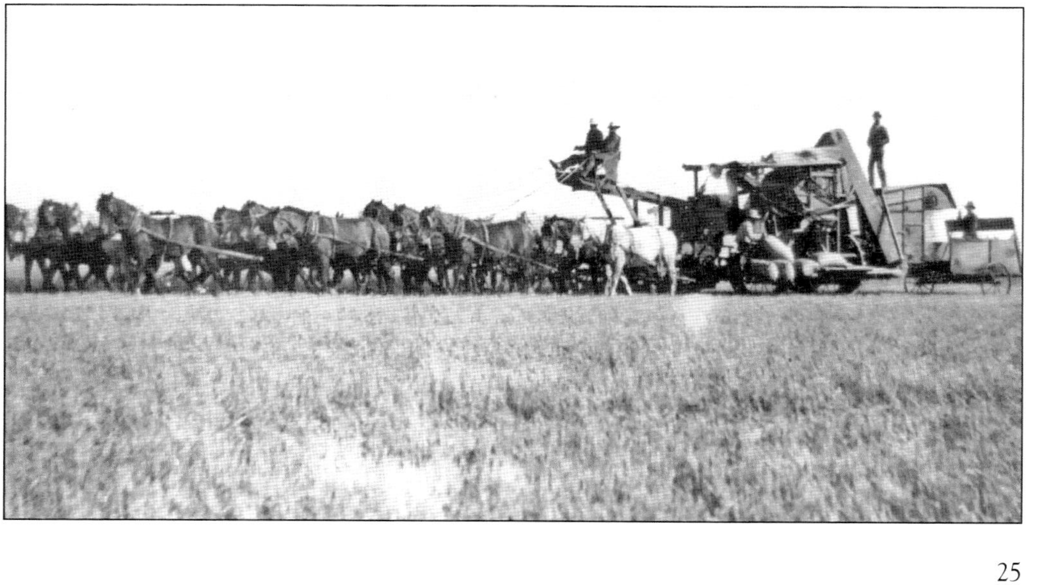

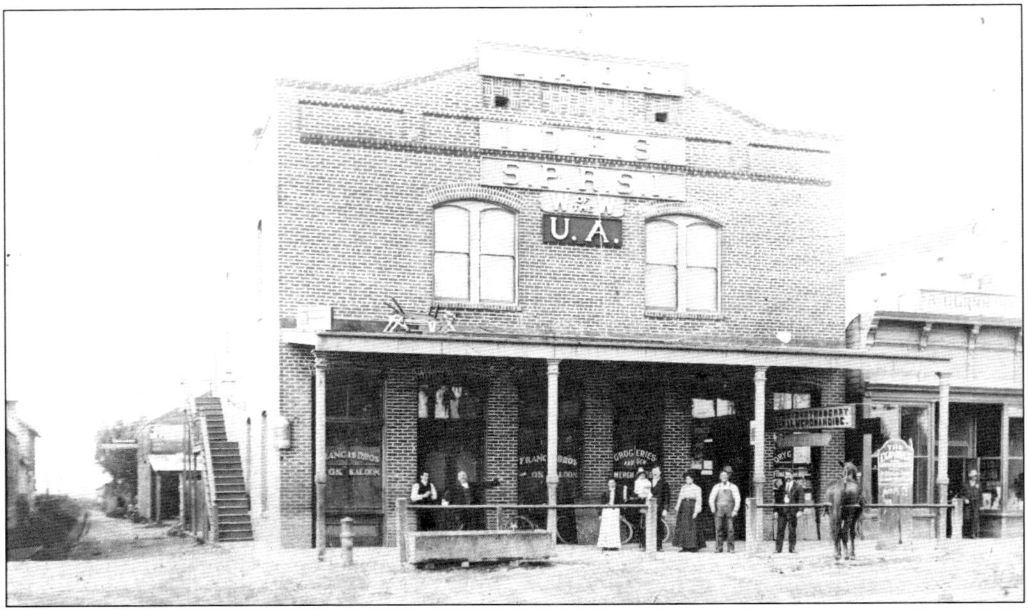

The Centerville Fraternal Building hosted Portuguese organizations and secret societies Irmindade do Devino Espirito Santo (IDES), Sociedade Portuguesa Rainha Santa Isabel (SPRSI), Woodmen of the World (WOW), and the Order of United Americans (UA). Located downstairs was the Francis Brothers OK Saloon.

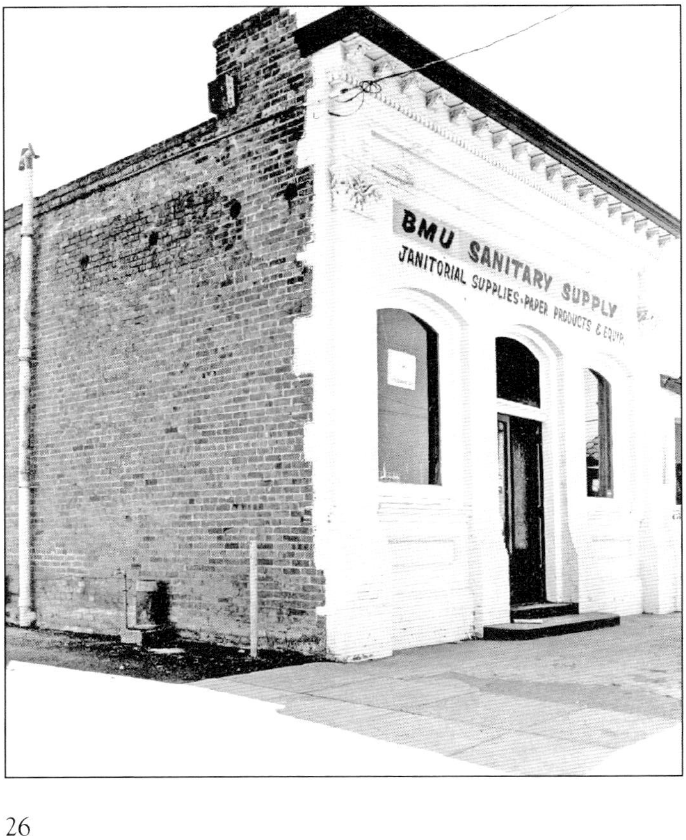

The first bank in town, photographed here in 1966, was built in 1906 with brick from Remillard brickyards in Pleasanton. The Bank of Centerville was established in 1905; its first president was John G. Mattos Jr., an immigrant from Fayal, Azores. He was also a road overseer, notary public, justice of the peace, school board member, county deputy assessor for Washington Township, and twice elected at the state level representing Washington, Eden, and Murray Townships.

The first courthouse in Centerville was on Main Street, pictured behind the Lernhart, Hansen, Hawes, and Salz Building around 1920. Later the courthouse was relocated to Peralta Boulevard at the Alameda County Office Building, where the library was also housed.

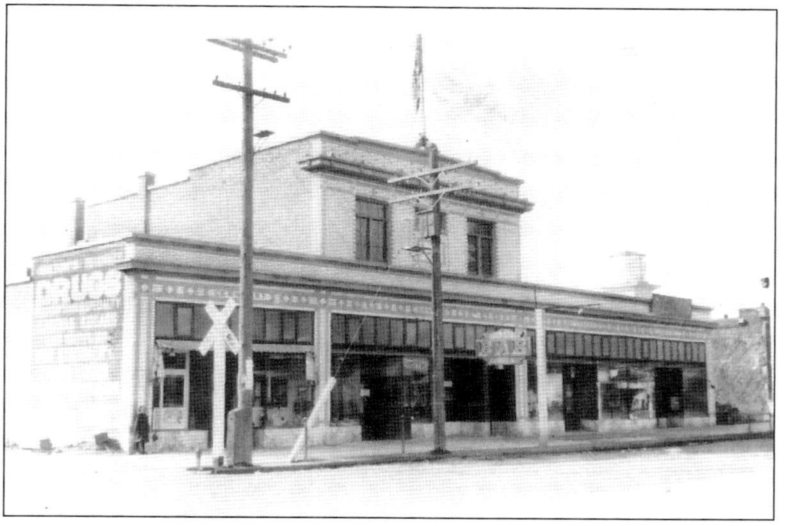

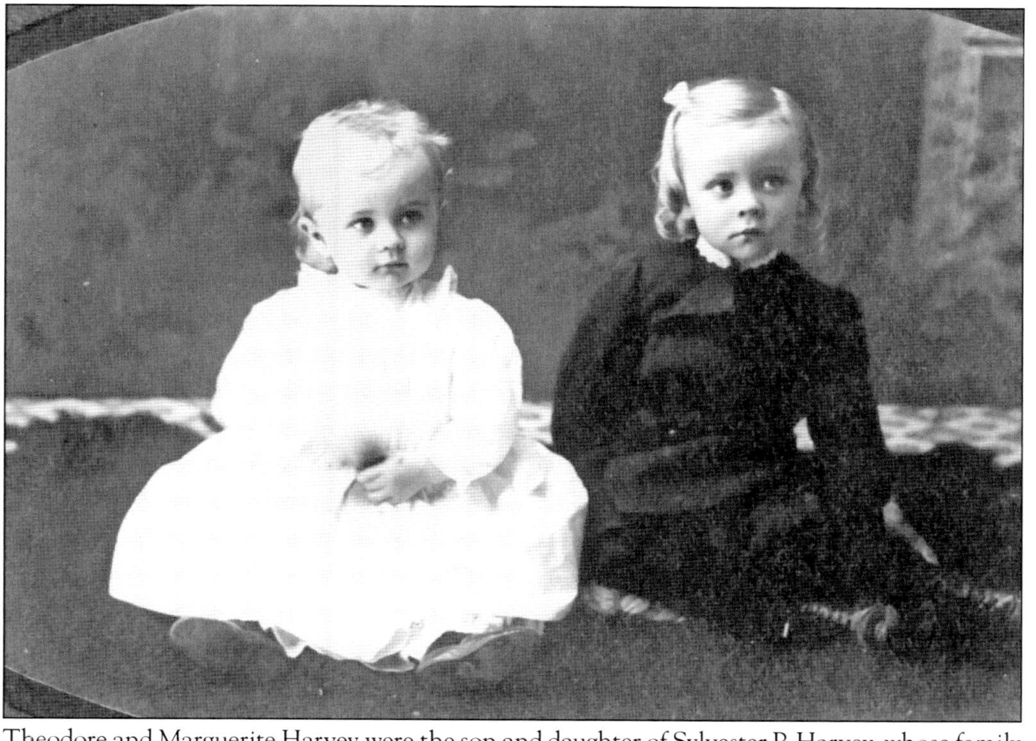

Theodore and Marguerite Harvey were the son and daughter of Sylvester P. Harvey, whose family farmed north of Centerville. The Harvey house was built 1868 and in 1877, when the railroad came through, Hall's Station was across the road. The Harveys farmed 100 acres and ran a dry goods store in Alvarado, the partial records of which are in the archives of the Museum of Local History. The house still stands in a City of Fremont park on Alvarado Boulevard.

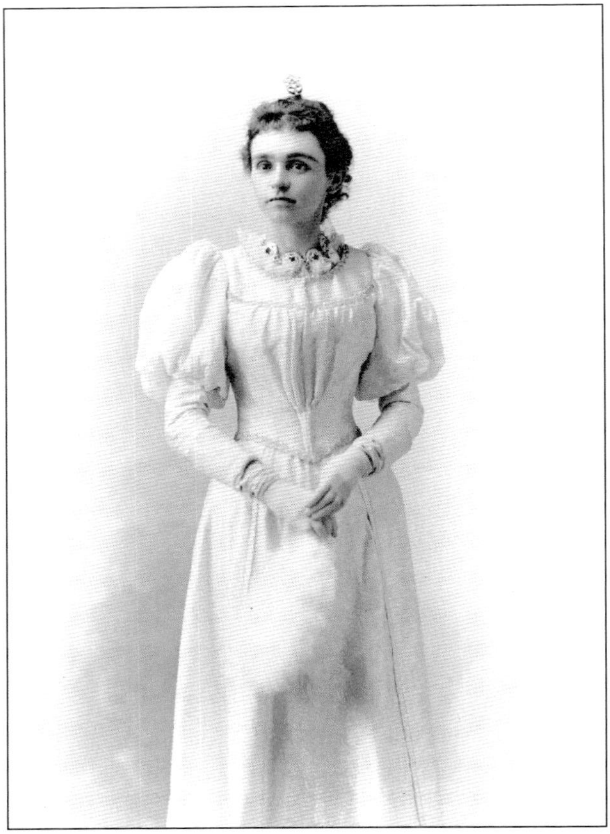

Miss Riley (pictured) taught Elma Salz at Centerville Grammar School around 1890. In those days, teachers were hired annually. According to the Union High School records of June 1897, the executive school board would meet then and elect the principal, vice principal, and teachers for classics, languages, and mathematics for the following school year. That year, Miss Reynolds resigned from the classics position because she had obtained a scholarship to Bryn Mawr College.

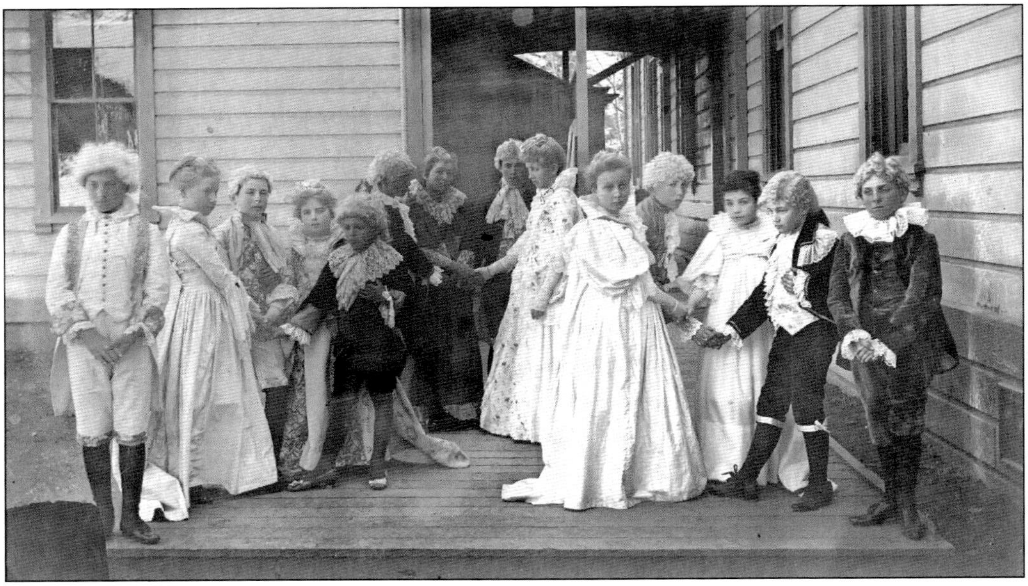

Centerville Grammar School students performed a George Washington play in February 1893. School pageants and operetta at graduation became traditional. When the school district unified in 1964, the school became Centerville Junior High School.

According to a 1925 issue of the *Hatchet*, "Thirty-three years ago, in 1892, the old Masonic Hall served as the first high school of this district. The first story was rented and fitted with about forty desks, necessarily placed in double rows, as the room was not large. A hall five feet wide, which extended across the building, had seats placed at one end for recitation. A small zinc box with faucet and drain served as laboratory equipment. A three foot cupboard contained laboratory apparatus and the library."

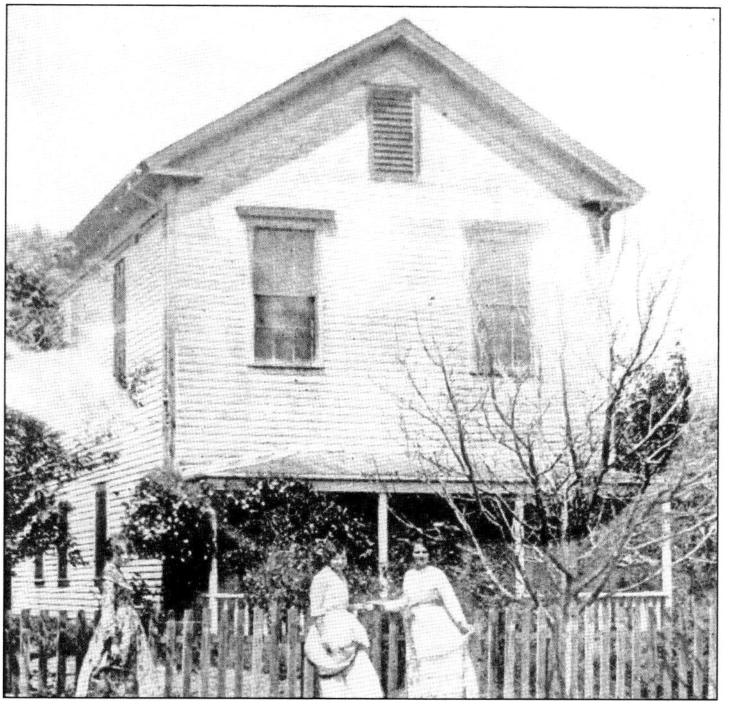

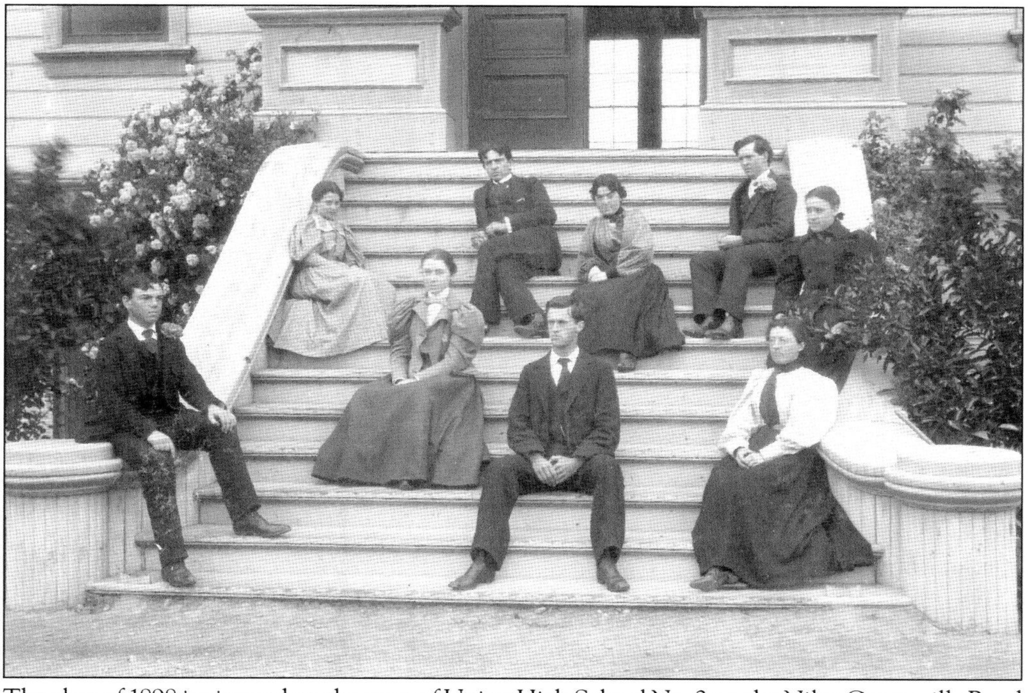

The class of 1898 is pictured on the steps of Union High School No. 2 on the Niles-Centerville Road (now Peralta Boulevard). Pictured in no particular order are Mary Alice Connors, Rob Roy Denny, Gertrude Gibbons, Francis Girard, Florence Hudson, Elbert Mugill, Florence Mayhew, Kenneth Reynolds, and Mila Rix. Rix is at the upper left and Florence Mayhew is at the lower left.

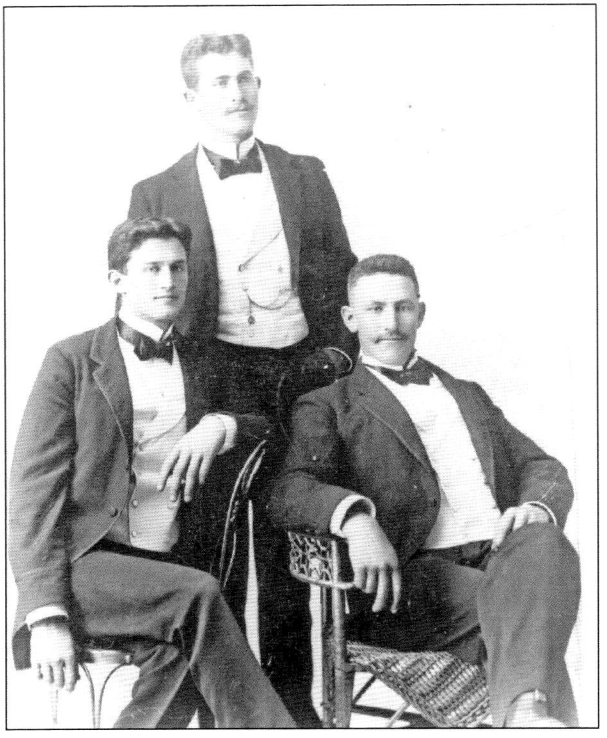

The Crosby brothers pose in the mid-1890s. From left to right are Henry, a contractor; Peter, the eldest brother and a lawyer; and Daniel, a surgeon. Daniel was born in Centerville on September 28, 1874, graduated from Cooper Medical College in 1898, and later practiced at the Alameda County Hospital. Henry Crosby acquired the well-drilling, tinning, and plumbing business on Centerville's Main Street from John Bunting. All the Crosby brothers were athletes at Washington College and in the Centerville Athletic Club. Daniel Crosby taught a year of school and coached sports at Washington Grammar School at Irvington in 1894. The Crosby brothers' parents were Edward and Mary. The family's property was located across Niles Road from their cousins, the Overackers.

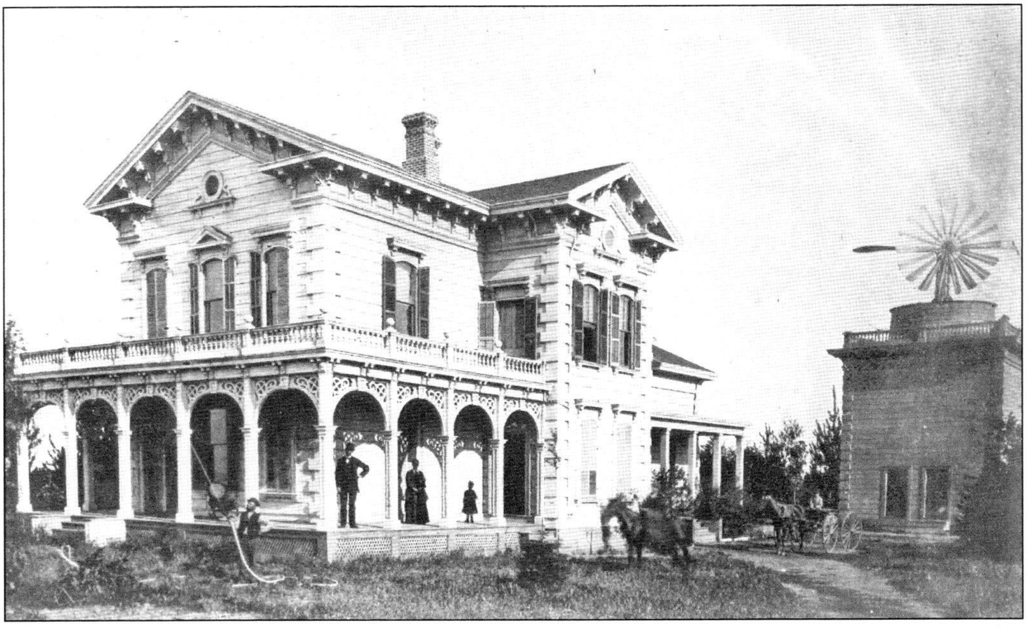

Howard Overacker's elegant residence was erected in 1867. Overacker was a forty-niner who came to farm at Centerville in 1852. He was the rare survivor of a grizzly bear attack while deer hunting, as he described in an interview with Charles Shinn in the 1880s. He recovered the use of his torn limbs and went on to be county supervisor from 1862 to 1880, a position in which Henry Dusterberry would succeed him.

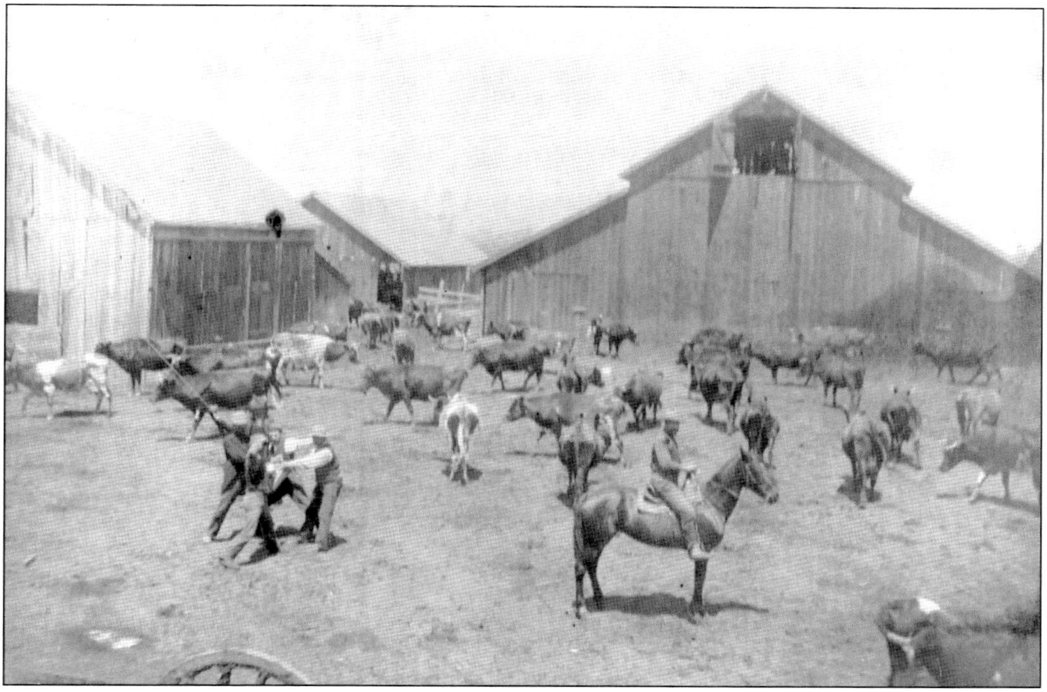

John Thomas Stevenson and his wife, Jane, came to the area in 1852. They lived in a one-room log cabin owned by E. L. Beard and finally saved enough money to buy a 380-acre ranch north of Centerville between the Alvarado Road and Alameda Creek (pictured). The ranch prospered and expanded to include the area presently occupied by American High School and the Brookvale Shopping Center and housing development.

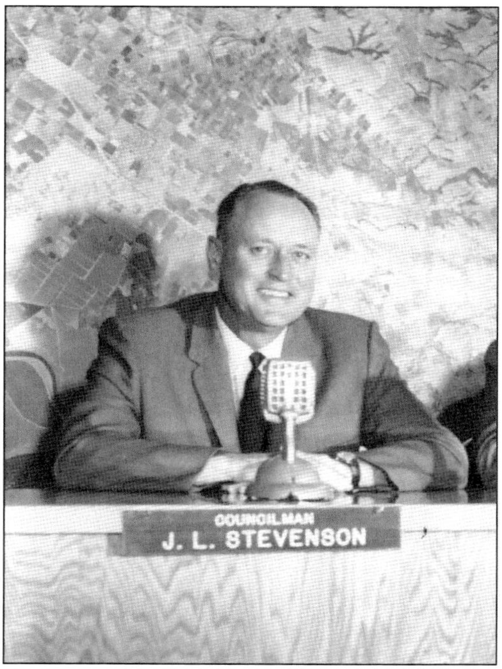

John L. Stevenson (son of John William Stevenson and grandson of John Thomas Stevenson) was the family property manager, a practicing attorney who was elected the first mayor of Fremont in 1956. He also served as mayor from 1960 to 1962 and was a councilman from 1960 to 1964. John L. Stevenson also developed Mowry East and Mowry West Shopping Centers on Mowry Avenue.

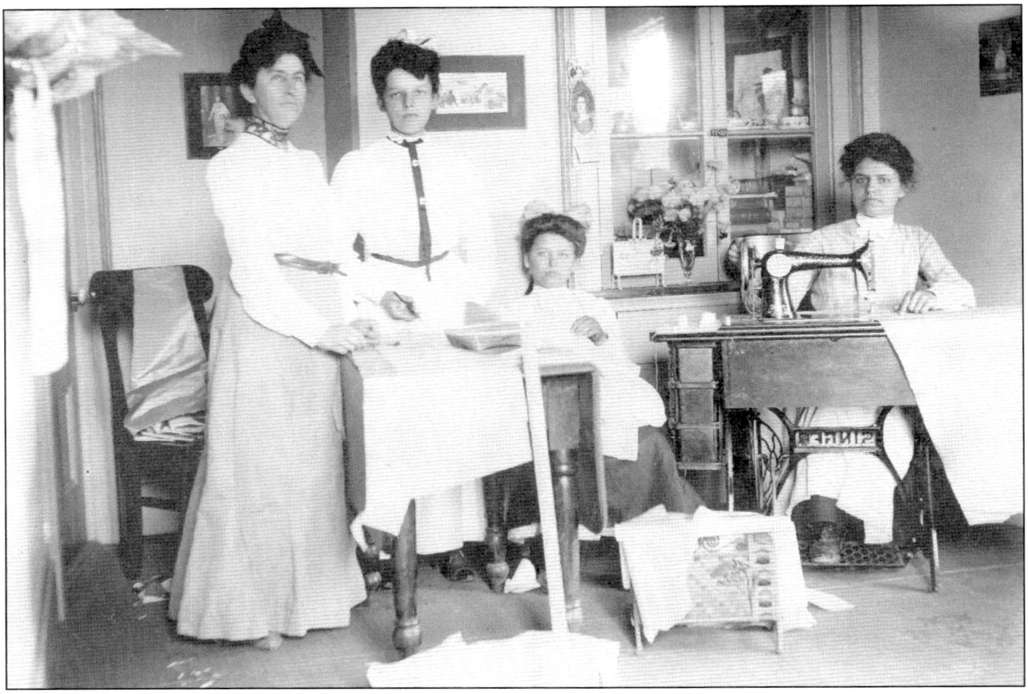

Sewing circles were very popular in Washington Township. They provided a reason for women to gather to make items for worthy causes. This sewing circle in Centerville includes Rose Pires, pictured second from the left. (BLB.)

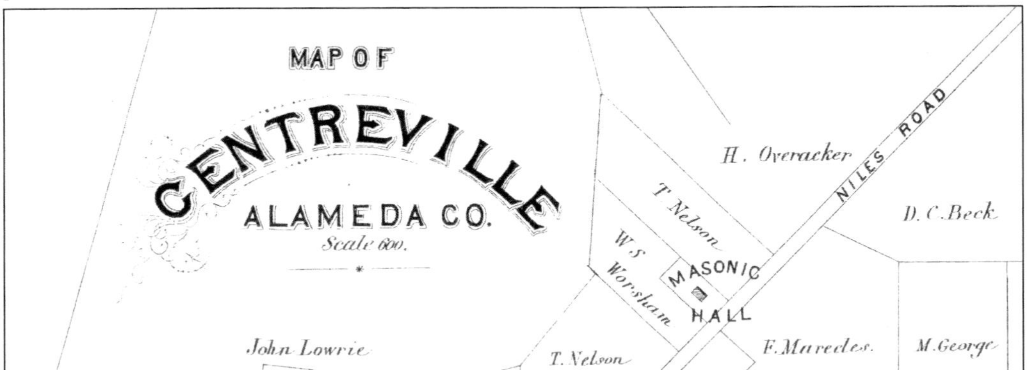

A Centerville sketch map in the Thompson and West Historical Atlas of 1878 shows George Bond's central parcel. According to Charles Shinn, "The first store in Centerville was kept by Captain Bond. It was in a 20' x 40' building, which stood on the road where the Sutherlands now live, near the little [post] office. The office was built by James Starr in 1853. Captain Bond afterwards had Mr. Clemens as partner, then Captain Valpey. Clemens, who was a relative by marriage of the late B. B. Redding of San Francisco [former secretary of state] went across the street and opened another store."

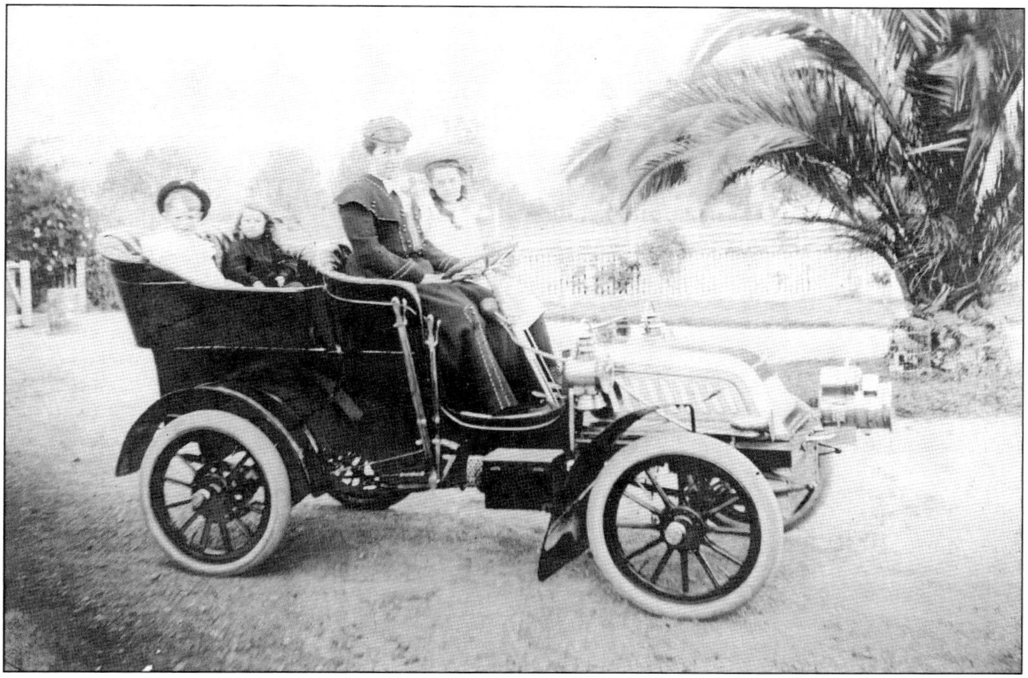

Marie Elizabeth Horner and Helen Blacow are pictured in an electric car in Centerville in 1906.

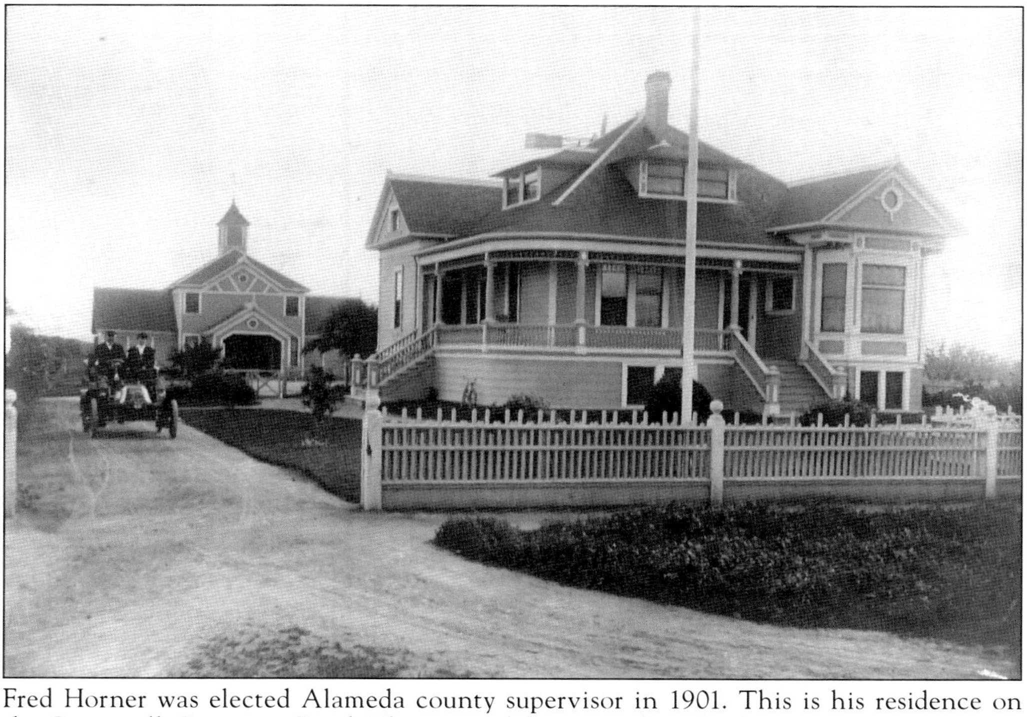

Fred Horner was elected Alameda county supervisor in 1901. This is his residence on the Centerville-Irvington Road. The automobile pictured in the driveway is apparently his one-cylinder Thomas.

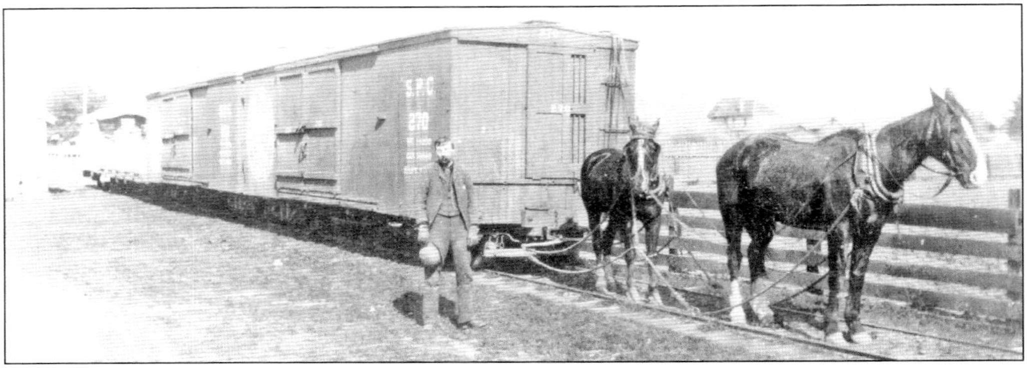

This horsecar was photographed leaving Centerville with freight, such as bushels of vegetables. In the 1870s, potatoes were harvested on the Machado ranch beginning in May and delivered by wagon to the Jarvis Landing Warehouse. Other crops that were harvested were corn, tomatoes, and apricots. By the mid-1880s a wood-frame house replaced the adobe structure as the main Machado family home. Alviso School was a 1-mile walk north on the Oakland Road, on the corner of the James Beard ranch.

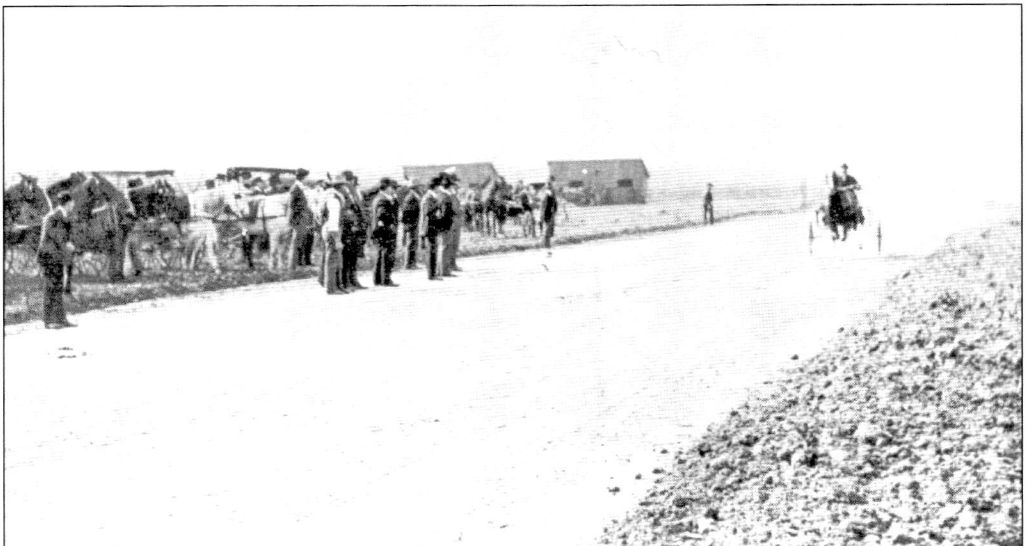

George Machado's blacksmith shop was located at the corner of Oakland and Decoto Roads. He developed an expertise in shoeing racehorses at local sulky races such as the Walton track, pictured here, and in the harness racing circuit of the 1920s, where he skillfully shoed the horses he trained and drove for George J. Giannini. Machado's travels took him to racetracks from Salem, Oregon, to Riverside, California. Giannini was the friend who, in 1935, introduced Charles Howard to trainer "Silent Tom" Smith, later of Seabiscuit fame.

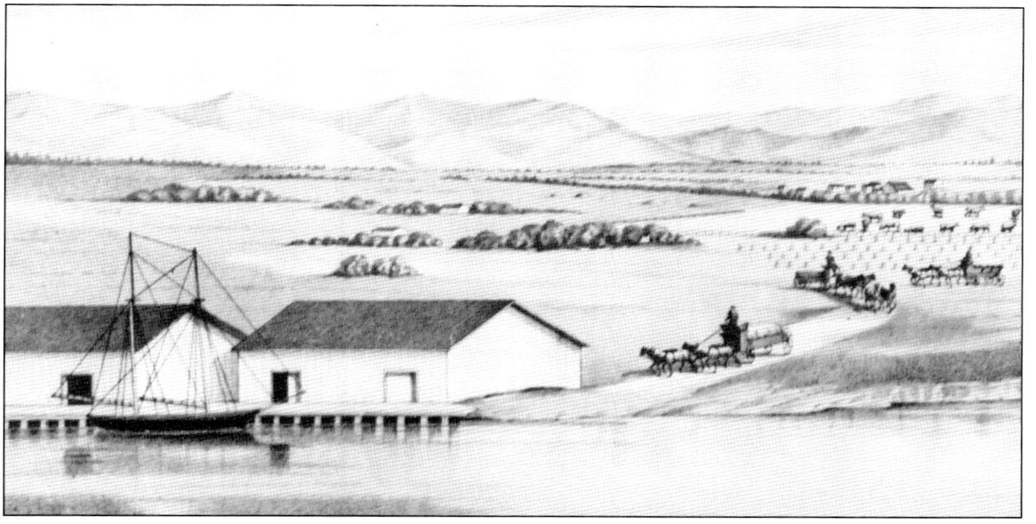

Patterson Landing was portrayed in the Thompson and West Historical Atlas in 1878. Essential to the Patterson ranch enterprise from early days, acquiring Anderson Landing at the mouth of Alameda Creek was critical for the shipping of hay, grain, and other crops directly to San Francisco. Later known as Patterson Landing, the waterway was beneficial because of its adequate draft and short hauling distance to and from the loading areas.

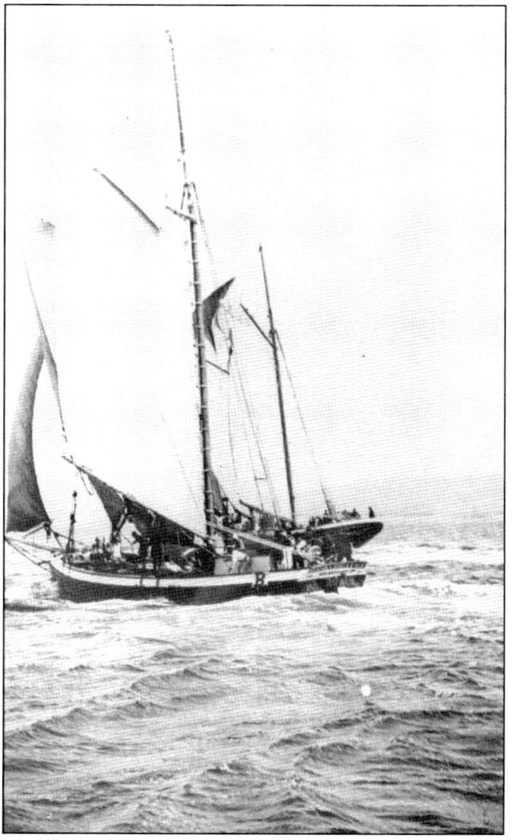

The Patterson scow schooner, called the *Broadgauge*, was purchased on August 4, 1878, for a price of $3,950 that was paid to the boat's builder, George D. Weaver. The flat-bottom scow schooner design was customized for the San Francisco Bay and the shallow landings typical of the bay's muddy perimeter.

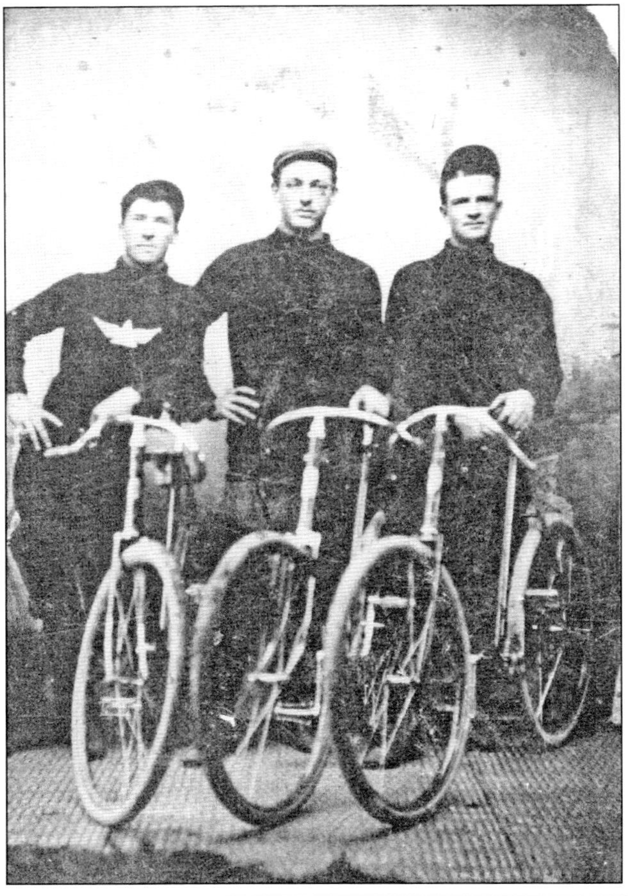

Frank and Henry Dusterberry pose on bicycles. On April 21, 1896, the *San Francisco Call* reported "A three lap dirt track has just been completed at Centerville by the Centerville Athletic Club. The northerly curve of the track is banked six feet and has a radius of ninety feet. The southerly and westerly curves are banked five feet and have a radius of 150 feet. Inside the track enclosure are baseball, football, tennis and trap-shooting grounds. . . . It has a membership of 200 and also a club building thirty by sixty feet, well supplied with athletic appliances. The officers and directors are: F. T. Smith, President; F. Dusterberry, Secretary; N. Leonhart, Treasurer; H. C. Gregory, W. W. Walton, J. D. Norris, Frank Hawes, Joseph Ritter and H. Emerson, directors." Frederick Dusterberry came to California from Germany in 1852. He purchased the home below from Capt. Samuel Marston in 1860. It was restored in 1970 by Josephine Marion.

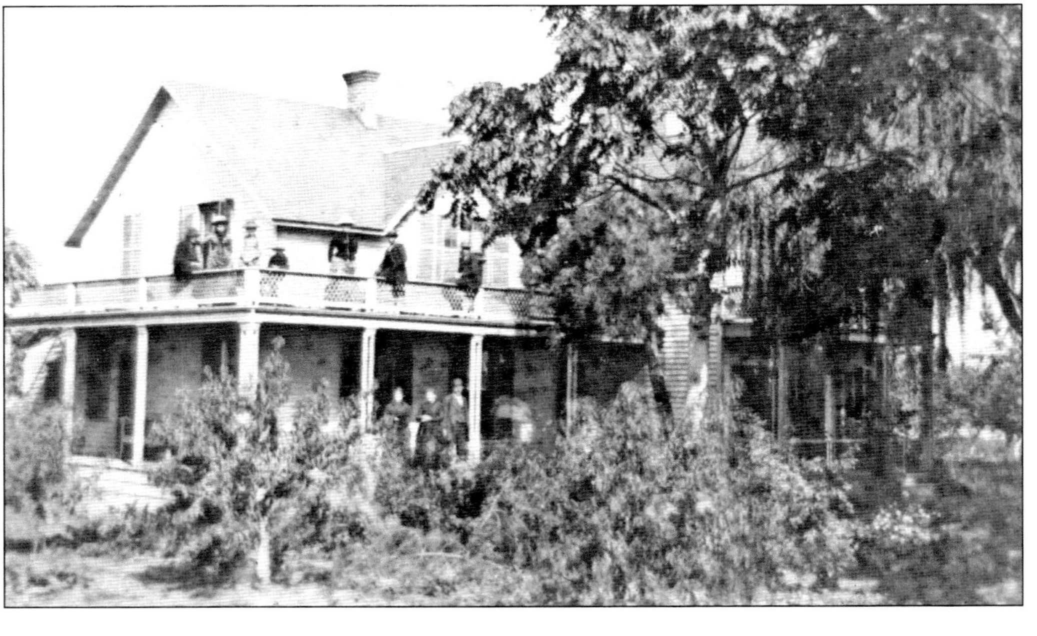

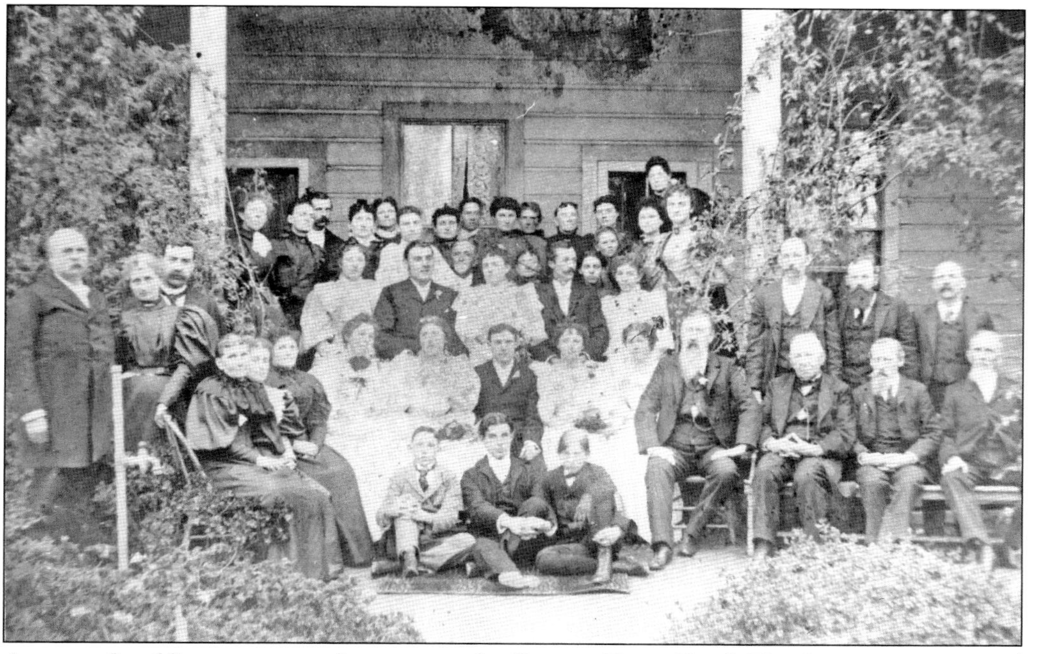

A group of wedding party attendees poses at the Gregory House Hotel. The Gregory House Hotel advertised itself in an 1897 issue of the *Niles Herald Weekly* as the best hotel in the county, a fact verified by a number of sources. The hotel also advertised itself as a place for wedding gatherings, summer vacations, or a lunch destination for cyclists on a day ride from San Jose or Oakland.

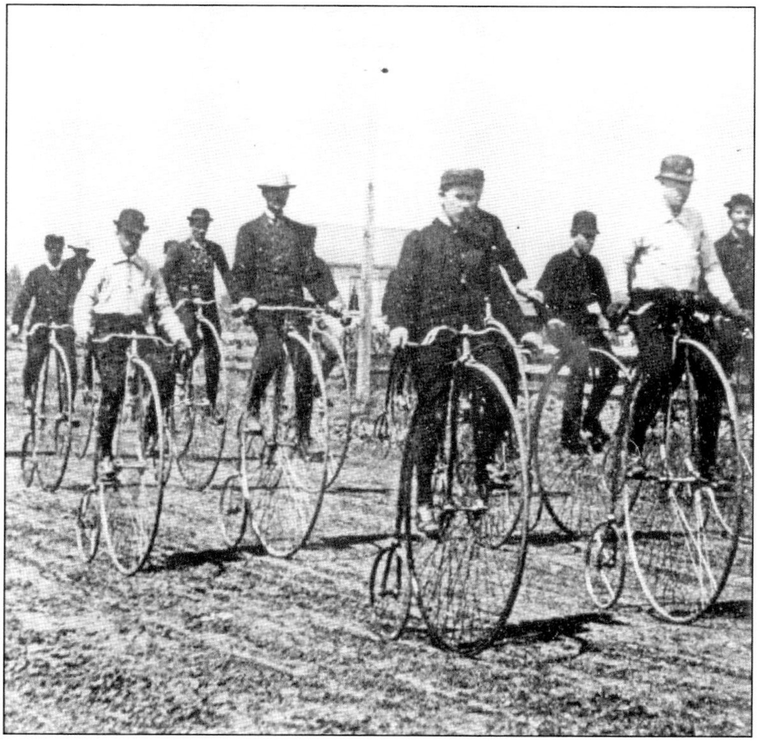

This Dusterberry brothers tintype photograph dates from the mid-1880s, based on the fact that the penny-farthing, or high-wheel, bicycle went out of fashion in 1885. The chain-drive transmission and inflatable tires of later bicycles were first popularized by John Kemp Starley's Rover safety bicycle. Advertisements at Centerville's bicycle event, held on May 24, 1896, advertised the Victor bicycle, made by the Overman Wheel Company, which had a showroom in San Francisco.

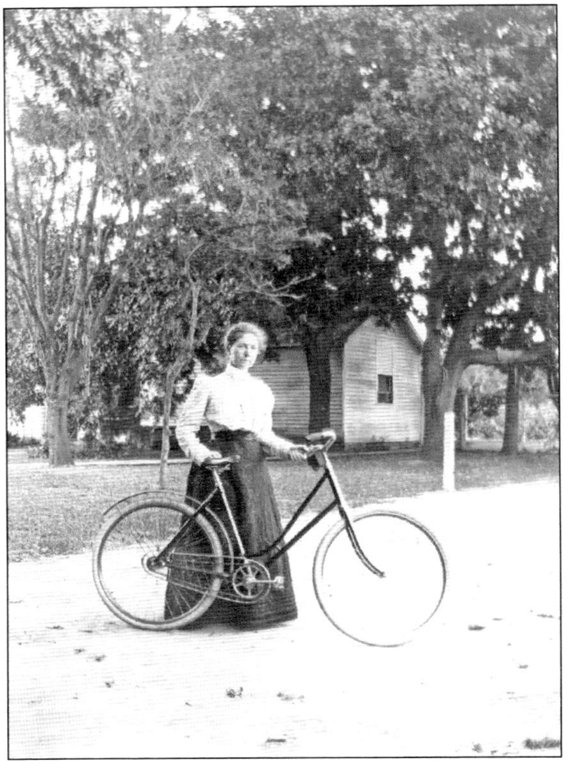

Clara Patterson is depicted with her lady's safety bicycle in the mid-1880s. Her sons were born in 1878 and 1880. Bloomers were not brought into bicycle fashion until the 1890s, by which time Patterson was widowed and her sons were high school students. She was 24 years old and a qualified teacher when she married 55-year-old neighbor George Patterson in 1877.

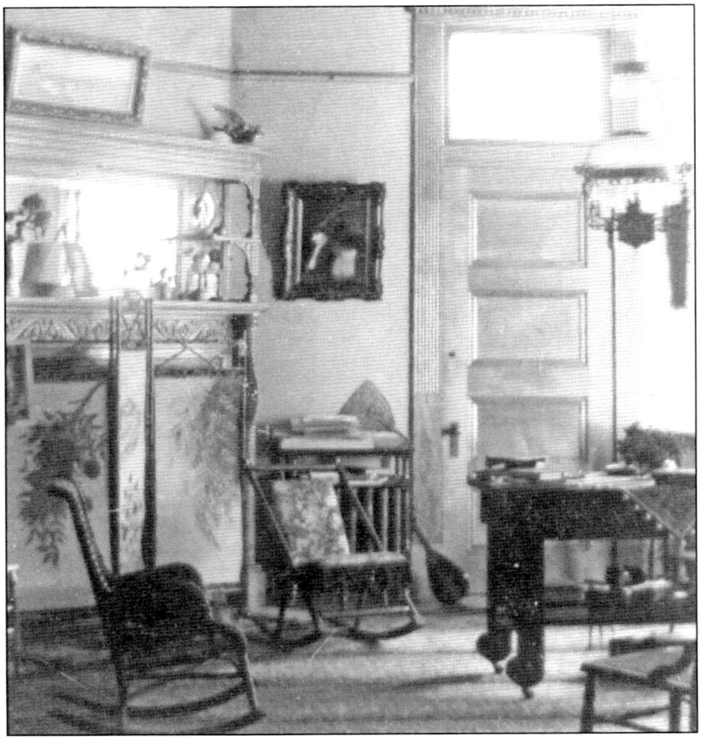

Clara Patterson's new front parlor was designed by the Newsom brothers in the portion of her farmhouse that was added in 1889. The original foundation was built in 1857. The Queen Anne addition was rich in Victorian details, with a great arching entryway. This room was to the right of the front entrance, opening to the side porch with a hanging porch swing. The transom above the porch door allowed cross breezes and airflow between rooms.

Three

All the World's a Stage 1898–1919

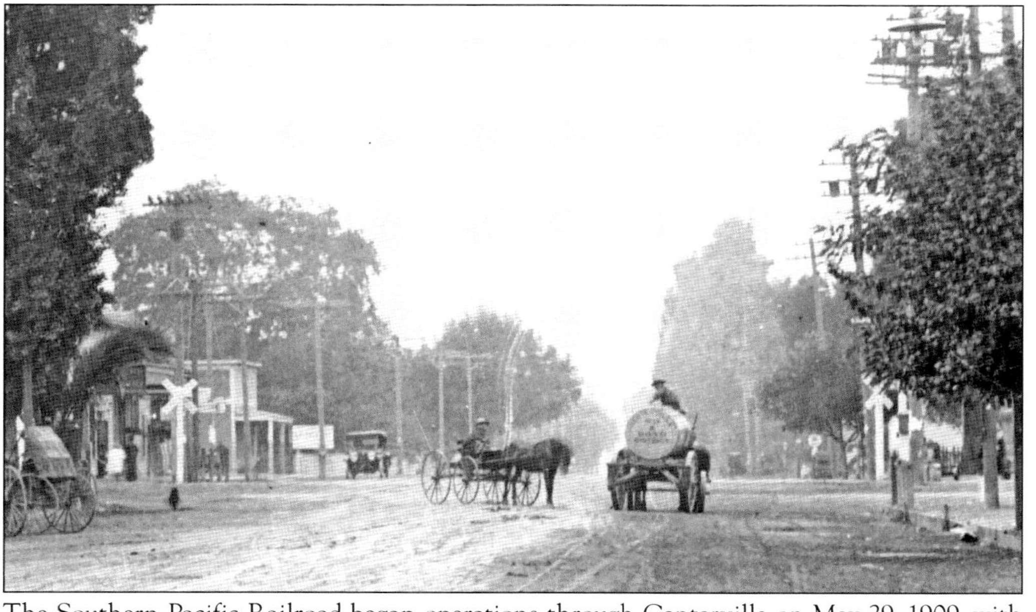

The Southern Pacific Railroad began operations through Centerville on May 29, 1909, with fanfare crossing over Main Street. In 1910, there was more to celebrate—a new station was built on the south side of the tracks, just west of the 1891 high school. A new station provided many benefits, including ease of transport to urban jobs and for sports matches with other Bay Area high schools.

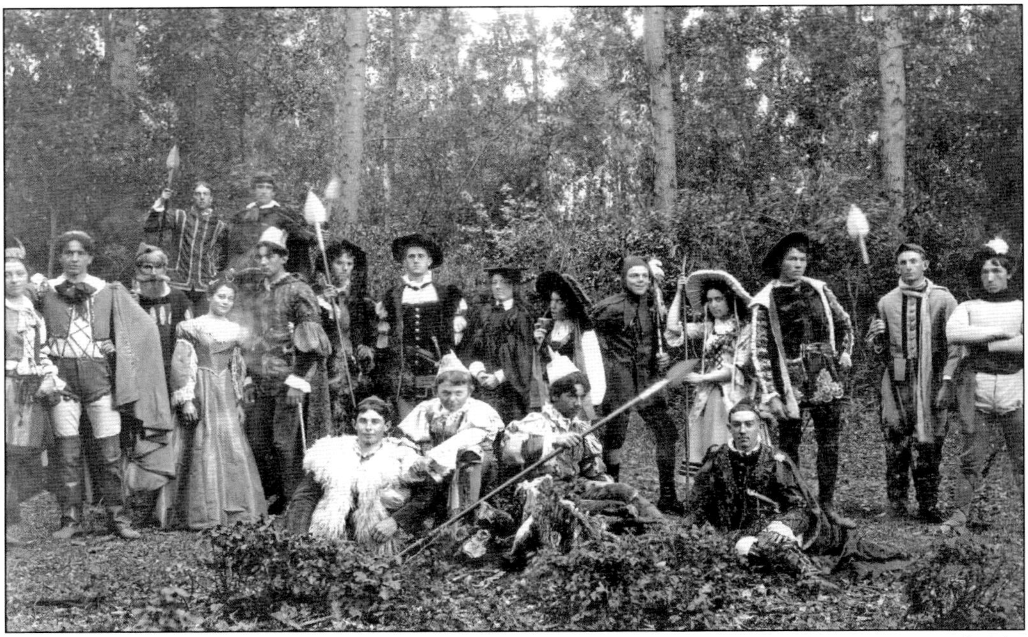

Shakespeare's *As You Like It* was performed in a grove at the Patterson ranch in 1898, much like the Arden described in the play from which the quote "All the world's a stage" is derived. One of the performers, William Patterson, is pictured at the far left. The director was Ella Castelhun, who was licensed as California's second woman architect in 1905. "It was long remembered by all who saw it," according to a 1924 article in the *Hatchet*.

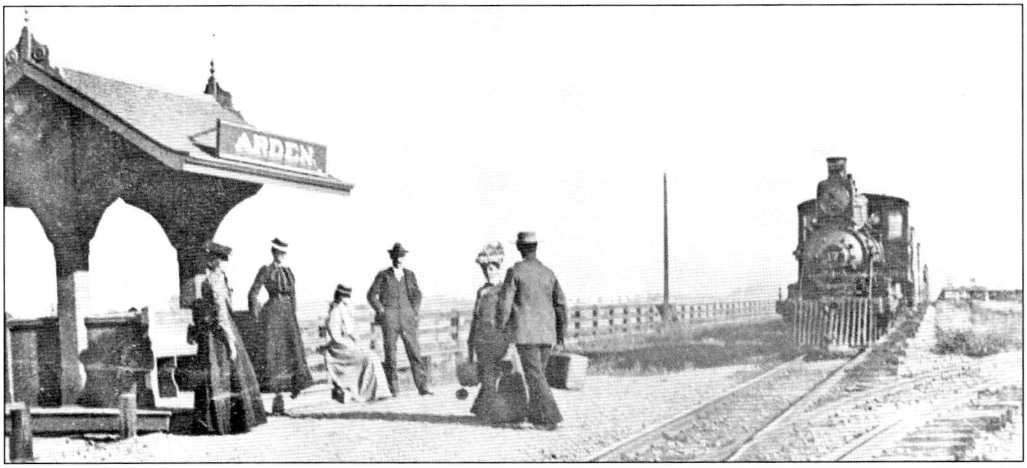

The South Pacific Coast Railroad used a right-of-way for its narrow-gauge track through the Patterson ranch in 1877, during the same time when George Patterson was away in Sacramento getting married to his neighbors' daughter, Clara Hawley. In the 1890s, Clara commissioned a small railway shelter for the stop, both for passenger travel and as a loading point for taking specialized crops to market or for the delivery of household items.

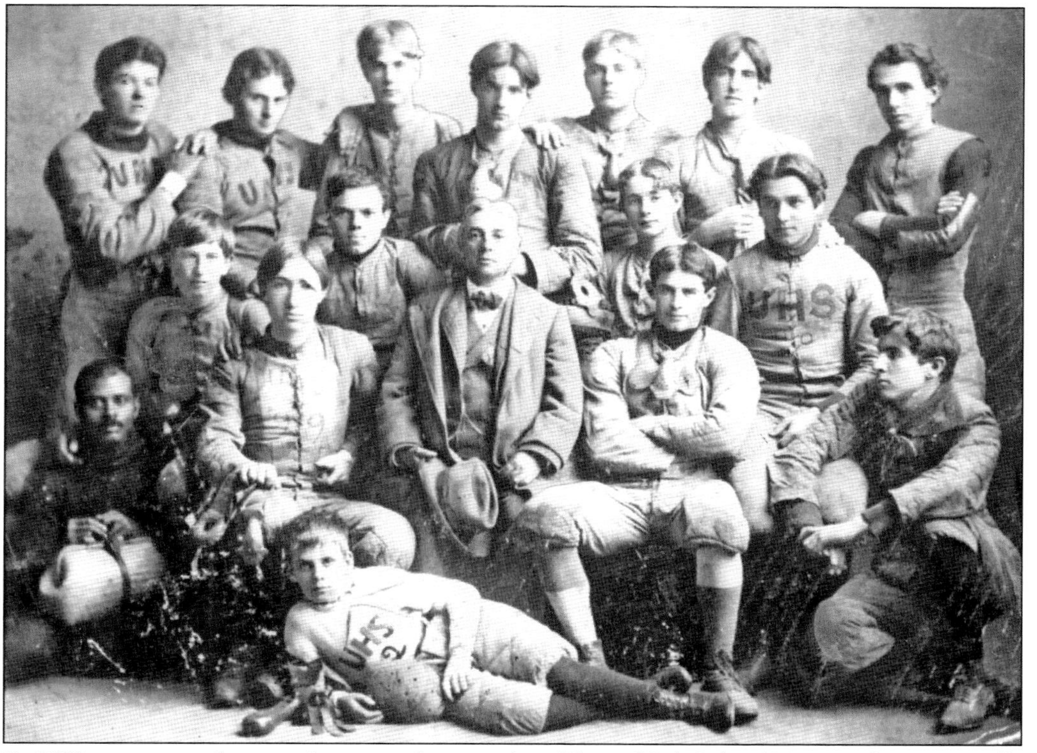

By 1899, newspapers began referring to the team from Union High School No. 2 as the Centerville High School team, and by the new century the players' wool sports jerseys sported a large orange C on a black ground. The name Centerville High School would hold true until the high school relocated in 1924 to the present site, when the school became more widely known as Washington High School.

The Patterson boys, William and Henry, took over a part of their father's barn to use as a sort of den. Hosting the high school drama group here led to the first outdoor Shakespeare performance at the ranch, which in turn led to the ranch's train stop and local salt works both being named Arden. Typical of the late Victorian era, the teenage hang-out included hanging lanterns and exotic items from the Far East, romantic draperies, and popular notions of a Turkish den.

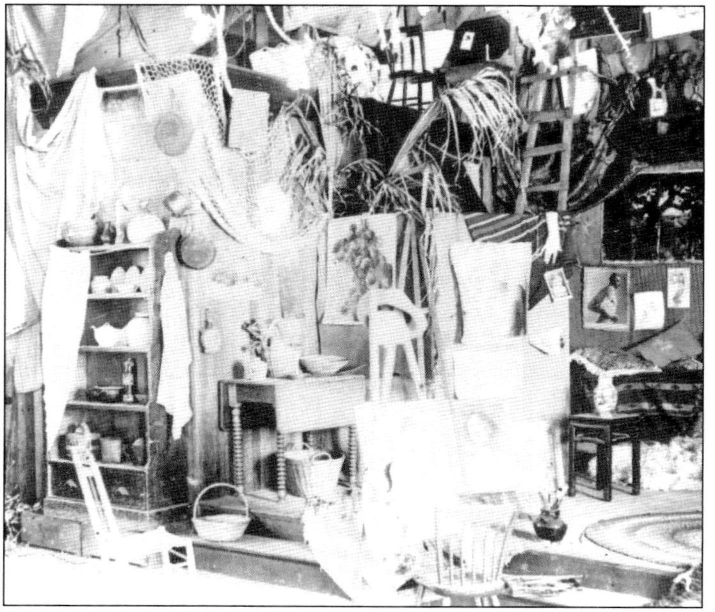

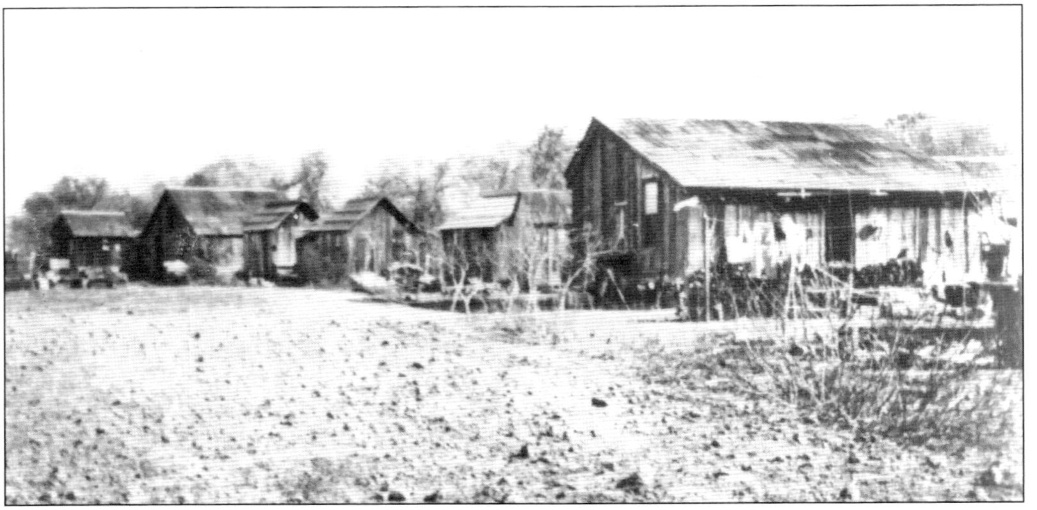

This is a rare photograph of the Chinese camp at Patterson ranch around 1900. Farm worker camps near Alameda Creek in Washington Township in the late 1800s were bunkhouses with a cookhouse, such as those at the California nursery, Shinn ranch, Stanford ranch, and Patterson ranch. Later Chinese immigrants, such as Wah Sing Cheng, rented a farmhouse and a plot of land from one of the ranches and grew vegetables like tomatoes, cabbage, cauliflower, and bok choy for wholesale distribution.

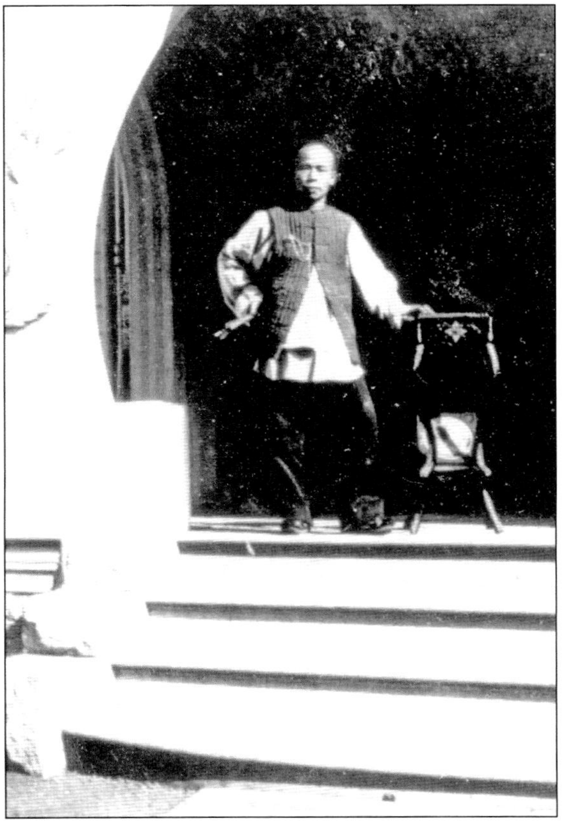

A Patterson family photograph records their cook, Skuga, known to the family as "Harry." Few Chinese women immigrated to North America, or "Gold Mountain" as it was called during the Gold Rush and railroad building eras. Later on, a series of exclusion acts were passed to limit immigration from China; these were variously in place between 1882 and 1965.

The yacht *Starlight* was commissioned for the Patterson family for ease of travel across the bay and up to yacht clubs in Alameda, Marin, and San Francisco—all of which were accessible from Patterson Landing. In the development stage for planning Coyote Hills Regional Park in the 1970s, a marina at the mouth of Alameda Creek in the location of Patterson Landing was much debated. The flood control channel in the south arm of Alameda Creek was completed by 1972, and an understanding of silt buildup in potential moorage basins may have stalled the marina idea.

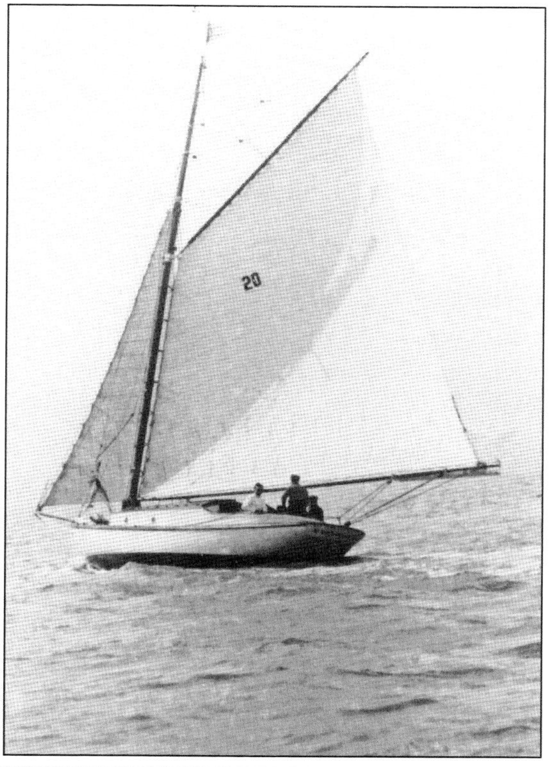

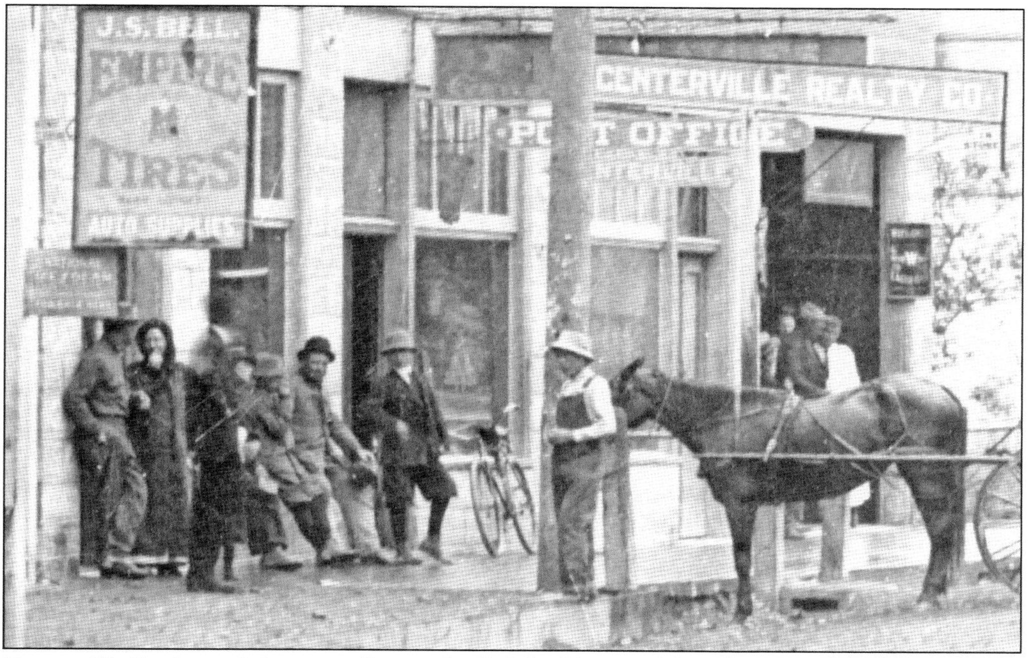

Centerville Realty and the post office at the Salz building on Main Street, pictured here around 1910, was the place to collect mail, look into property, and apparently, hire a day laborer—a common farm worker practice in Centerville up to the 1950s.

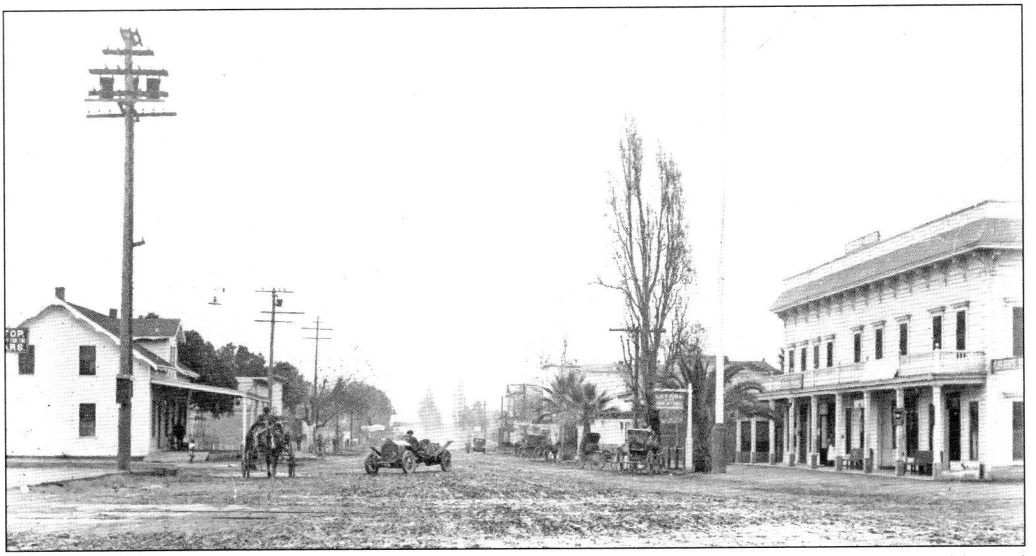

"Roadsters" was the term for these early two-seater motor cars, photographed in the muddy and rutted Main Street outside the Gregory Hotel around 1910. Brush, Packard, Oldsmobile, Overland, and many other companies designed and built roadsters in that decade. The single-cylinder models might have a top speed of 45 miles per hour. The Buick roadster of 1910 came with a choice of two- or four-cylinder engines.

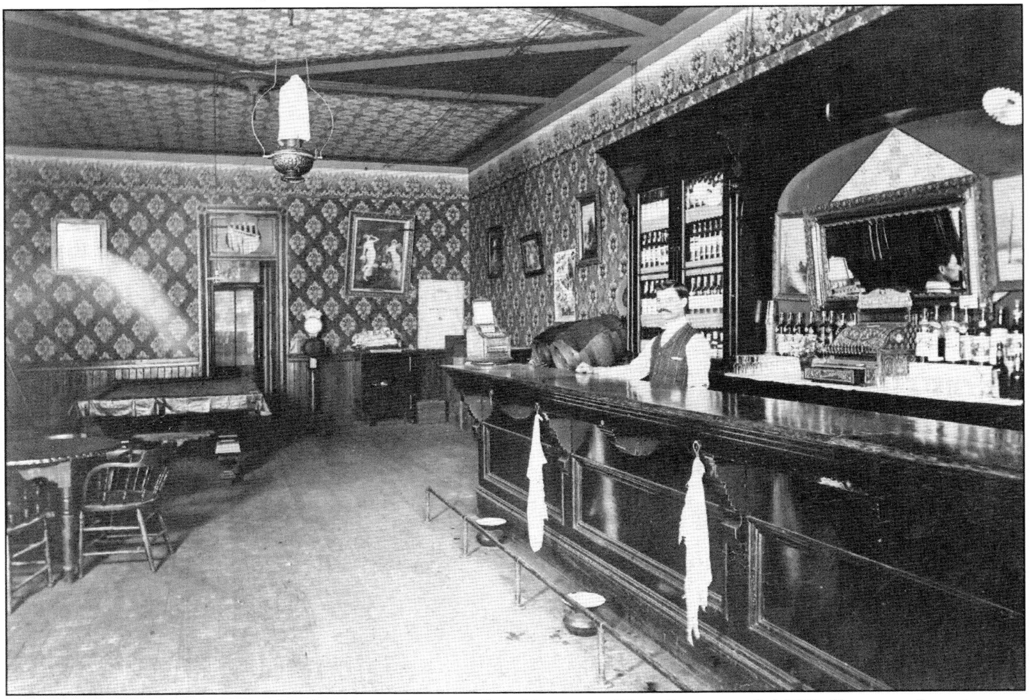

Manuel Simas photographs his new bar in the Gregory Hotel around 1910. Braunschweiger, a California distillery, produced brands with names like Bear Grass, Bear Valley, California Club, Extra Pony, Golden Chief, Old Pioneer, and Silver Wedding. There's no doubt that wine and brandy from the wineries at Mission San Jose and Irvington were also dispensed.

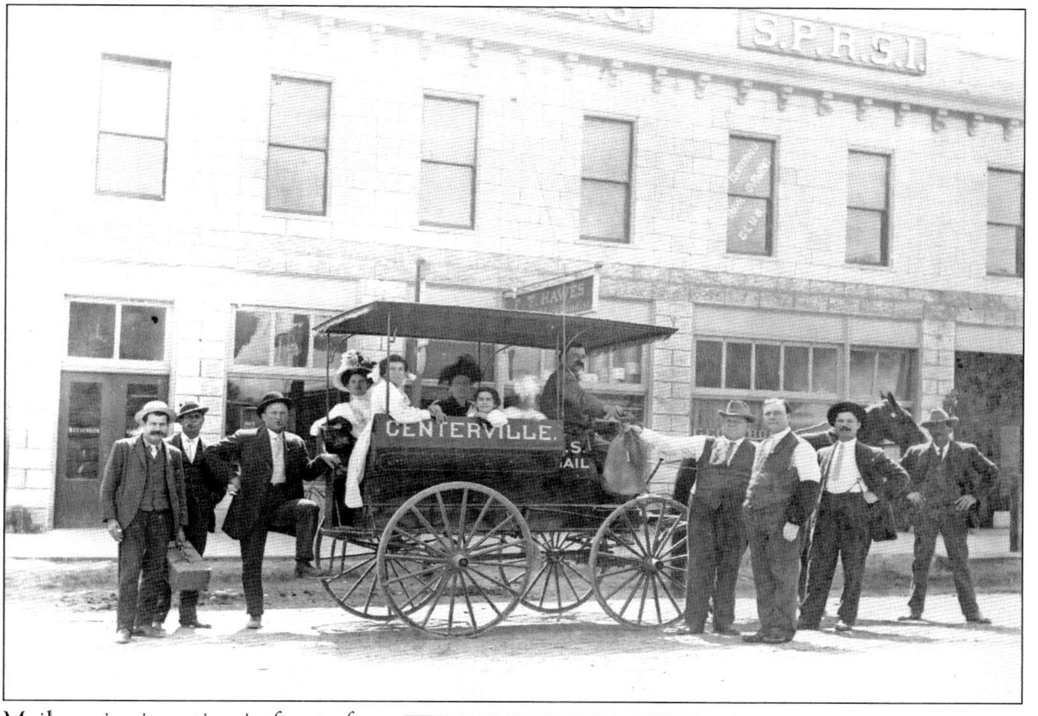

Mail service in action in front of the Centerville post office was caught by Santos photography on August 19, 1909. Parcel post delivery began in 1913.

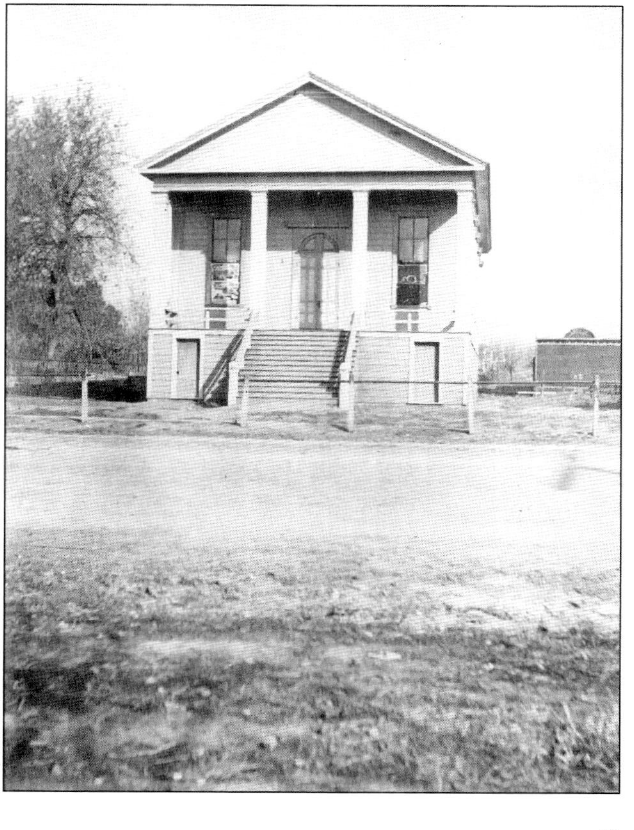

Centerville Town Hall was built in 1868 and was photographed here in 1904. It was described as a "diminutive Greek Temple" by historian Woodruff Minor in 2007. A bowling hall was built in the basement when 10-pin bowling became popular in the late 1800s. The hall was later leased to the Centerville Fire Department, which had formed in 1894. In 1954, the moderne-design fire hall was built on the parcel, opposite the funeral home. The latter is now known as Century House.

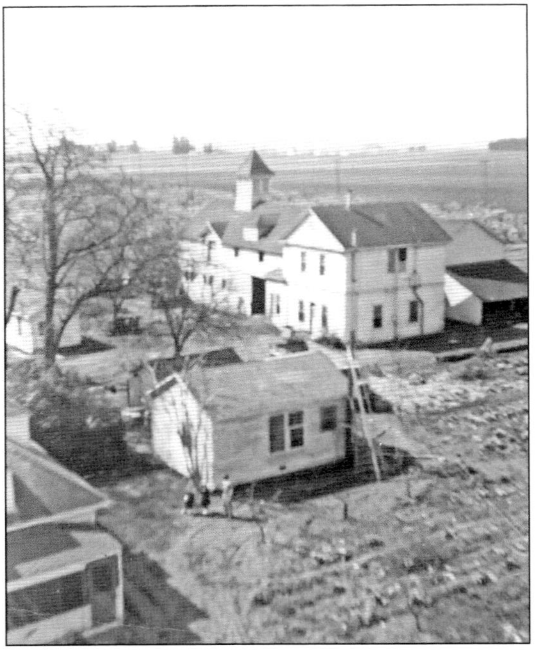

Model farm buildings at Sycamore Farm backed up to the narrow winding waterway Sanjon de los Alisos. This was the distinctive boundary landmark that once wound across the alluvial soils laid down by Alameda Creek between Centerville and the Coyote Hills. Another spelling of *sanjon* is *zanja*, closely allied to the Arabic root of the word, *zanqutan*, meaning "street" or "ditch-way." Wherever these great sycamore and Fremont cottonwood trees were found, there was certain to be great heronries and eagle aeries in the highest possible nesting places. (SB.)

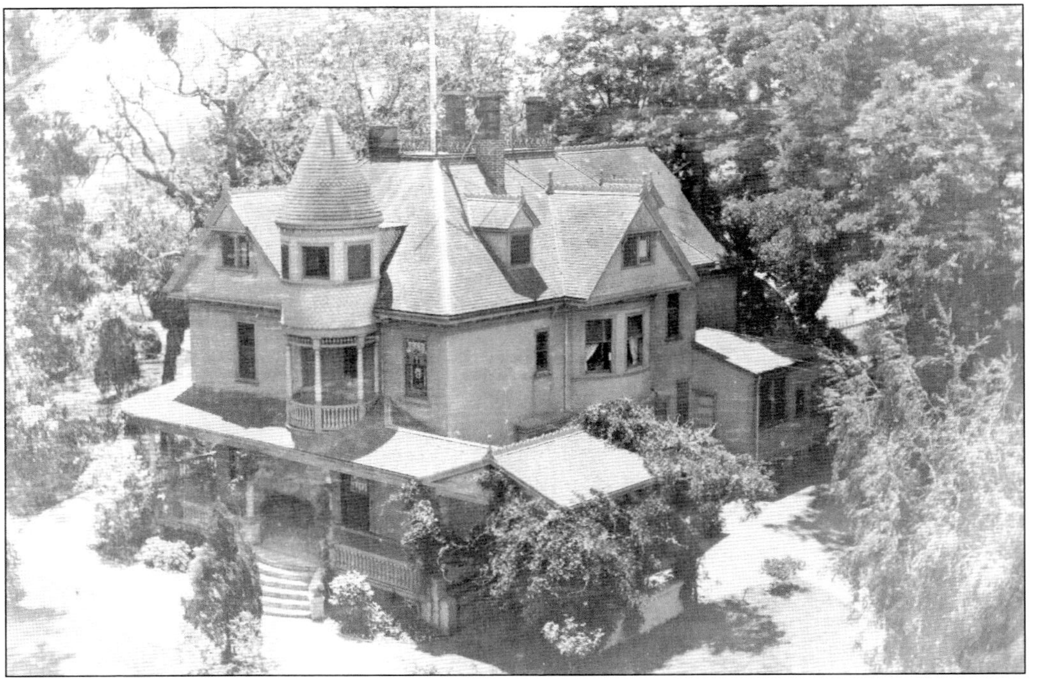

The Bunting mansion was completed in 1900. John McLaren, landscape architect for Golden Gate Park, planned the grounds using the principles described in his 1914 book, *Gardening in California, Landscape and Flower.* The double allée to the new mansion was lined with dozens of flowering locust trees and date palms and centered on a lawn with deep semitropical flowering beds and a goldfish pond in the center. In 1914, the Bunting sons began a farm wireless station (early radio) from the top of the great water tank, picking up the signal in the mansion. (SB.)

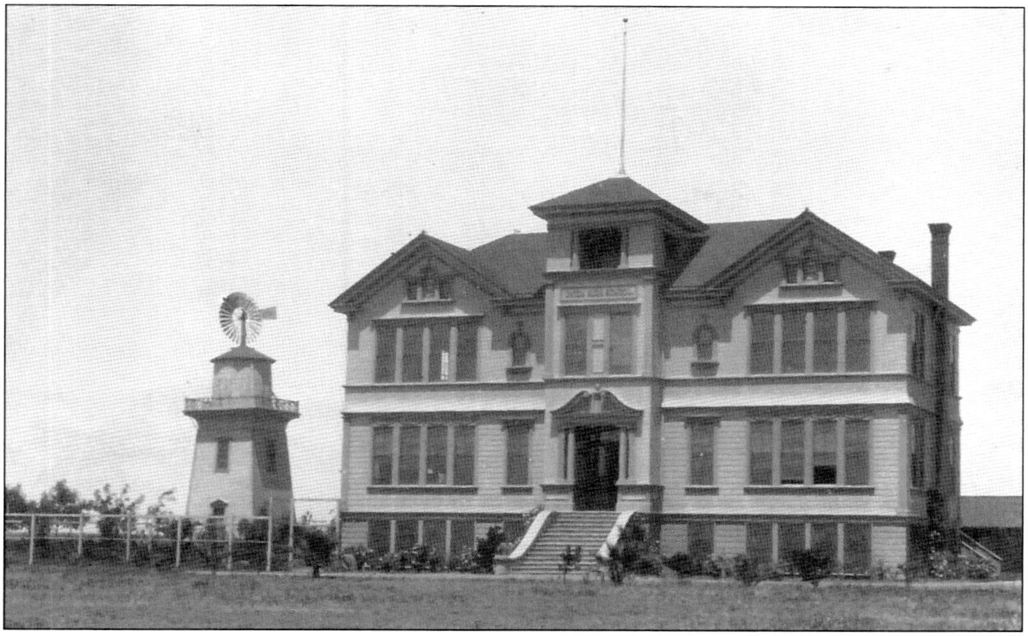

Bids for this new Washington High School (at times also called Centerville High School and Union High School), located on the present Peralta Boulevard, were opened November 5, 1892, and the contract was awarded to Anderson and Greig for $6,582. In spite of a wet season, the construction was rushed and students moved into their new building in March 1893. The school became fully accredited and was giving "preparation for all university courses." Graduates in 1893 were Daniel Crosby and William Jarvis. This building served until 1924, when a new Washington Union High School was built at its present location on Fremont Boulevard.

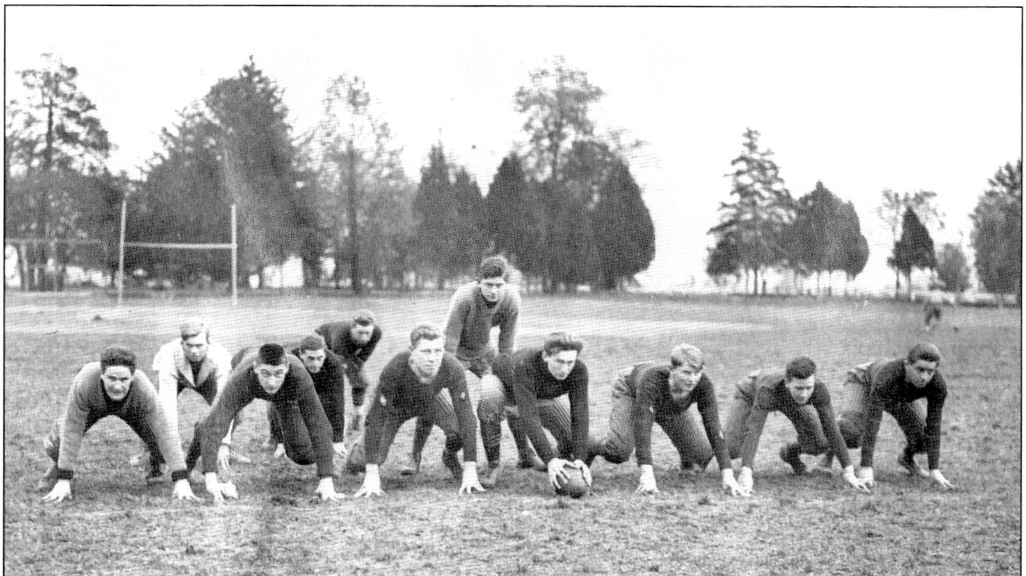

The Centerville High School football team practices on the Bunting fields around 1909. Lawrence Bunting, son of Fleda and John A. Bunting, was on this team.

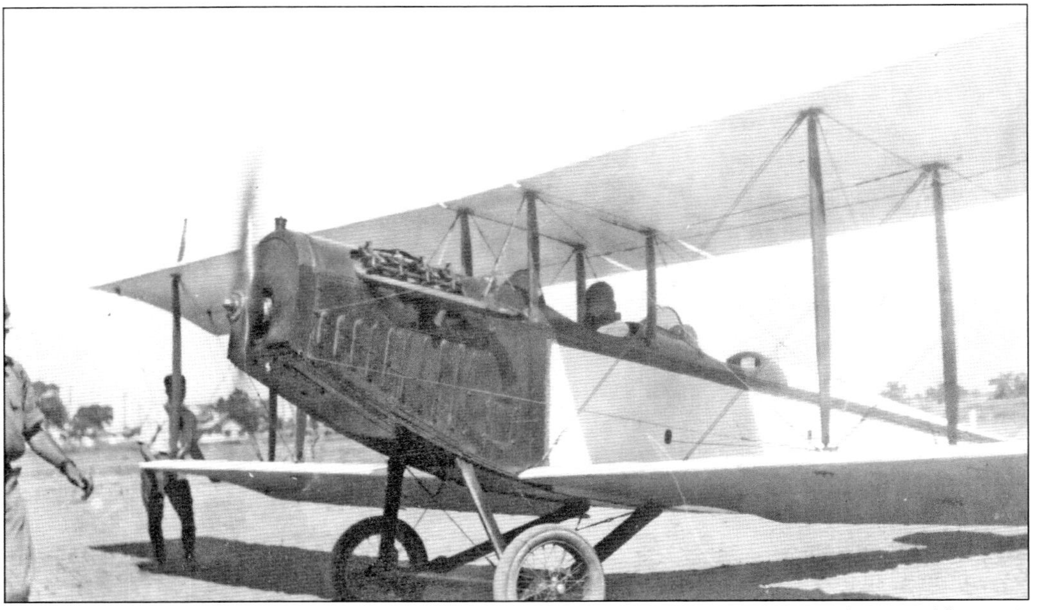

Fleda and John A. Bunting are photographed in their sons' flying machine after World War I. The landing field was the Sycamore Farm cattle pasture. (BJB.)

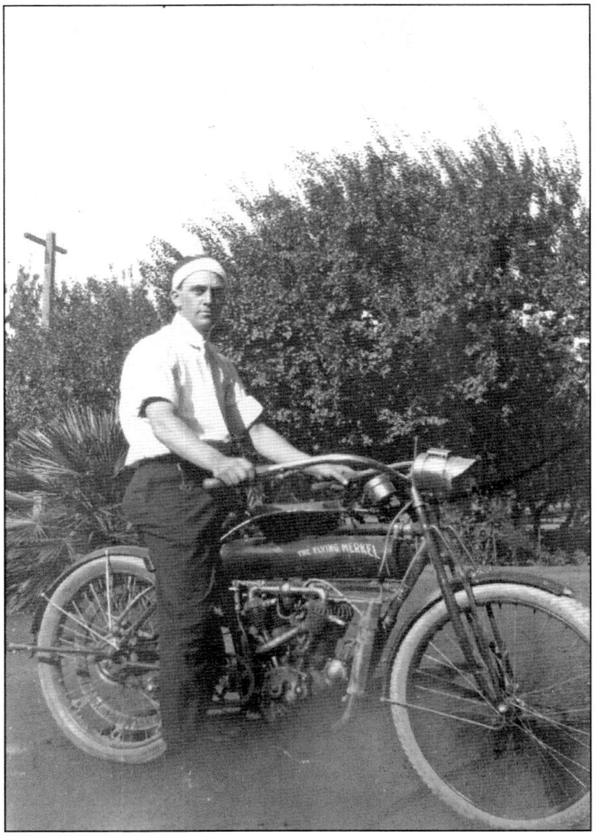

Lawrence "Laurie" Overacker Bunting is pictured with his Flying Merkel. He was injured on this motorcycle in 1912, and after being laid up for months, he married his nurse, Genevieve Garvey of Berkeley. A natural machinist, Bunting worked for the Hall-Scott plant in Berkeley, the F. E. Booth cannery in Centerville, the Schuckl cannery in Manteca, and then as plant superintendent at the Niles sand and gravel company. In World War II, he was a crane operator who helped build C2 cargo ships in Oakland; afterwards he ran the Rhodes-Jamison gravel plant at Centerville. (BJB.)

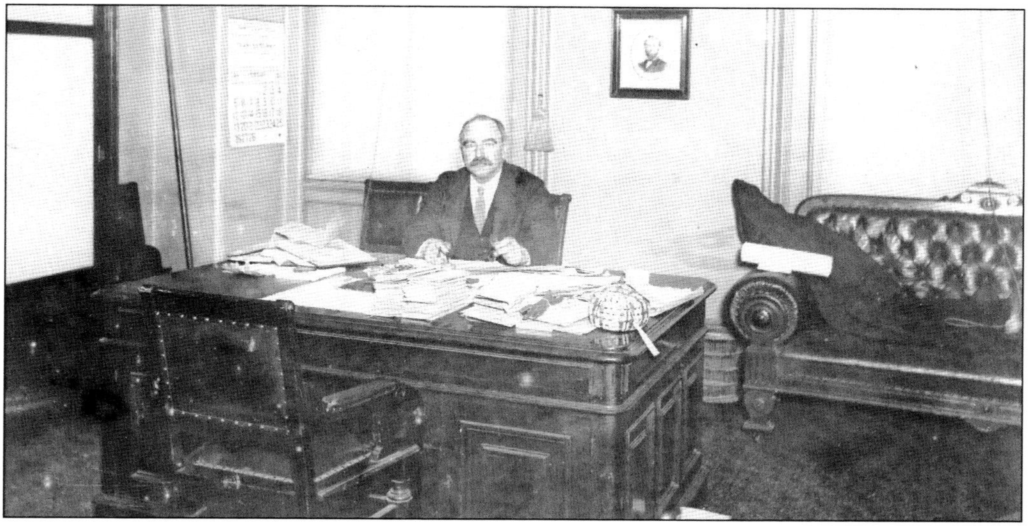

Judge John Mattos Jr. was photographed in his offices in1912. Among his many roles, he was justice of the Centerville court from 1914 to 1922. He and Frank Dusterberry were the founders of the Bank of Centerville in 1905 with a capital stock of $35,000; the stock was valued at of $700,000 in 1913. The John G. Mattos Jr. family home was on Central Avenue, not far from the home of his father, John Mattos Sr., and from the Frank Dusterberry home, which is still standing.

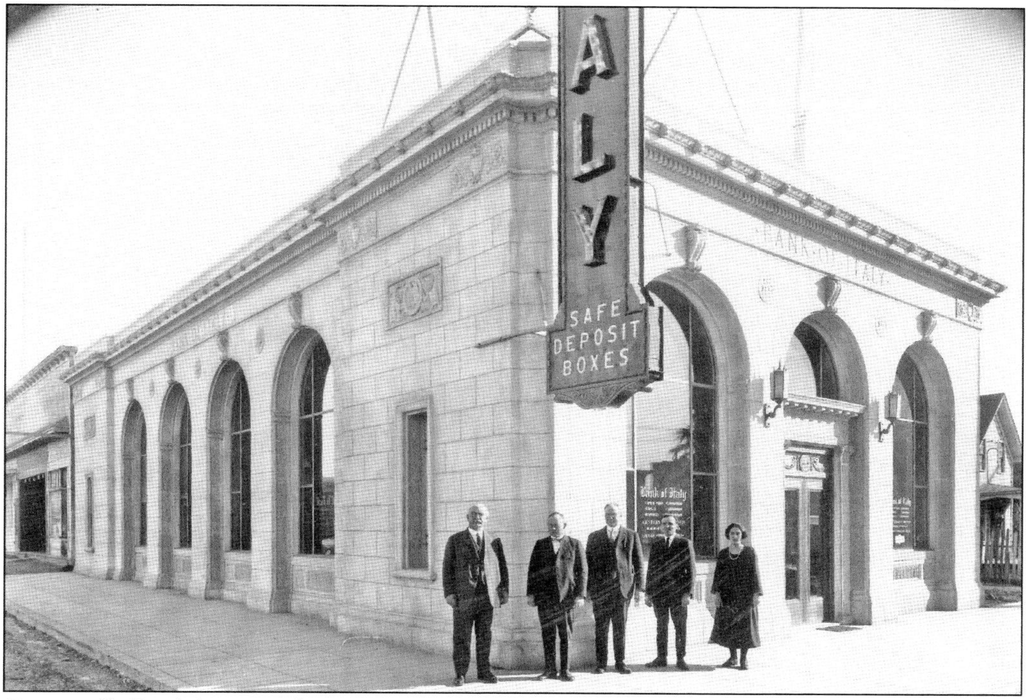

Centerville Bank became the Centerville branch of the Bank of Italy in 1921, then one of the very first branch banks for what would become the Bank of America in 1930, back when branch banking was a new concept in the United States. Amadeo Giannini founded the Bank of Italy in 1904 to provide banking services to immigrants refused service at other banks in San Francisco. His produce background led to his business focusing on the banking needs of farmers.

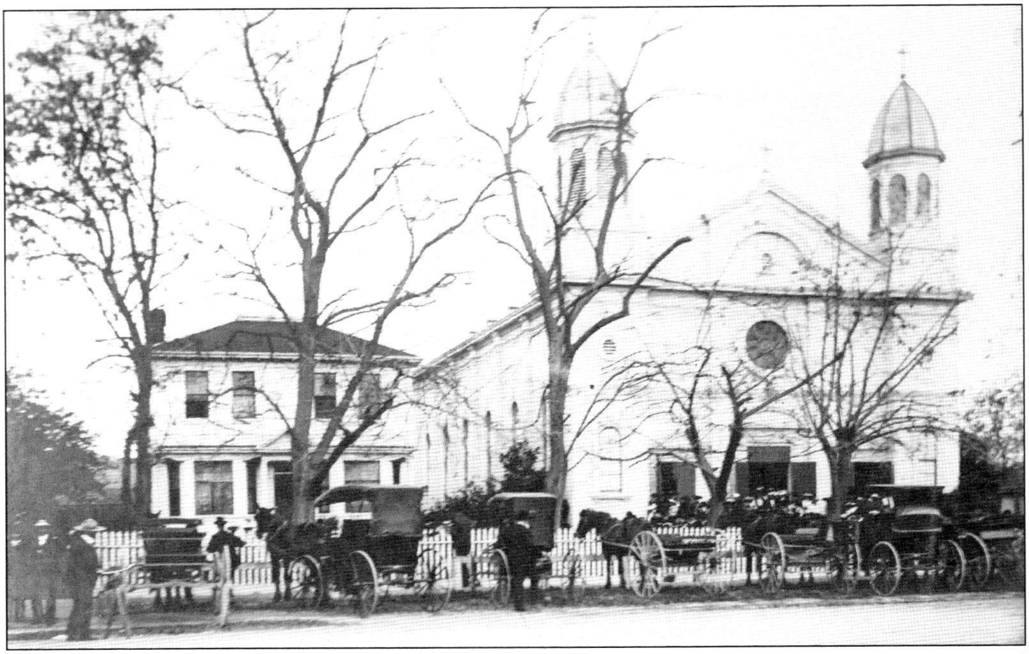

The Holy Ghost Catholic Church of Centerville was built in 1886, with the name later changed to Holy Spirit Catholic Church. Rebuilt after a fire in 1913, it was enlarged and then enlarged again in 1969. Emigrants from the Azores arrived on whaling ships during the 1849 Gold Rush. Until this church was built, they had to travel by horse all the way to Mission San Jose for christenings and other services.

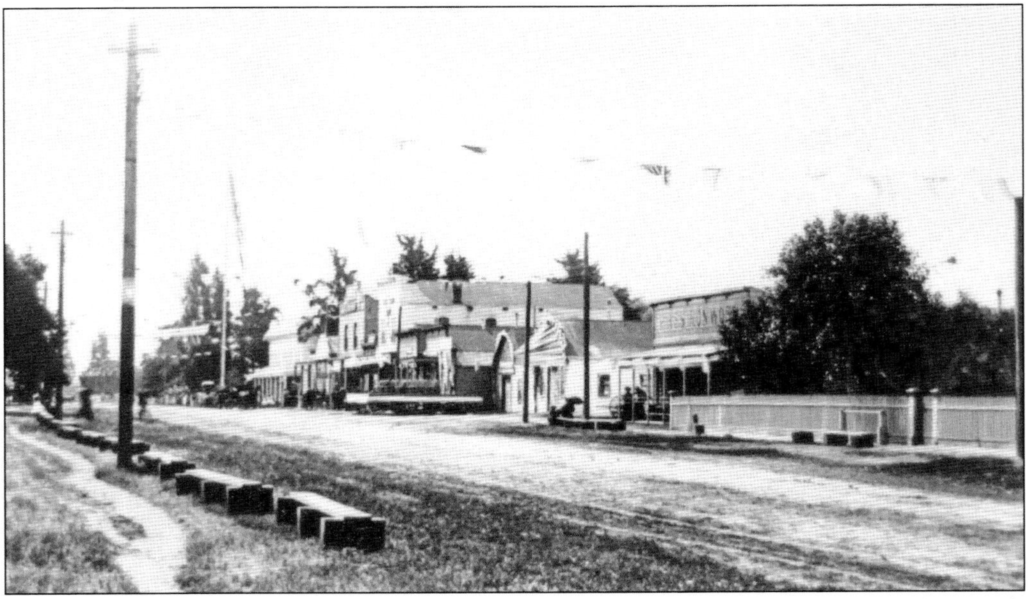

Centerville parade benches are set out in front of the Presbyterian church, ready for all the Fourth of July visitors in 1911. The Centerville Improvement Club had been meeting for over a year in the fraternal hall at the dry goods store. The parade celebrated not only Independence Day but also Centerville being home to a full-scale train station and regular train service.

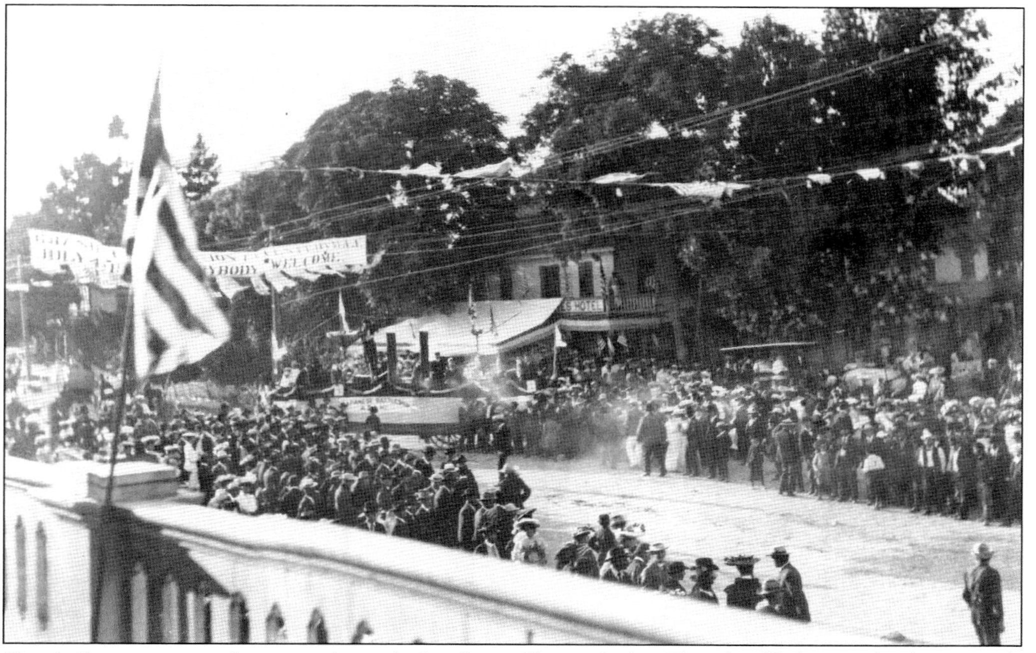

Carrie Emerson was the town doctor's daughter. She took this Fourth of July parade photograph in 1904 from the upper verandah of the Gregory House Hotel, looking toward the intersection at Niles Road.

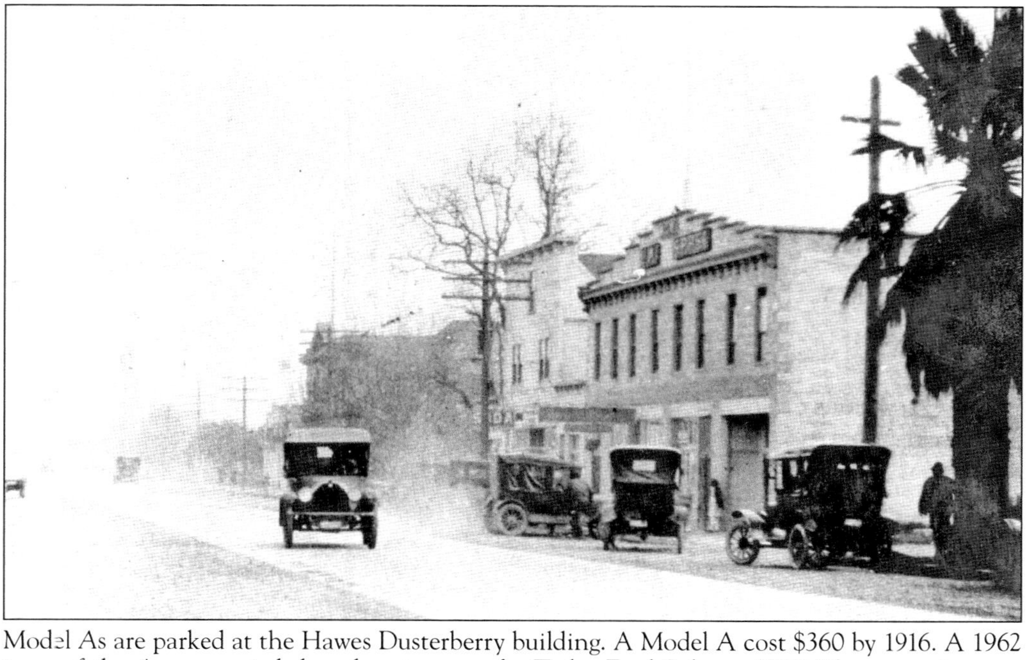

Model As are parked at the Hawes Dusterberry building. A Model A cost $360 by 1916. A 1962 issue of the *Argus* carried the advertisement for Tudor Ford Sales at 3909 Thornton Avenue: "From axle to axle, '63 Ford Pickups are built like big trucks. But they're mighty easy on you! Riding's easier with Ford's 2-stage springs and extra insulation. Driving's easier with Ford's new no clash transmission."

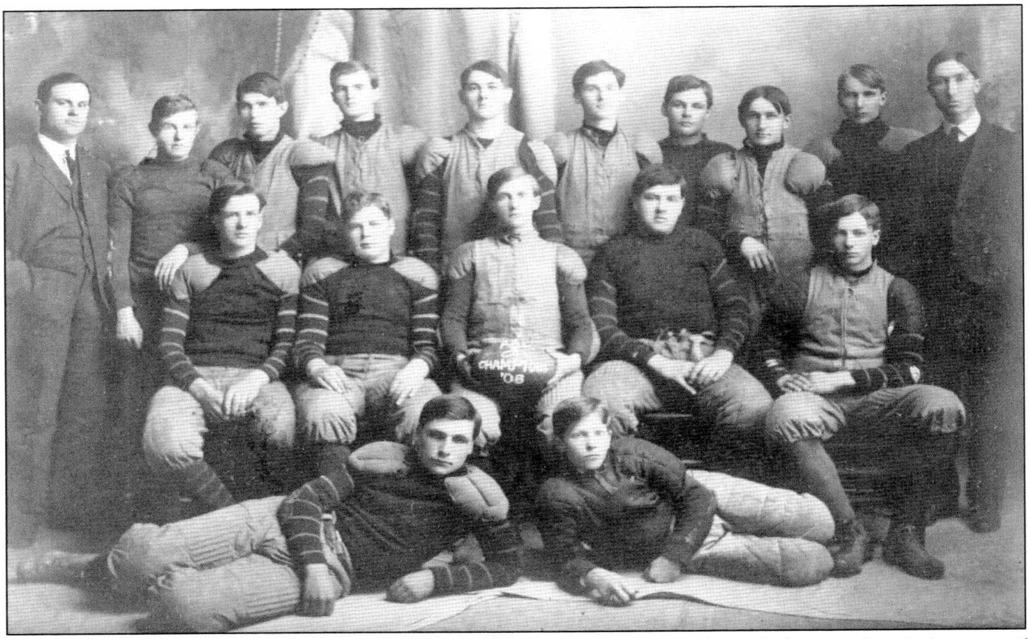

The Centerville High School football team won the championship of the academic league of Northern California and the state championship in 1906 under coach/manager Wolsey Shaw. In 1905, Pres. Theodore Roosevelt threatened to shut down college football after a number of fatalities. Stanford University and the University of California switched sports from football to rugby, though after the forward pass of football was added to the rules of rugby, the game began to take on the modern form of football.

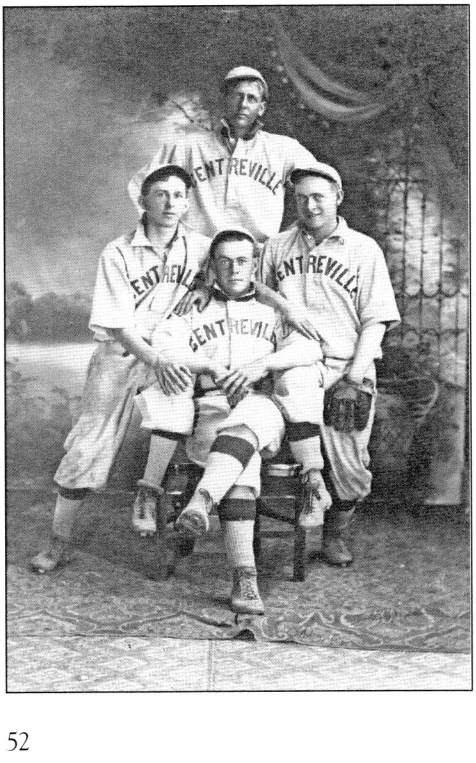

The Centerville baseball team took on Mill Valley at the fenced baseball grounds behind the train station for the 1911 July Fourth celebrations. Cyrus "Cy" Hanson is pictured standing at the back. Admission to the game was 25¢. At the same time, there was dancing in the town hall, also for 25¢. Throughout the afternoon, free entertainment included Japanese wrestling and fencing, fireworks, vaudeville performances, and a band concert.

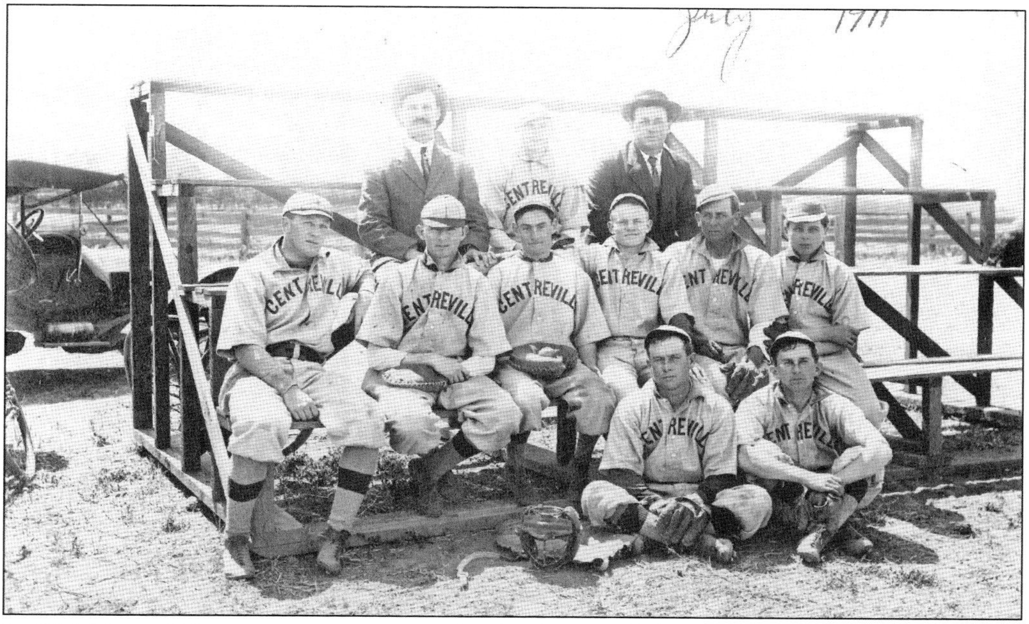

In 1911, Manuel Simas procured new suits for the Centerville baseball team for their July Fourth match against Mill Valley. He is at left in the back row in the team photograph. (MS.)

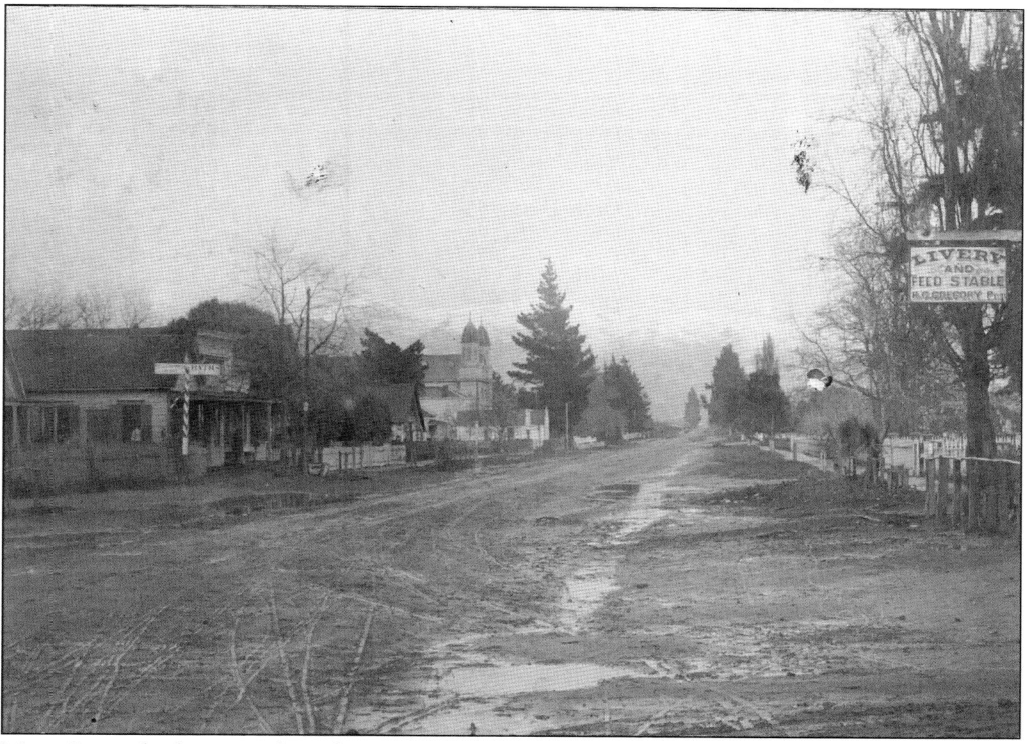

Main Street looking south with snow on Mission Peak. On the right is the "Livery and Feed Stable" sign at the Gregory Hotel. Further up the street on the left can be seen the spires of the Holy Ghost Church. (MS.)

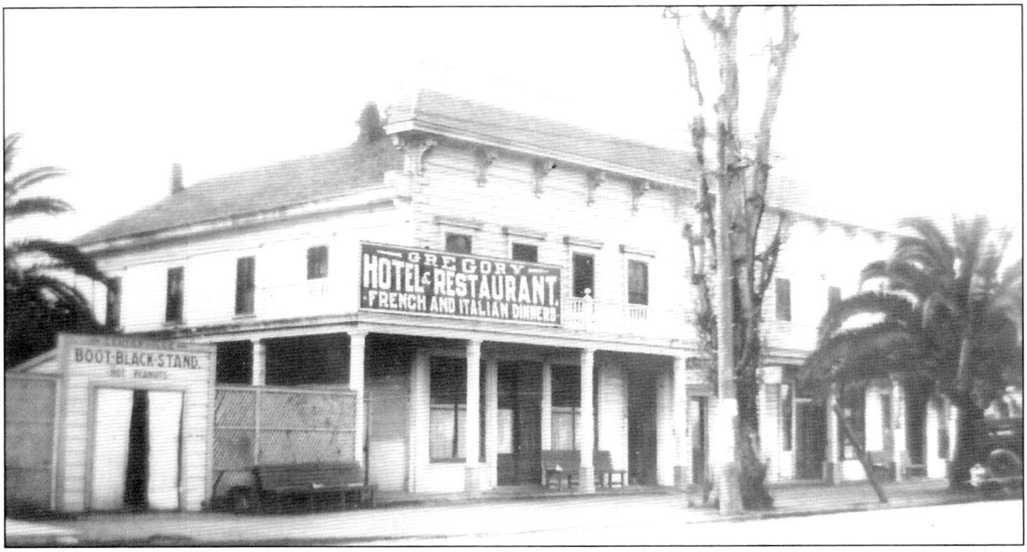

Henry Gregory built the Gregory House Hotel, which became famous for its French and Italian dinners, in 1869. He operated a livery stable in conjunction with the hotel. There were a number of proprietors after Henry's death. The hotel was razed in 1949.

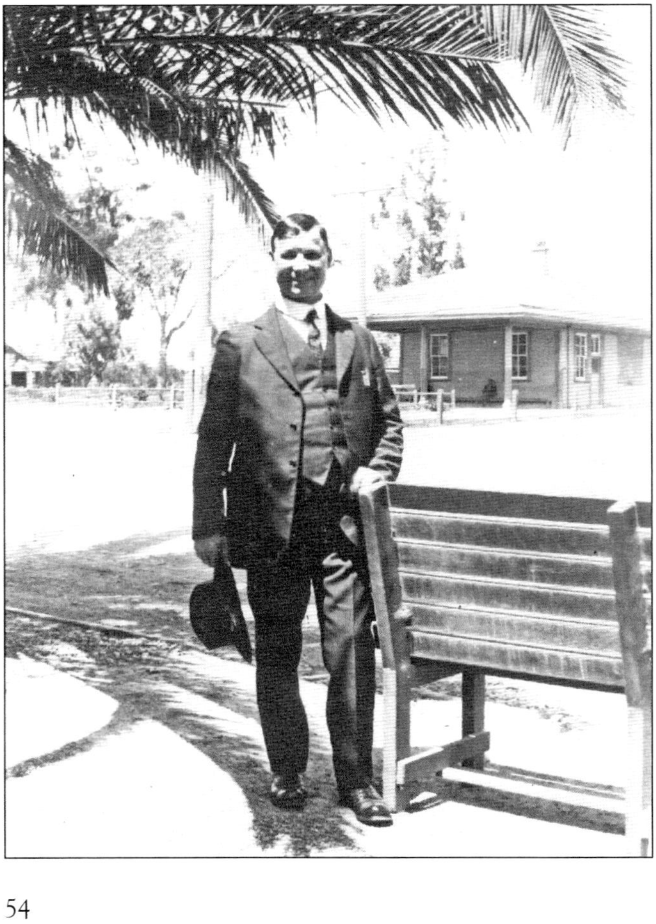

Manuel Simas stands proudly at the 1910 train station. The station was restored in 1999 and is now located on the opposite side of the tracks. The original site has been replaced by Bill Ball Plaza, named for the Fremont mayor (1989–1994) who lived and worked in the Glenmoor neighborhood of Centerville. (MS.)

At the Gregory House Hotel, a happy group with parasols enjoys the 1904 July Fourth celebrations. The day's events included remarks by Frank Hawes, followed by the reading of the Declaration of Independence by Thomas Power, a lawyer from Irvington. The "Star-Spangled Banner" was sung by Lida Thane, followed by the oration by the Honorable William Donahue, a graduate of Washington College and elected judge of the superior court. The assembly ended the ceremony by singing "America the Beautiful."

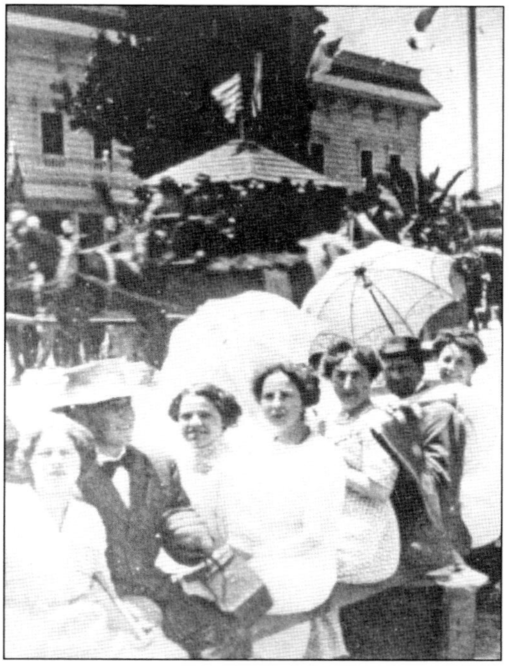

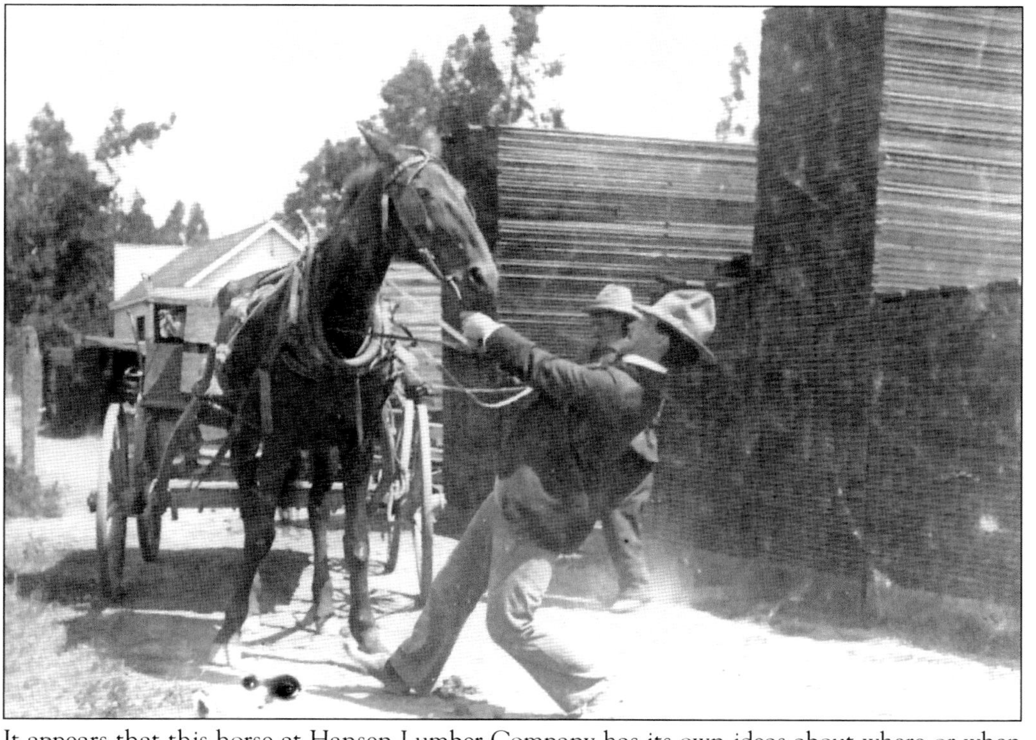

It appears that this horse at Hansen Lumber Company has its own ideas about where or when to go. P. C. Hansen founded his lumber company in Centerville in 1906. Later he established branch yards in other towns in Washington Township. Hansen died in 1935, but his son Earl carried on the business until the 1950s.

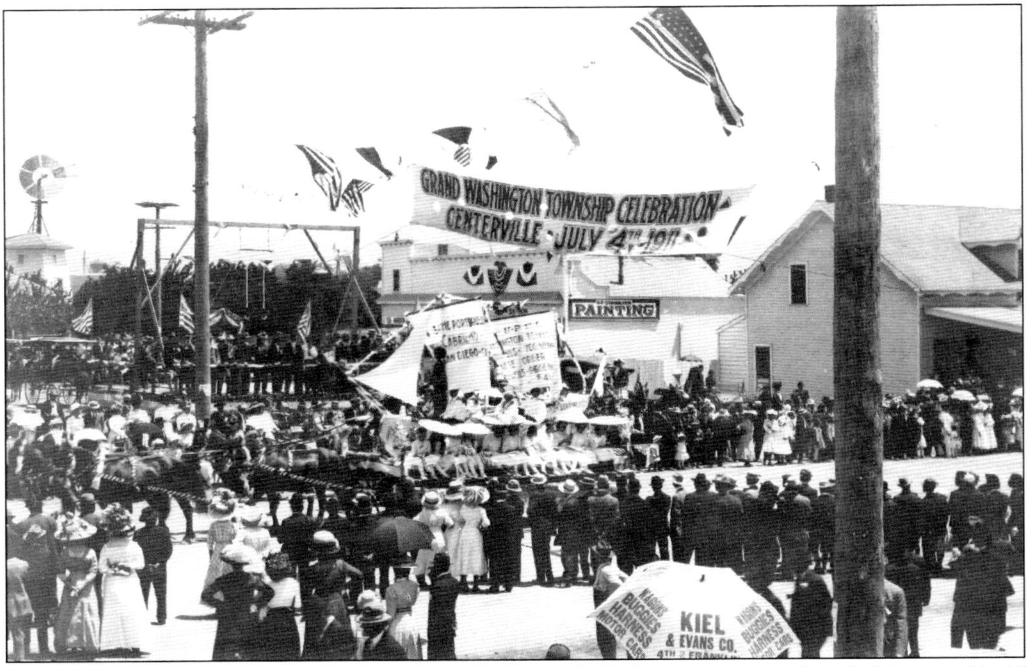

The banner in this photograph announces the "Grand Washington Township Celebration" held at Centerville on July 4, 1911. Spectators enjoyed the parade as well as the exhibition of athletic feats that included boxing and trapeze performances.

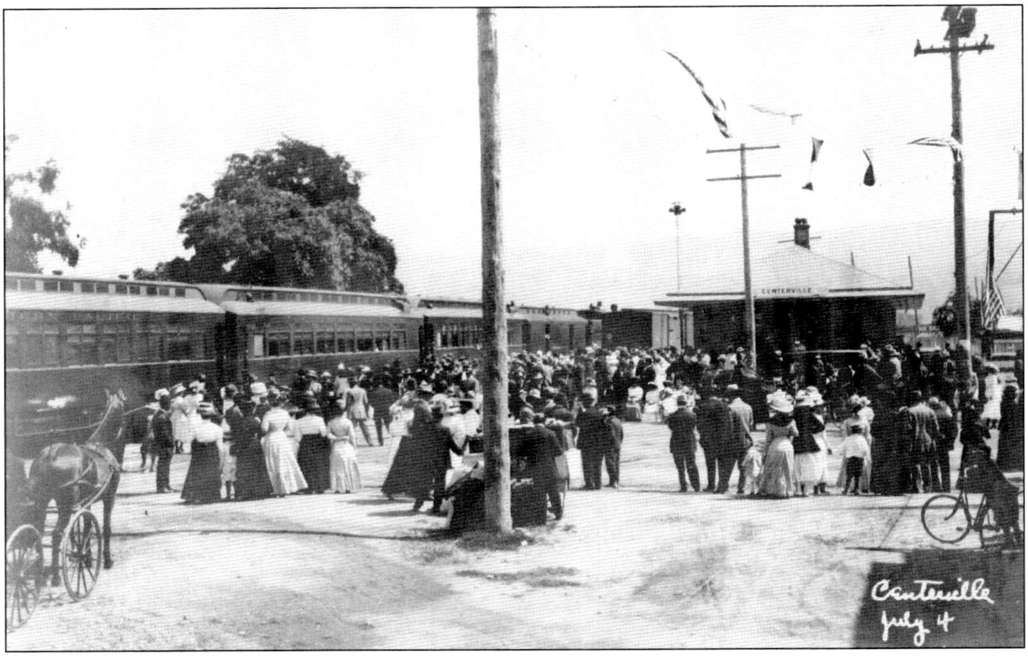

Here the parade passes in front of the train station. Participants included the San Francisco Concert Band and the Centerville Brass Band as well as school and industrial floats. Many fraternal orders marched, and there was a large contingent of automobiles.

The Yankee Doodle Band was created for the 1911 Fourth of July celebrations because there was not a band program at Washington High School until John Kimber began one in 1927. The parade printed programs describing the stages of the parade as "divisions," as if they were military units. The third division began with the Decoto band, ladies driving, family carriages, other floats, and the Japanese and Warm Springs contingents. The fourth division was led by the clown band, ladies riding horseback, cowboys, and automobiles.

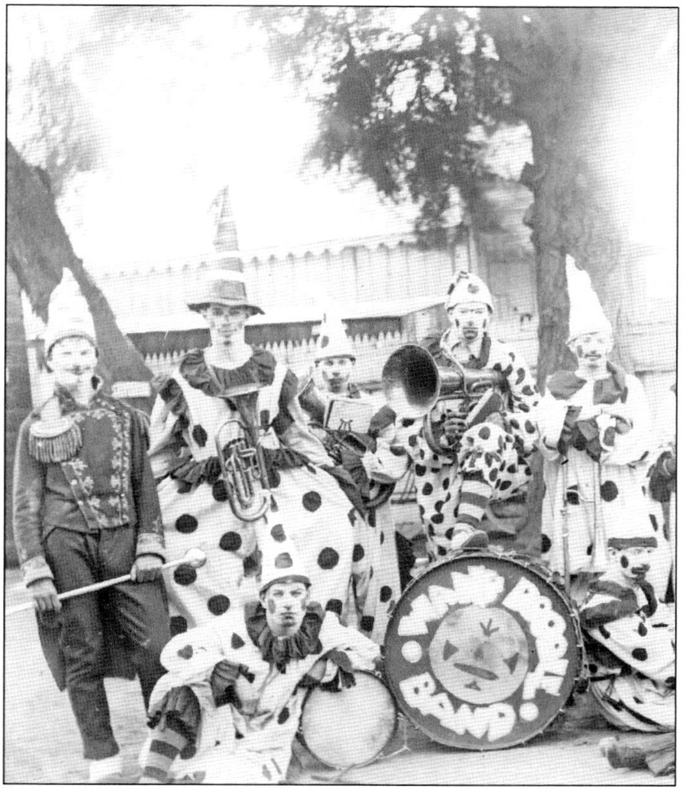

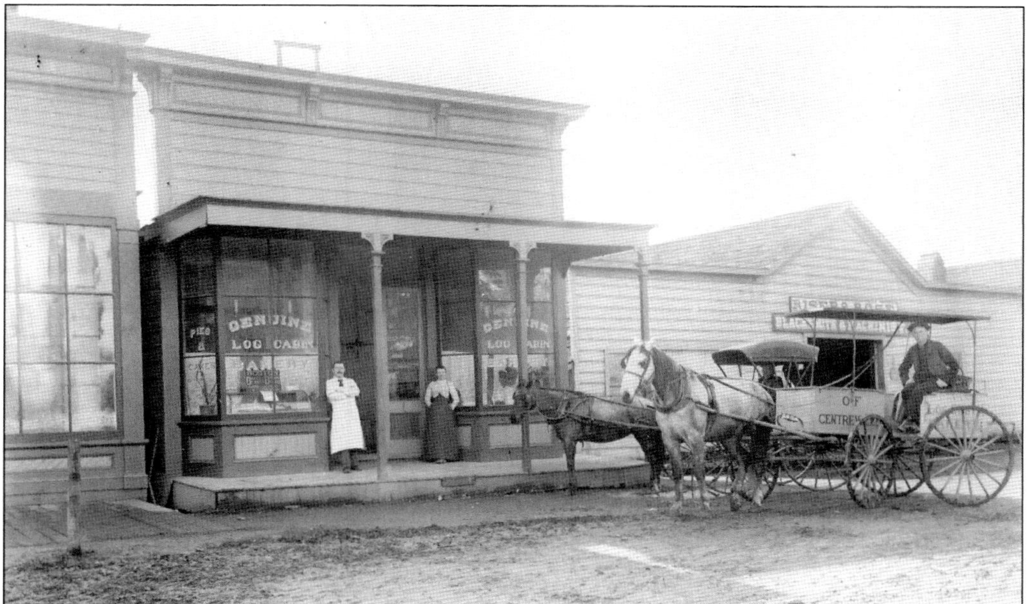

Proprietors of the Genuine Log Cabin Bakery stand in front of their business, which offers "Pies and Cakes" and "Boston Baked Beans and Boston Brown Bread Every Saturday." Their delivery wagon, equipped with bells, stands in front of Riser and Rose Blacksmith and Machinist. (BLB.)

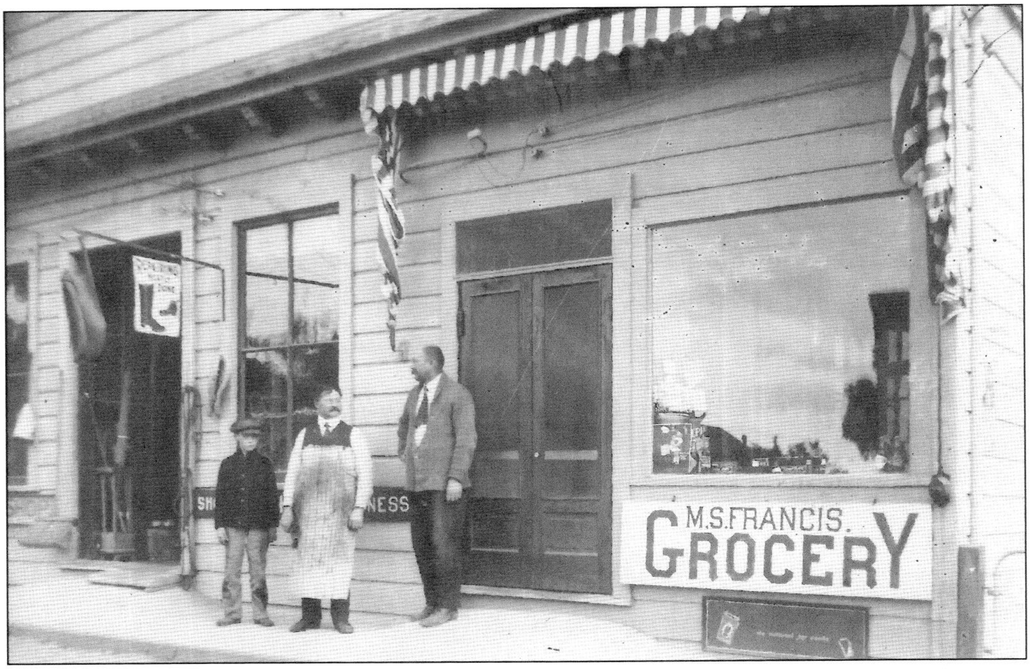

Commercial enterprises on the east side of Main Street, south of the town hall in the early 1900s included M. S. Francis Grocery and the Centerville Soda Works.

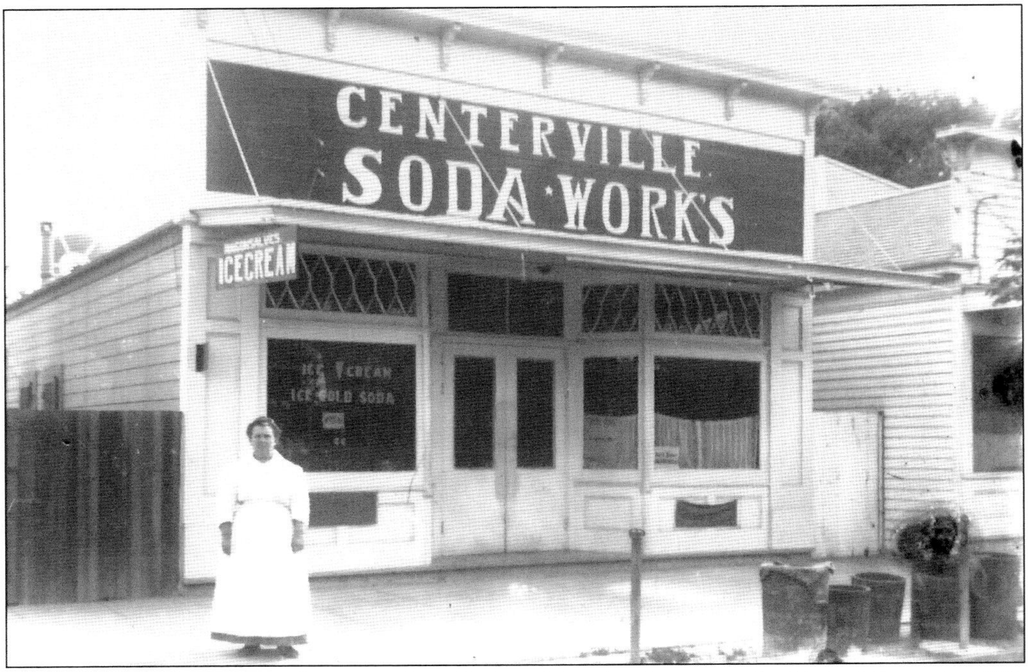

The term "soda water" was first coined in 1798, and bottling began in the United States in 1835. Soda became very popular, and soda works appeared everywhere. By the late 1800s, many flavors were being enjoyed. The beverage was sold in bottles bearing the maker's name and delivered in horse-drawn wagons. The Centerville Soda Works operated on Main Street in the early 1900s.

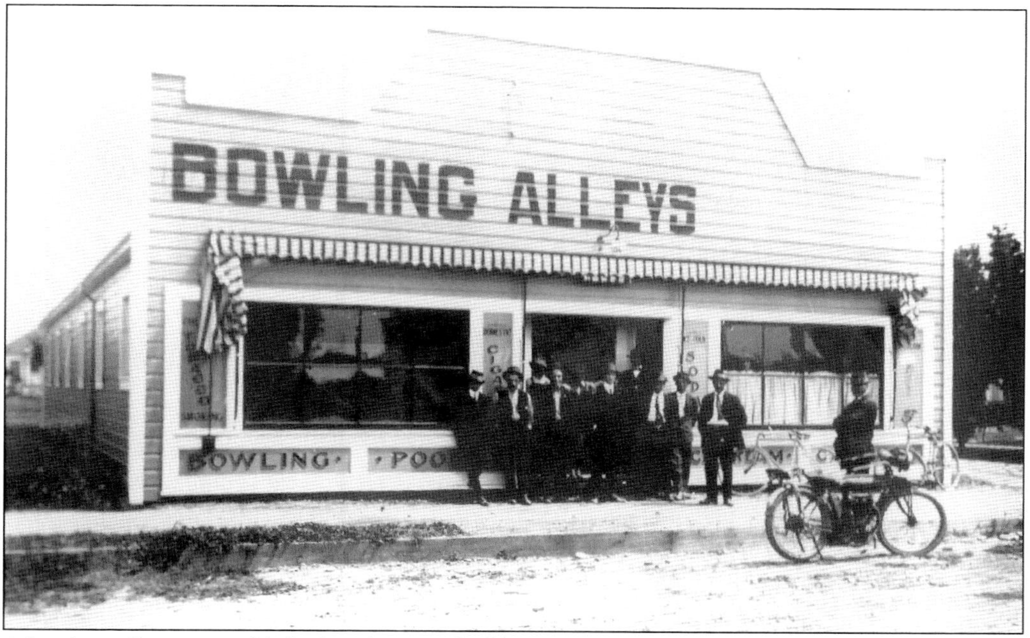

A bowling alley was established in the town hall basement, and some years later a new bowling alley was constructed by Randall, Maul, and Herman, as pictured here. A large crowd of onlookers was reported at a 1916 bowling tournament between Irvington and Centerville at the "new Centerville Bowling Alley." Details about this match are not available, but Dr. Elmo Grimmer was a member of the Irvington team and Ralph Emerson was on the Centerville team. Apparently, Irvington and Centerville were frequent competitors.

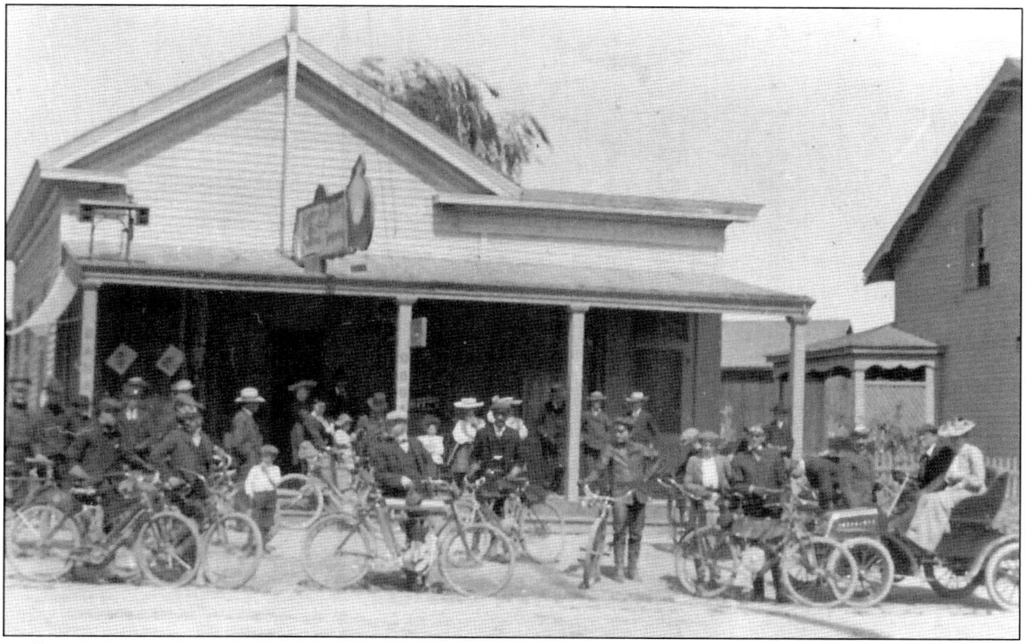

Bells Ice Cream and Cycle Shop was a popular meeting place for cyclists. Writers noticed that "the bicycle was what made the Gay Nineties gay and did much to liberate women."

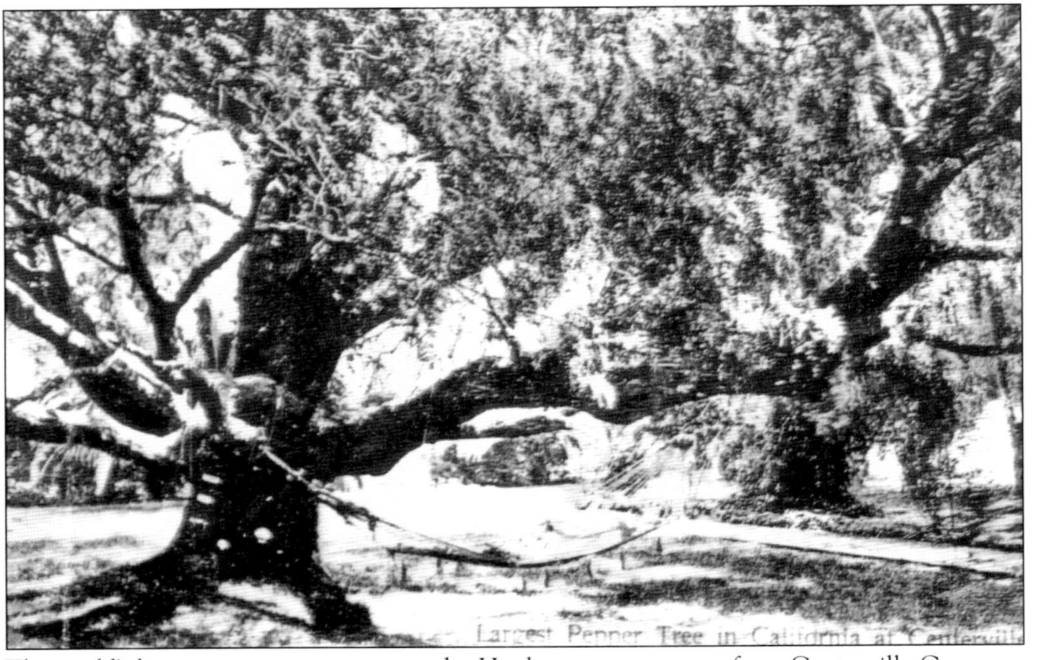

The world's largest pepper tree grew on the Huxley property across from Centerville Grammar School. The tree was planted for decades before the Huxley's built their home in 1880. Often called the California pepper tree and admired for its delicate leaves and sprays of tiny pink peppercorns, Schinus molle is actually native to western South America. Brought to California in the Mission era, these trees have provided shade here ever since. The tree continues to prosper at the Pepper Tree Apartment complex.

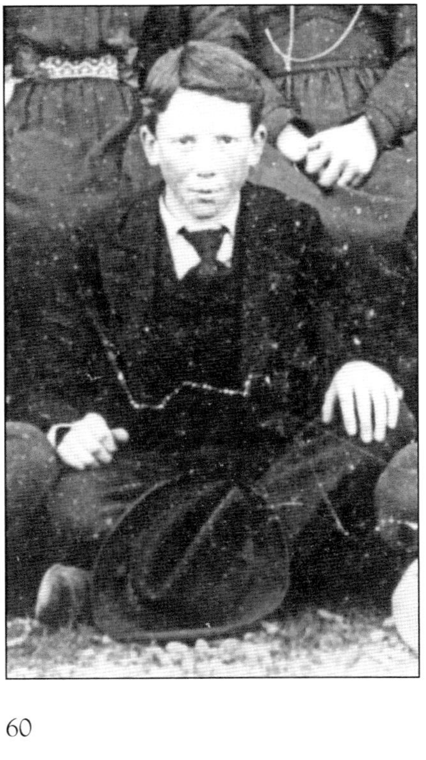

This schoolboy at Centerville Public School in 1910 is Arthur Yates, grandson of Lorenzo Gordin Yates, 1837–1909. Lorenzo Yates was a part-time dentist and full-time fossil-collecting scientist who lived east of Sycamore Farm in the 1870s. Yates published numerous ethnology, conchology, and botanical papers and retired to Santa Barbara in the 1880s to pursue these interests by running a botanical garden there.

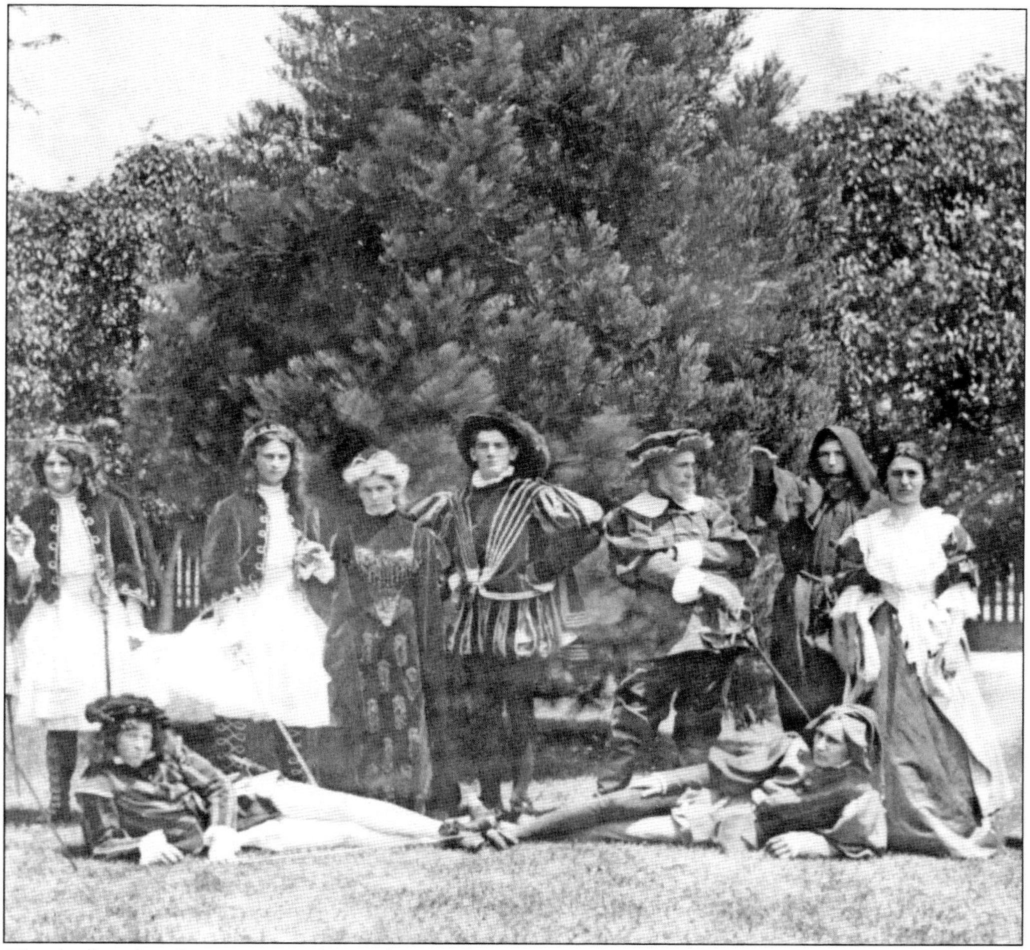

The high school seniors performed *A Midsummer Night's Dream* at Patterson ranch in 1908. According to the *Hatchet* in 1925, "The Class of 1904 produced *Everyman*, an old English morality play. Under Mr. Mayer several other Shakespearean plays were produced. . . . Later it became the custom to produce modern comedies and farces."

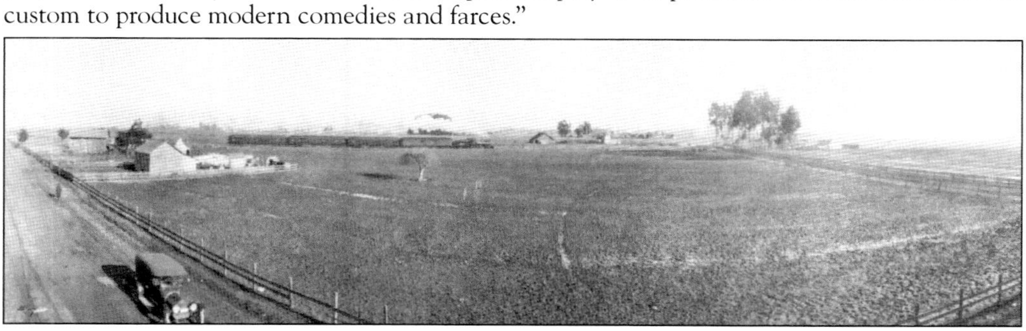

This Swiss dairy was photographed near Coyote Hills. An American investor, Reverend Briggs, bought and leased Coyote Hills to tenants. One of them in 1906 was Louis Zwissig, owner of the Denver Dairy. Briggs also leased the area above the visitors center to F. M. "Borax" Smith for a duck hunting lodge in 1883. Smith developed the marsh below the lodge to attract ducks. In 1916, the Pattersons expanded the duck pond and built their own lodge.

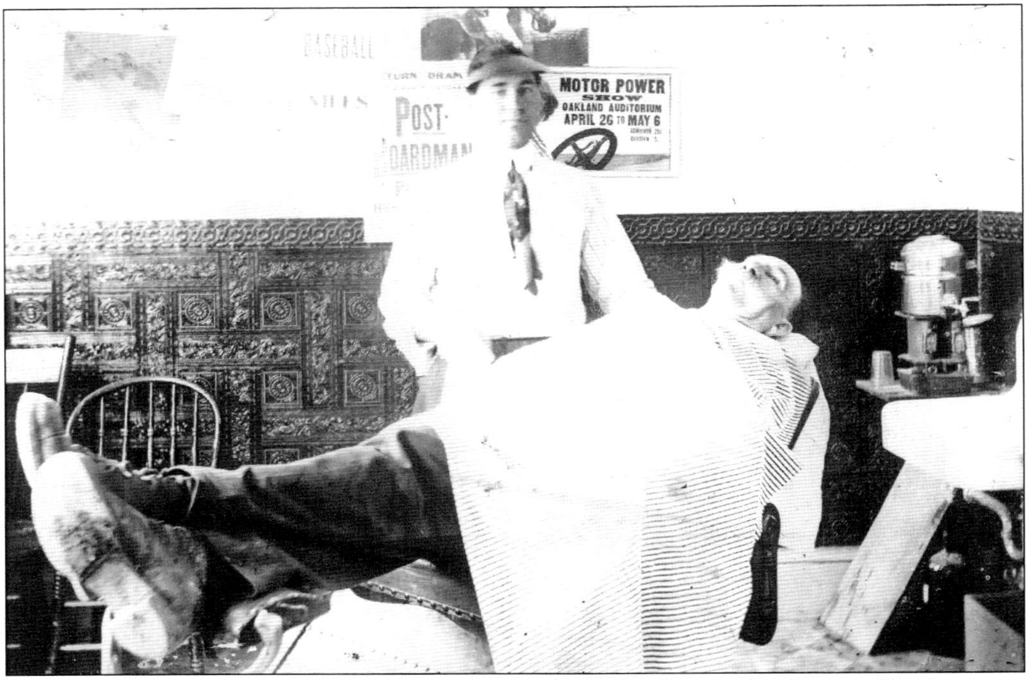

This *c.* 1880 photograph was taken at the Centerville barbershop in the Gregory Hotel.

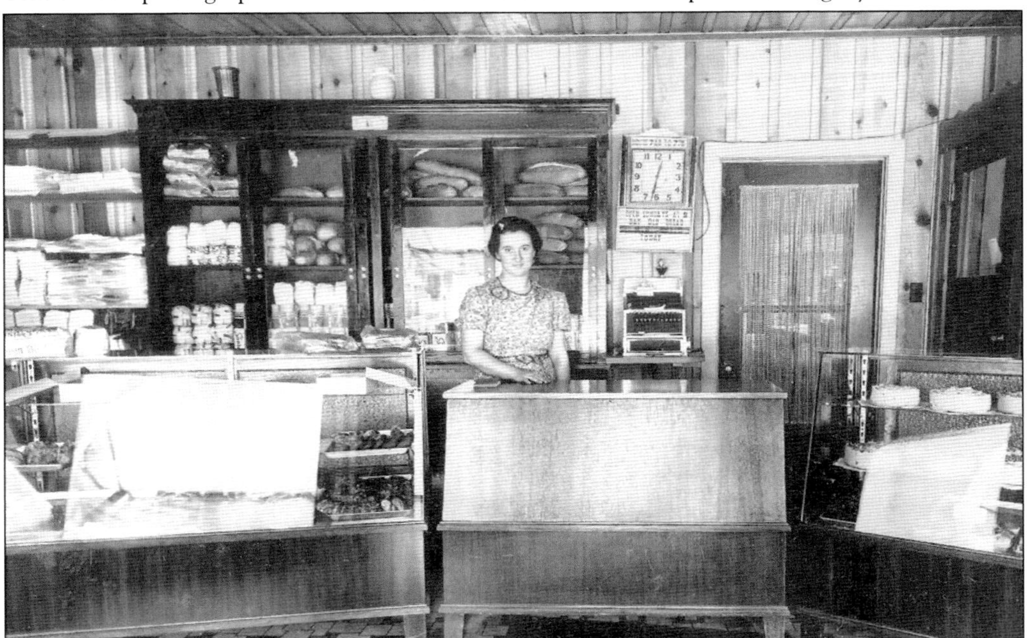
Lawrence and Emiline Rose opened the Sunrise Bakery at 161 South Main Street in 1937 (as pictured). They started the business with two used trucks and used bakery equipment. Their first bread cost 7¢ a loaf. They expanded and operated their business until they retired in 1974. (Courtesy Emiline and Lawrence Rose.)

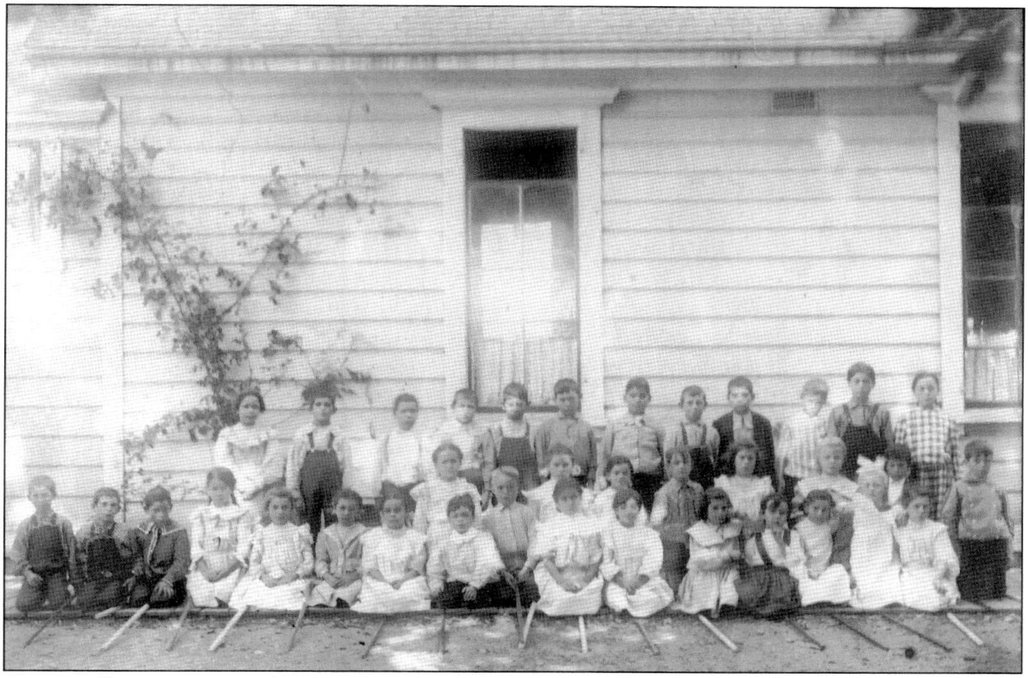

Centerville Grammar School students pose in front of the building in 1907–1908.

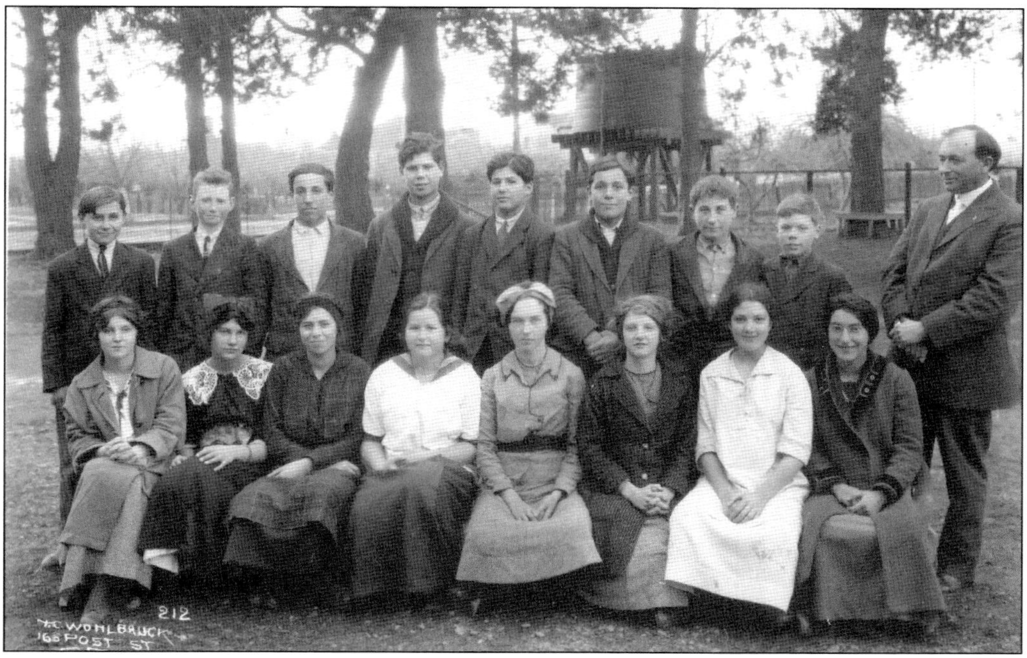

Centerville's eighth-grade graduates gathered for this photograph in 1915. Standing on the right is principal Joseph Dias. Front row center is teacher Irma Bond. Students include, from left to right, (first row) Byrd Thompson, Rilla Bell, Christine Vierra, Sara Blacow, Irma Bond (teacher), Bernice Thompson, Irma Vargas, and Carrie Oliveira; (second row) Frank Pine, Allen Norris, Fred Lewis, John Vierra, Alphonso Silva, Manuel Lewis, Tom Furtado, and George Wright Jr. .

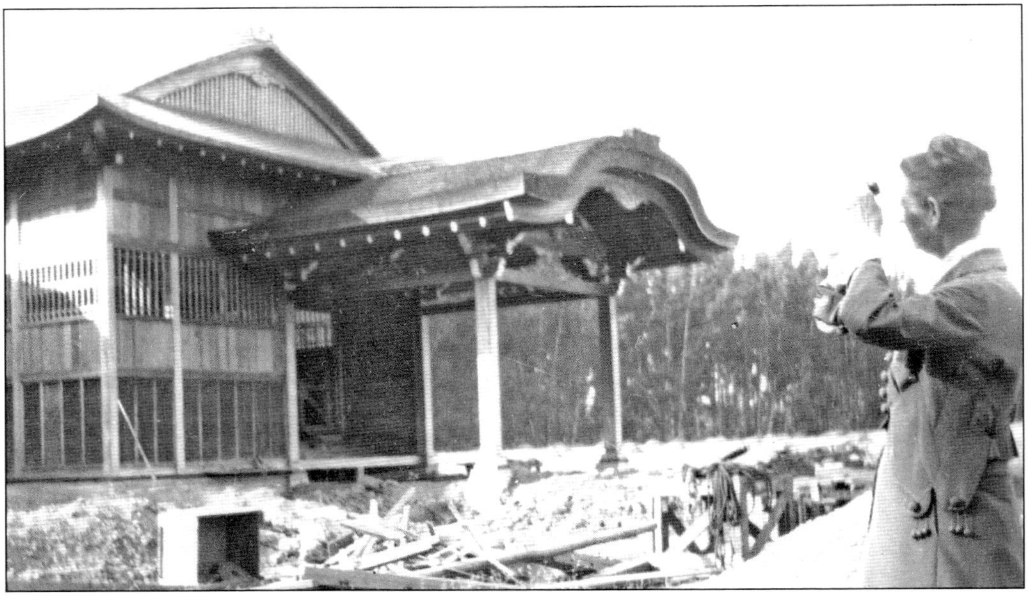

The relocated Japanese pavilion's officer quarters are inspected by architect Julia Morgan for remodeling. The structure was purchased from the 1915 Pan-Pacific International Exhibition, barged across the bay to Patterson Landing, and transported to a site east of the Patterson house. Clara Patterson Layton intended to use the structure for her home, but she died in 1917, before the completed building plans could be put into action. The empty building was burned after news of the attack on Pearl Harbor on December 7, 1941.

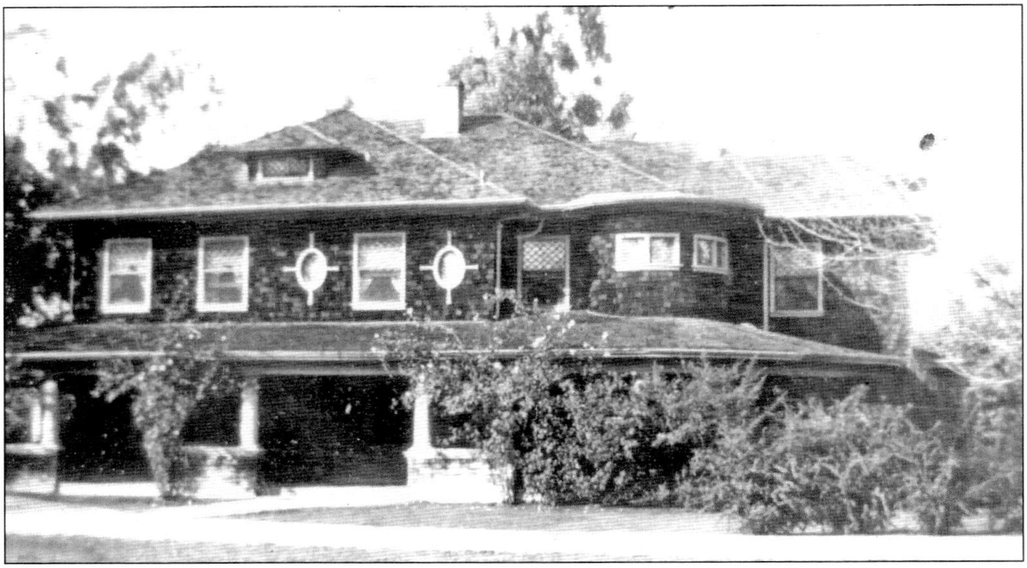

William Patterson married May Bird in 1903, and they built this large shingle house in a Bay Area style with local materials and sweeping rooflines. It was constructed for $12,000 and located about a mile east of the main Patterson house. Patterson helped found the Alameda County Water District and was a board member of it from 1914 to 1958, serving as president for 22 of those years. He died in 1961, and by the heirs' request, the house was burned as part of a Newark fire department training exercise.

Four

Tennis, Anyone?
1920–1939

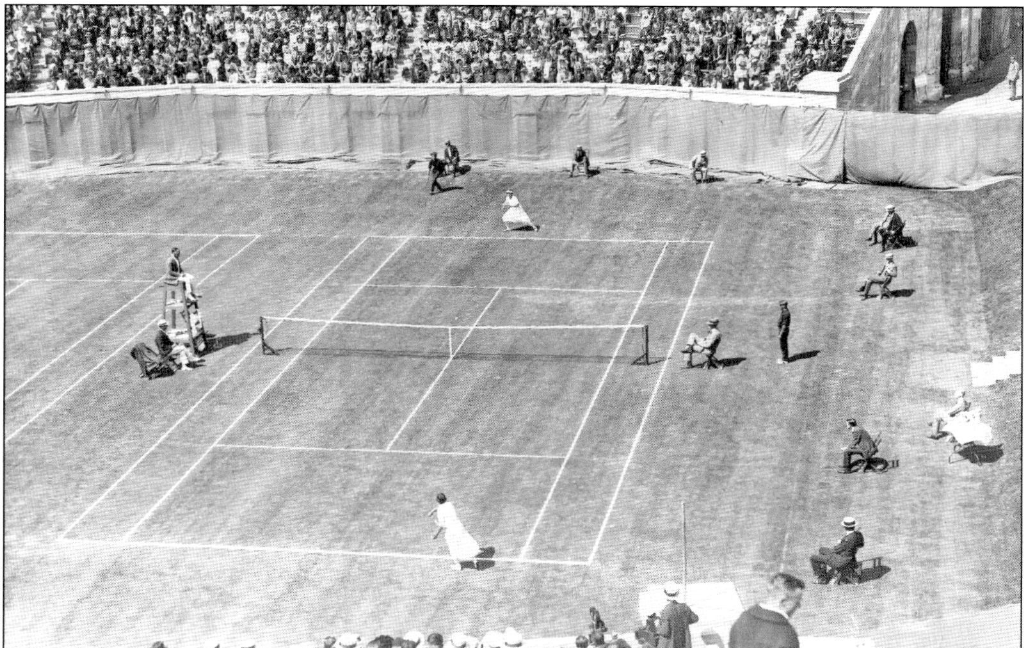

On July 13, 1972, the *Oakland Tribune* reported, "Known as 'Little Miss Pokerface,' Helen Wills Moody from Centerville won her first title in 1921 and went on to become a world champion tennis player for more than a decade." The article was part of a series remembering famous people from the Bay Area. The dry nickname bestowed by sportswriter Grantland Rice later gave way to others. As her string of titles accumulated, she was known in England as *La Belle Hélène*.

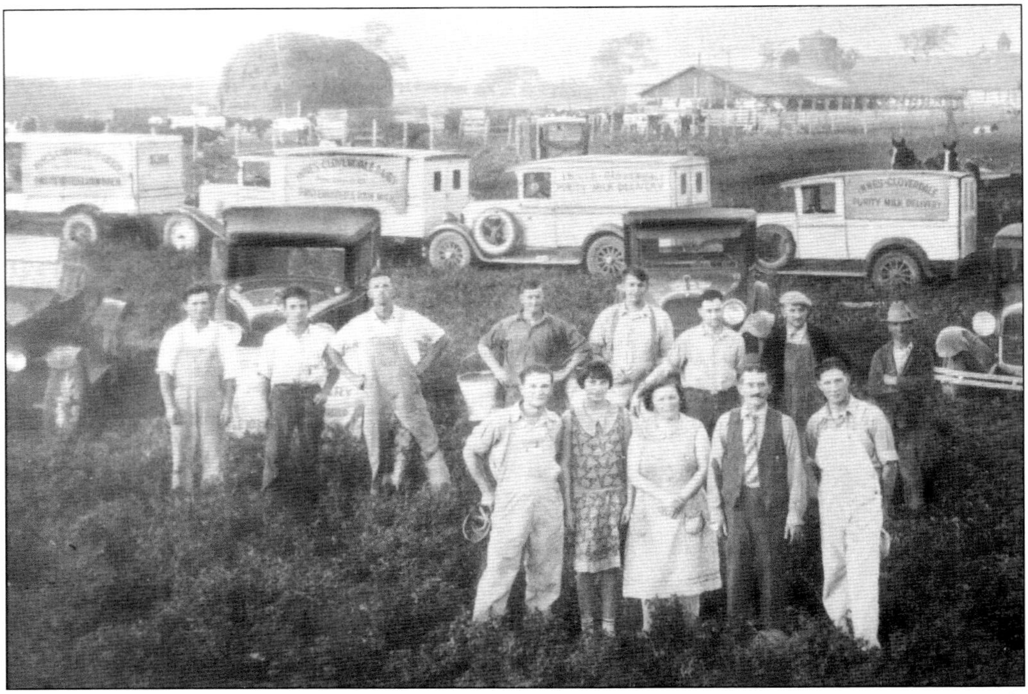

The Bauhofer family (first row) moved to Centerville in 1927 to operate the Innes-Cloverdale Dairy on the Chadbourne Ranch. Family members and hired hands (second row) farmed about 127 acres of land that is now the Hub, put up some 600 tons of hay, milked 120 cows by hand twice a day, made home deliveries of milk, and started the first processing center in Washington Township. The workers and the two brothers slept upstairs in the old carriage house. The Bauhofer family members pictured in this 1927 photograph in the foreground include Joe Jr., Lily, Emma, Joe Sr., and Bill. (BF.)

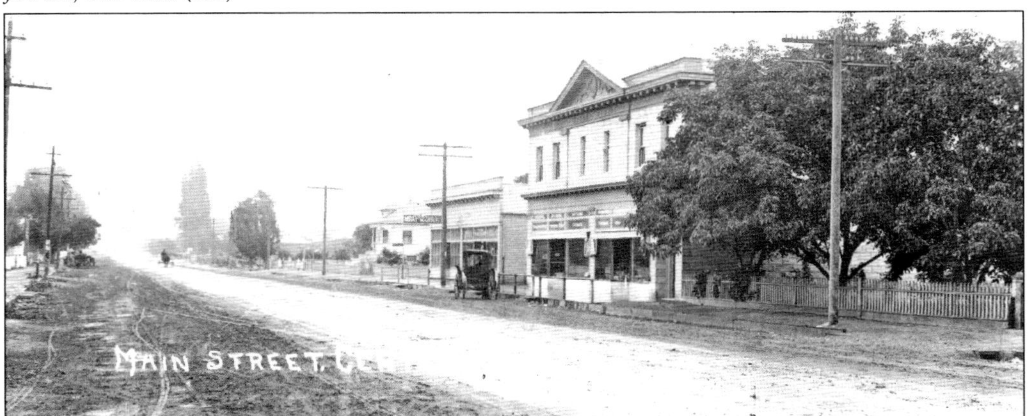

This is a southern view of Main Street. According to the *Hometowns in Southern Alameda County* in 1936, "Situated centrally in Washington Township and deriving its name from that position, Centerville is located 27 miles from Oakland on a State Highway leading to San Jose through Niles and Mission San Jose, or through Irvington and Warm Springs. . . . It is the home of the township's half million dollar union high school, the justice court and constabulary, and several organizations which serve the township as a whole."

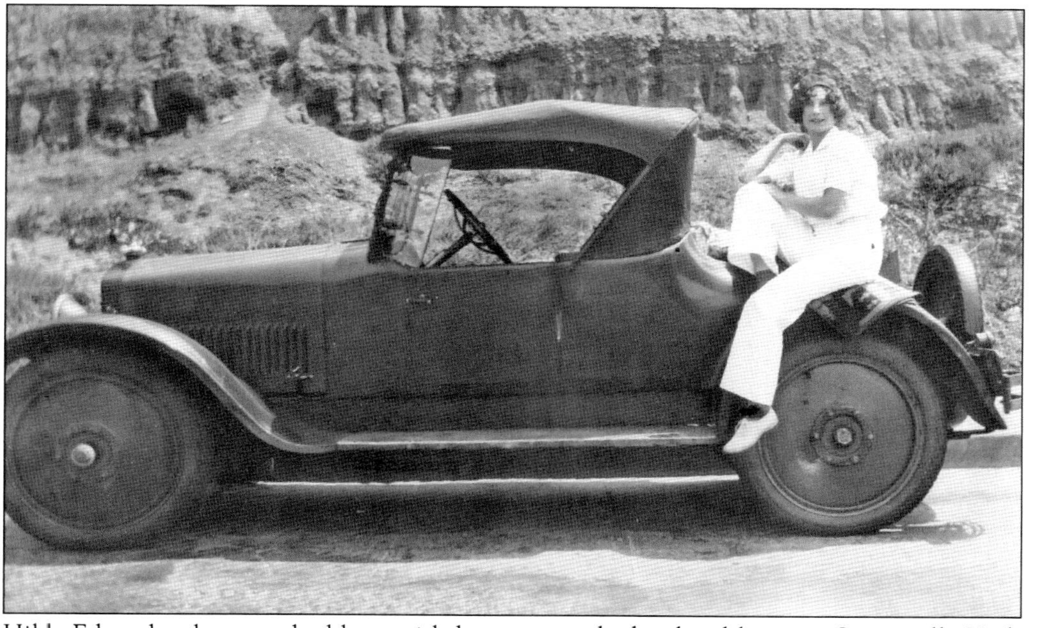

Hilda Edwards, photographed here with her car, coached girls athletics at Centerville High School in 1923, during a time when such sports were new. Helen Wills Moody was likely the first internationally celebrated female athlete born in the United States. She won 31 Grand Slam titles in tennis, eight wins at Wimbledon, and two gold medals at the 1924 Olympics. Her first national win occurred when she was just 17 years old.

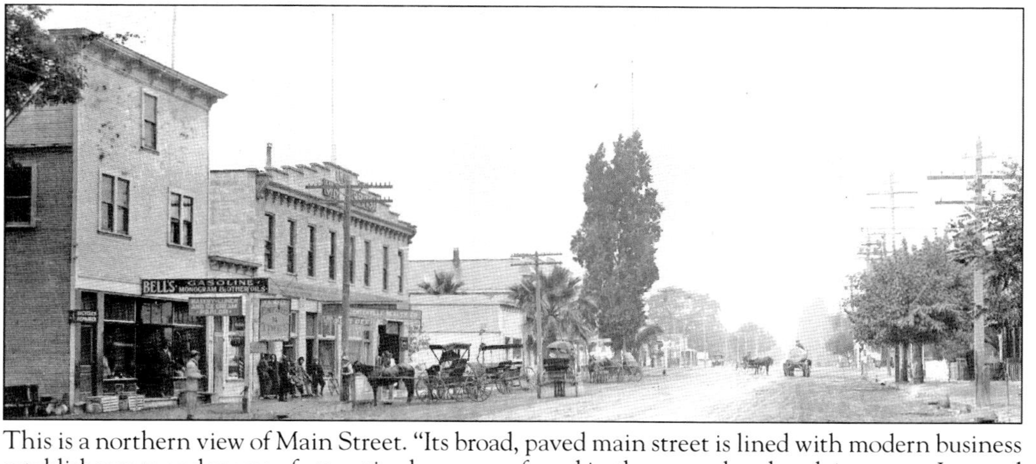

This is a northern view of Main Street. "Its broad, paved main street is lined with modern business establishments and scores of attractive homes are found in the central and outlying areas. Located here are several fruit and vegetable packing plants, a cannery, a metal products company, a hotel, a bank, several lodge buildings, three chain stores, a bakery, one of Southern Alameda County's largest machine shops, a nursery, a modern mortuary which also furnishes emergency ambulance service, municipal water company and volunteer fire department." Quote from HTSAC, 1939.

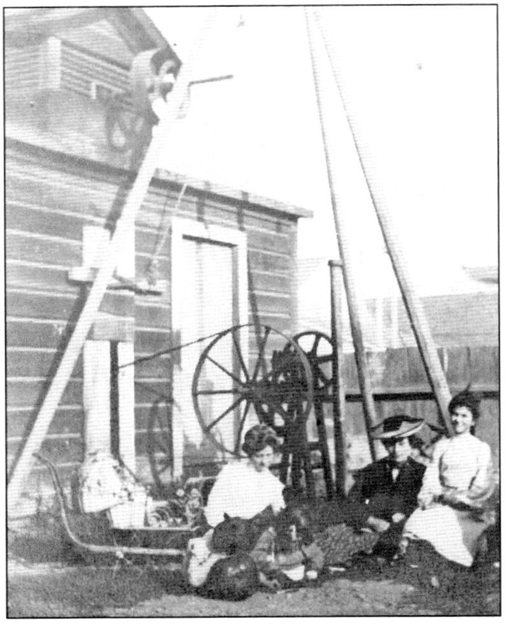

The Centerville Water Company was founded by Manuel S. Pires in 1896 to furnish water to Centerville and Newark. A local paper reported in 1898 that "excellent service is given at very reasonable rates." By 1913, many wells were dry and the company had to enlarge the system to supply water to new areas. The company was incorporated in 1916, and Pires continued to operate it until 1934. Pictured are Rose G. Pires (center) and daughter Elsie Pires Silva (right). (BLB.)

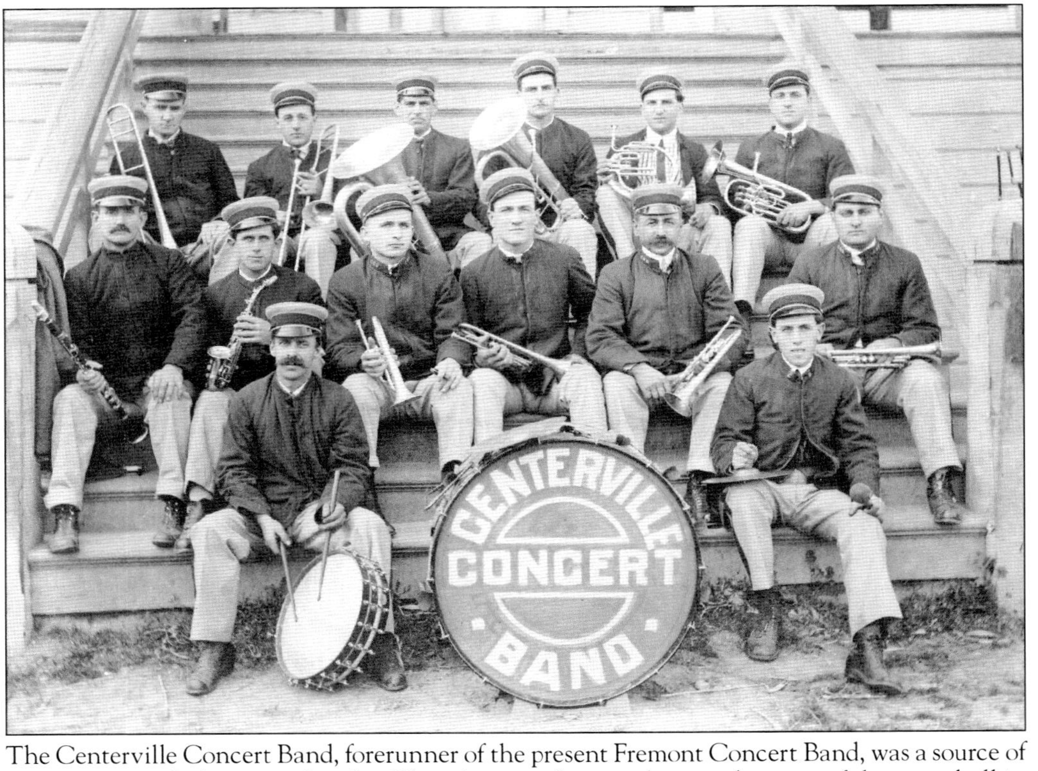

The Centerville Concert Band, forerunner of the present Fremont Concert Band, was a source of community pride for many decades. This photograph was taken on the steps of the town hall in 1915. From left to right are (first row) Manuel Goulart and Manuel Rose; (second row) William Maffey, John Rose, Frank Veit, Tony King, Frank Calhoun, and Anthony Clark (band leader); (third row) Earl Ingram, Manuel Silva, Joe Clark, Tony Silva, Clarence Silva, and Frank King. (BLB.)

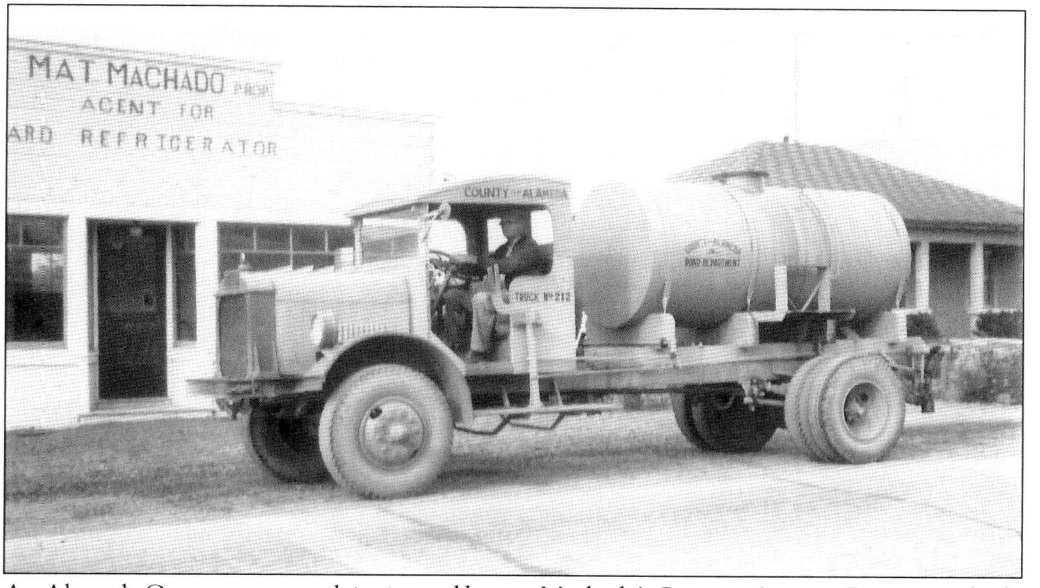

An Alameda County water truck is pictured here at Machado's Corners. Antonio Pereira Machado came from Fayal, Azores, in 1857 and settled on the Rancho Pacheco. He raised his family there and eventually purchased part of the rancho. Other family members acquired land near the crossroads of Alvarado and Decoto Roads, and that area became known as Machado's Corners.

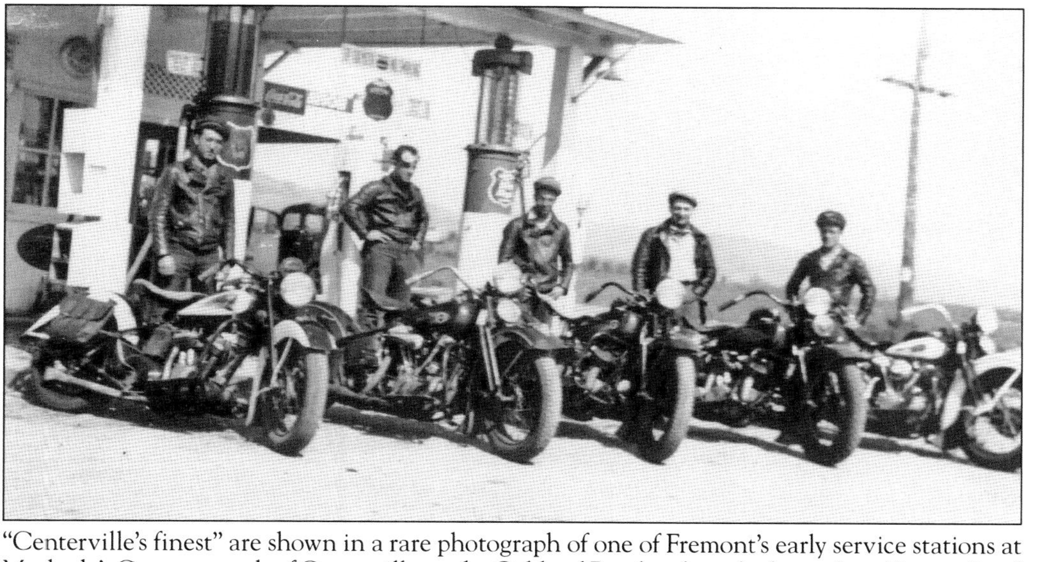

"Centerville's finest" are shown in a rare photograph of one of Fremont's early service stations at Machado's Corners, north of Centerville on the Oakland Road and not far from where Decoto Road crossed Alameda Creek with the Bell Ranch Bridge. The bridge was named for a bell taken from the church at Mission San Jose, used to call farm workers at the old Hawley Ranch. Bell Ranch Bridge was also the landmark for a favorite swimming hole used by the young men of Centerville and the surrounding area.

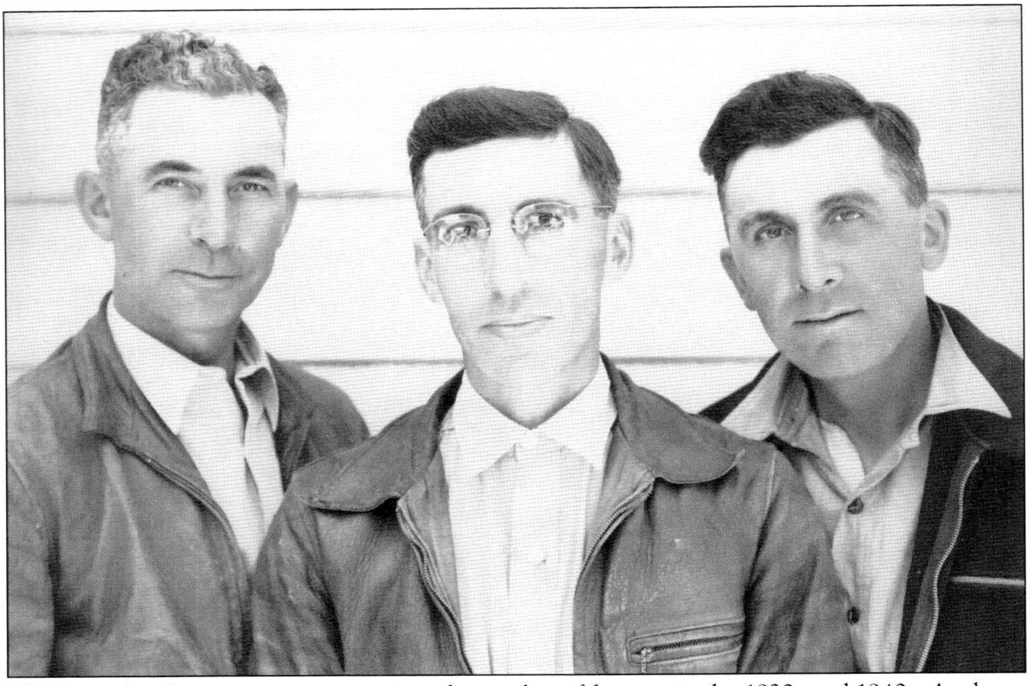

The Lewis brothers were representative of a number of farmers in the 1930s and 1940s. Anthony (Tony), Fred, and John worked many acres in various locations. They concentrated on cauliflower and tomatoes, usually bound for F. E. Booth Cannery, and sugar beets sold to the Holly Sugar Company in Union City.

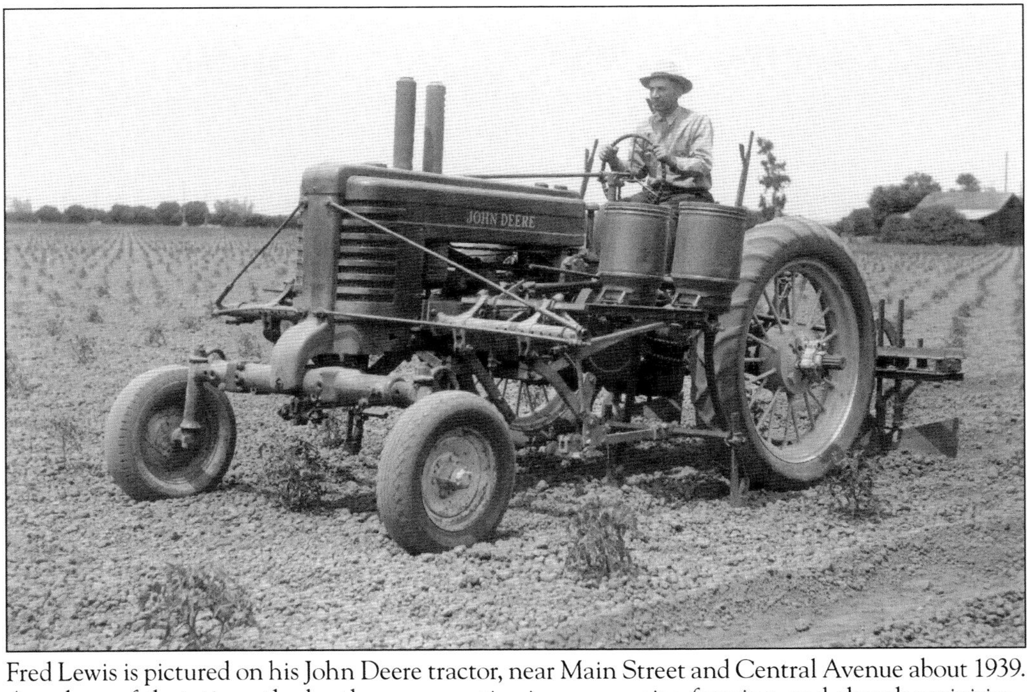

Fred Lewis is pictured on his John Deere tractor, near Main Street and Central Avenue about 1939. As others of their time, the brothers were active in community, farming, and church activities.

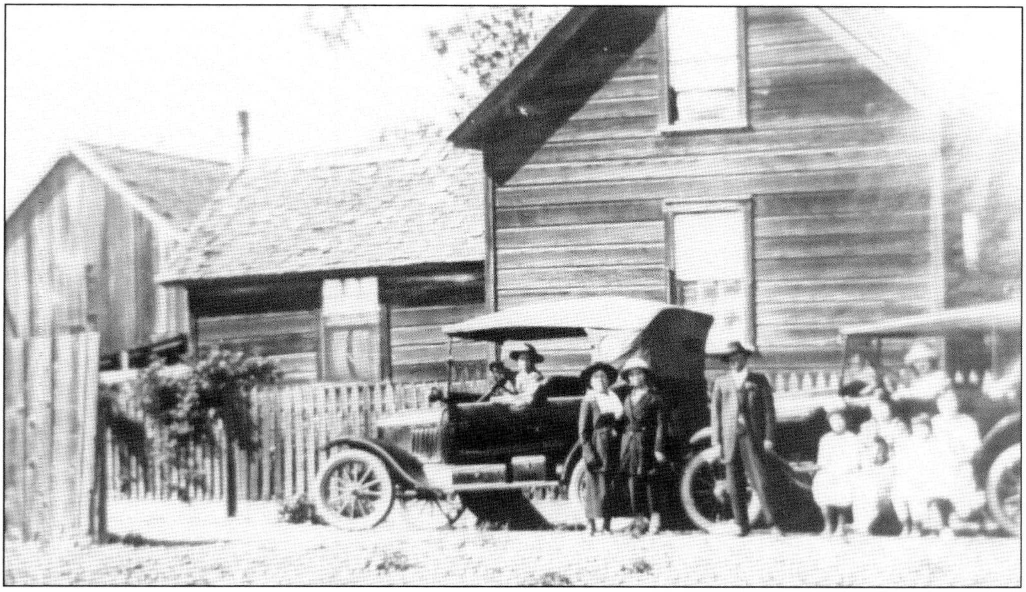

San Joaquin Oil and Development Company was the backbone of the Bunting family's wealth that supported Sycamore Farm as a model farm operation for a generation. After purchasing the farm, Clarence William Kolb and May Cloy used Sycamore Farm as a country home and retreat from their acting lives in Los Angeles and Hollywood for 27 years. The property managers for many years were members of the Asakawa family, who were also associated with the Patterson ranch.

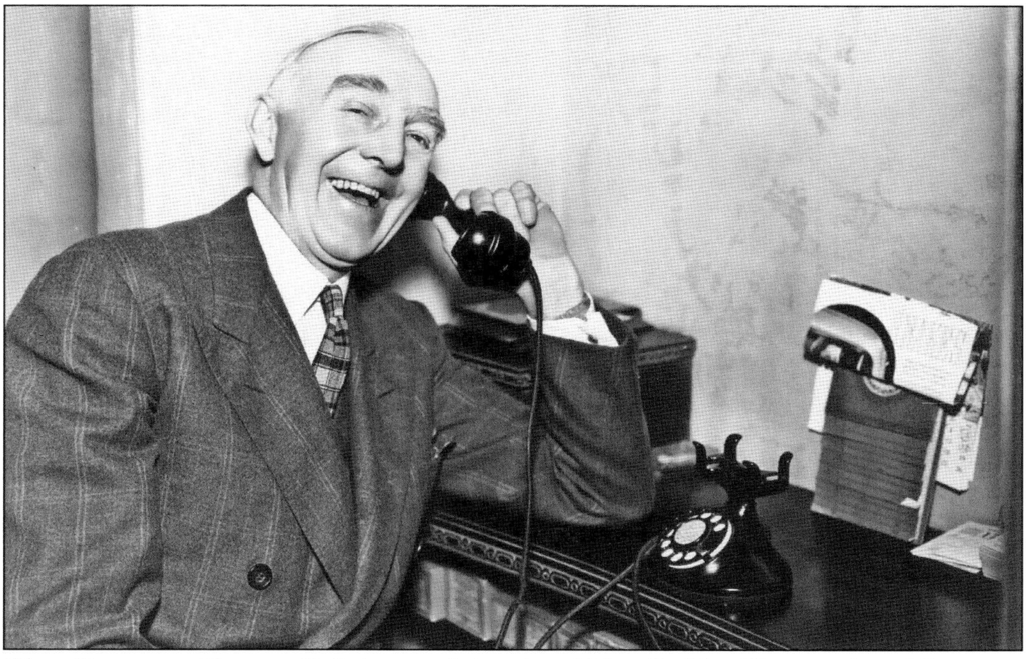

Silent film actors Clarence Kolb (pictured above) and his wife, May Cloy, purchased Sycamore Farm on July 10, 1918, from Fleda Bunting. Radio fans had the pleasure of hearing him on *Merrily We Live*, broadcast on March 3, 1938. Kolb was also a character actor in close to 60 feature films and television episodes during his career between 1938 and 1957.

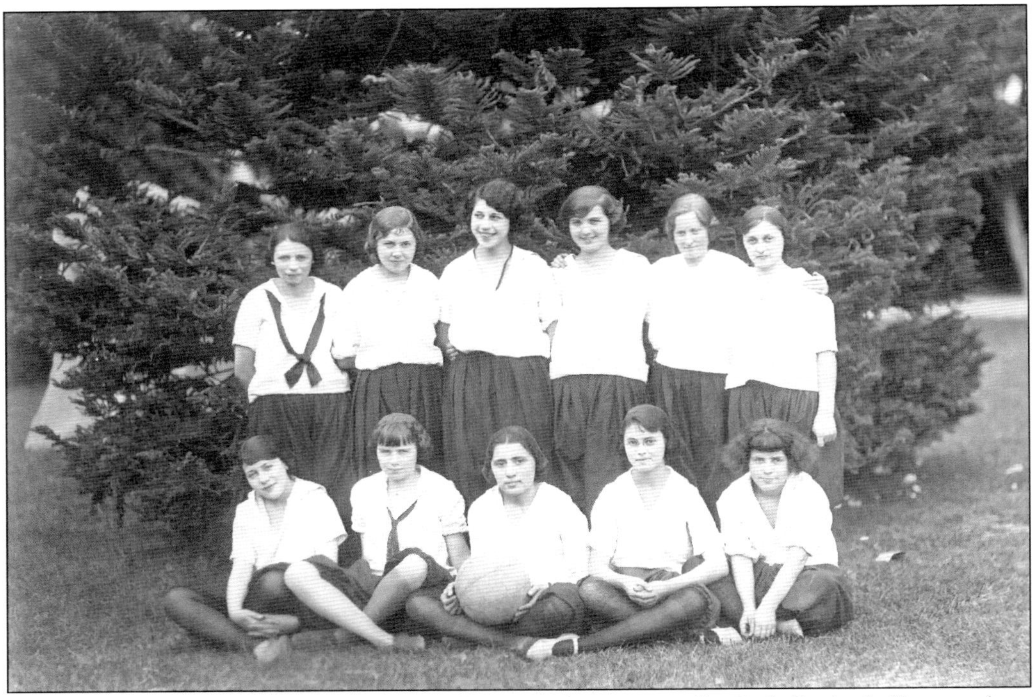

On April 17, 1910, the *San Francisco Call* reported, "Centerville Girls Basketball were close contenders in the championship game held on the grounds of Centerville High School. They won the first half 9 to 8 against Lowell of San Francisco, losing by three points with a final score of 22 to 19. The Centerville line-up included forwards Helen Blacow and Doris Jacobus, touch center Bessie Bailey, side centers Marion Lynch and Helen Baldwin, and guards Aloise Sinnott and Hattie Baldwin."

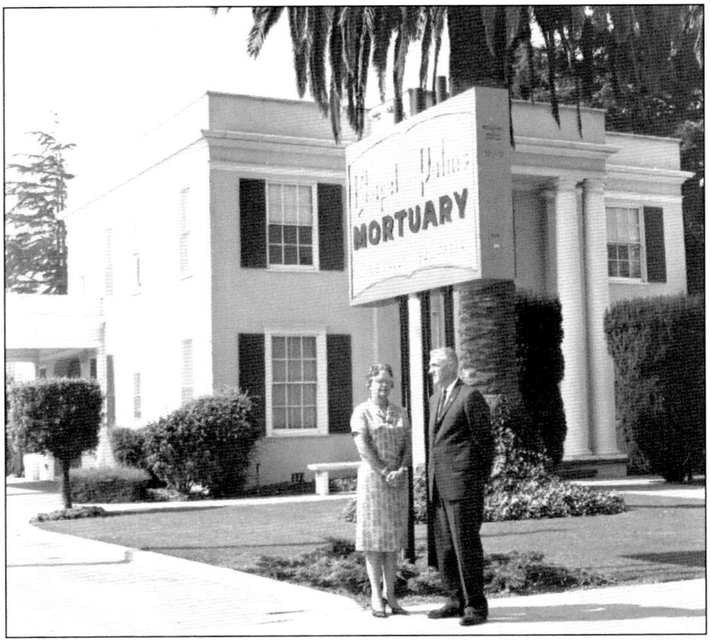

George Botelho established the first mortuary between Oakland and San Jose in Centerville in 1902. After his death in 1913, his brother Frank took over the business. A new building was erected next door in 1932, and Botelho held a public dedication naming it Chapel of the Palms. Lois and Dallas Paul (pictured) purchased the business in 1937. Bill Aboumarad bought the building in 1974. A number of businesses have occupied the building in recent years.

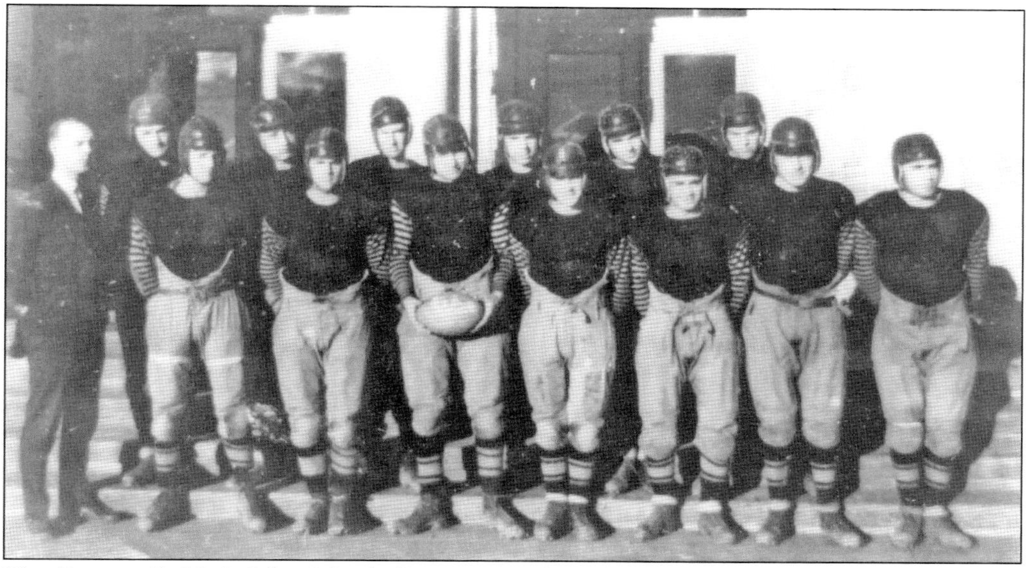

The Centerville High School football team poses for a photograph in 1924. Their great rival in these decades was Hayward High School, and any win over the team was much celebrated. On November 3, 1927, the *Hatchet* reported on the ongoing rivalry: "In 1912, Hayward High School was beaten 6-3 by Centerville High's rugby team. In 1912 the squad had black jerseys with a large C on them, and regular rugby pants. In that year they had the champion team of the CACAL." CACAL likely referred to the Central Alameda County Athletic League.

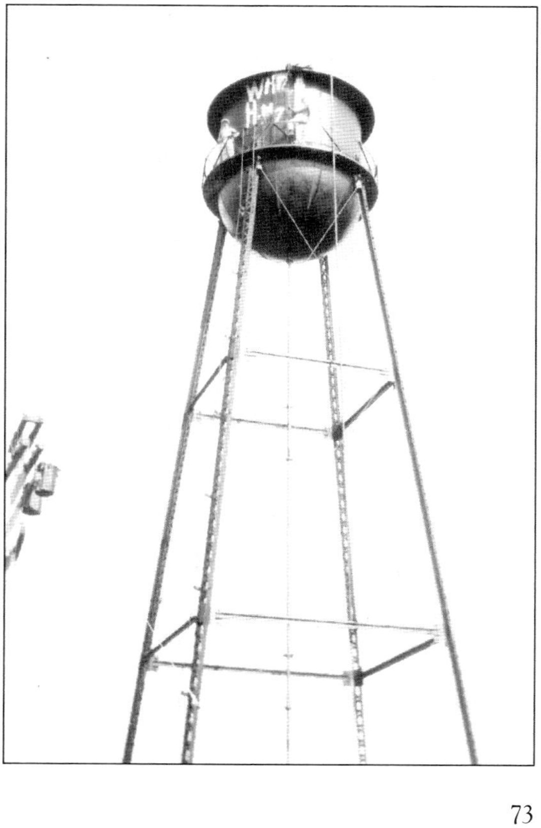

Centerville High School, known after 1924 as Washington High School, beat Hayward High School in a 1925 football game. That win was celebrated by decorating the water tank at the new Washington High School grounds. "The first football game that Union High School No. 2 participated in was with Washington College in Irvington on Dec. 16, 1893. The high school won by a score of 8-0. In 1894 regular football suits were secured."

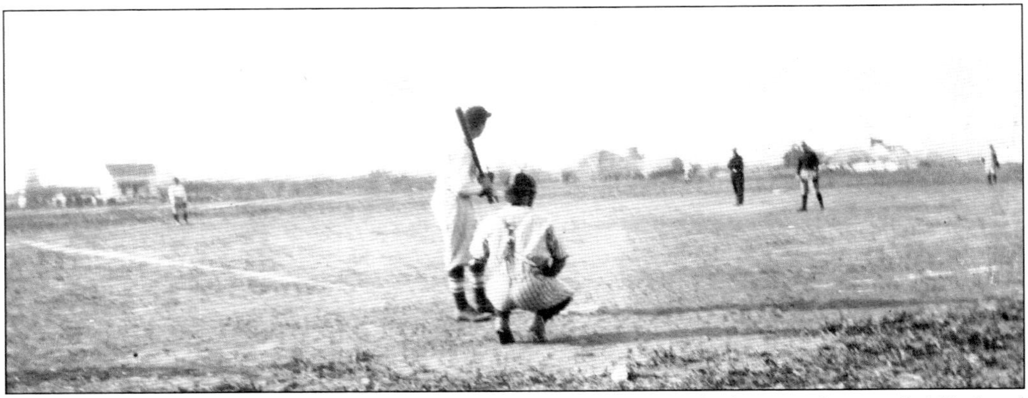

This Washington Union High School (WUHS) baseball game took place on the new field behind the new school in 1925. James Nunes (1908–1976) played baseball that year. He saved a baseball from the father-and-son game of 1924, wrote on it, and it is now in the Museum of Local History (MLH) collection. He also saved his school papers and other records, which are also in the MLH archives representing a slice of student life from the 1920s. Nunes graduated from WUHS in 1926, received a bachelor of arts from Stanford University in 1930, and received his University of California teaching diploma credential in 1934.

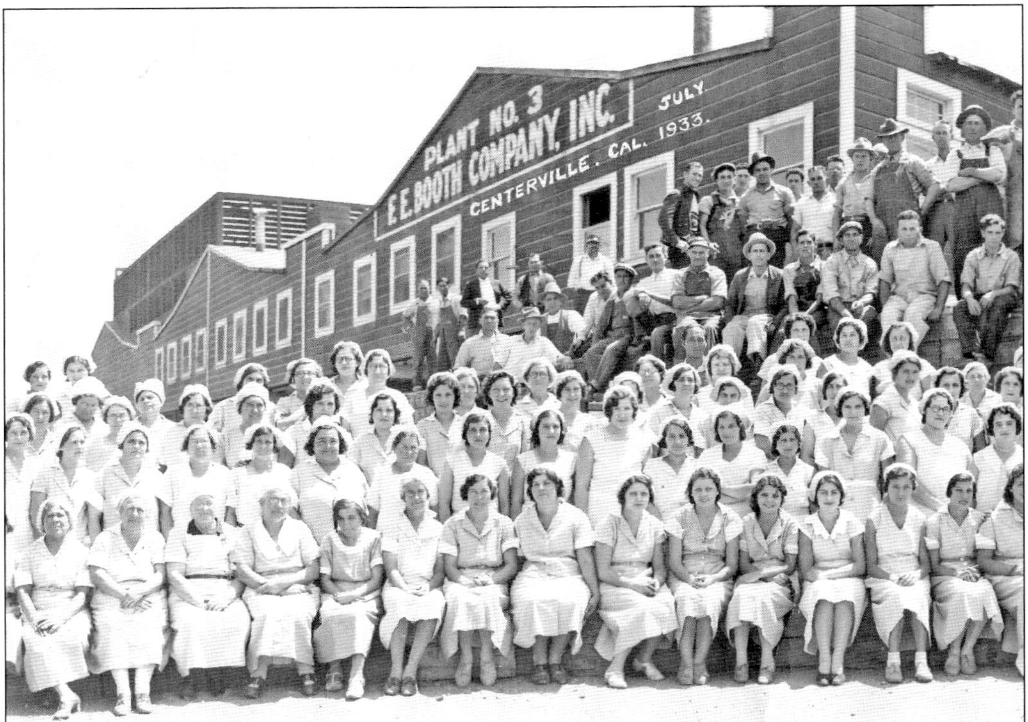

Booth Cannery workers are photographed here in 1933. In 1928, James Nunes met Mary Lucas when she was 16 and he was working at Booth Cannery to pay his way through Stanford University. She and her mother cut fruit as seasonal workers, and his job was carrying the boxes to the workers. They married in 1935.

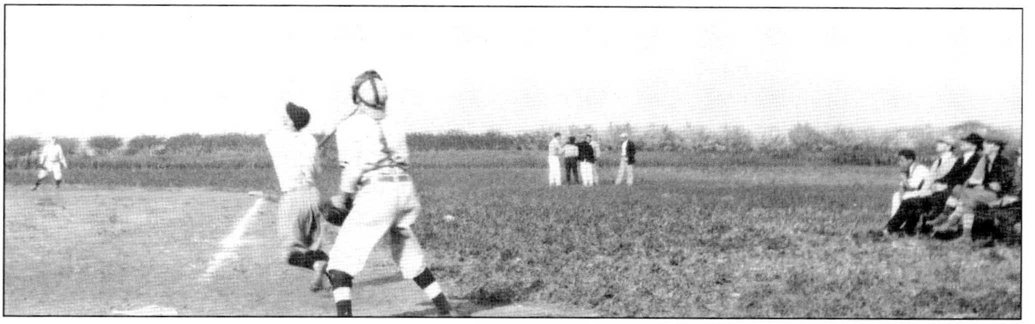

James Nunes was the son of Joseph Nunes, who came to Centerville from Massachusetts in 1875. Joseph had originally come to the United States as a 15-year-old stowaway from the Azores. James was the only child of Joseph's second marriage to Mary Clarice Pimentel, who came to the country from Pico in the Azores. After graduation, James worked for the Ferry Morse Seed Company in Salinas for two years. In 1932, he returned to Centerville, started his own seed business, drove to Berkeley for classes, and lived on the Nunes ranch in Centerville. James taught school from 1936 to 1966 at Alviso, Warm Springs, and Centerville Elementary Schools. He became principal at Alviso Elementary School when Elsie Madruga retired after 29 years of service. He and his wife, Mary, had one son. The five-acre Nunes apricot orchard operated until 1998.

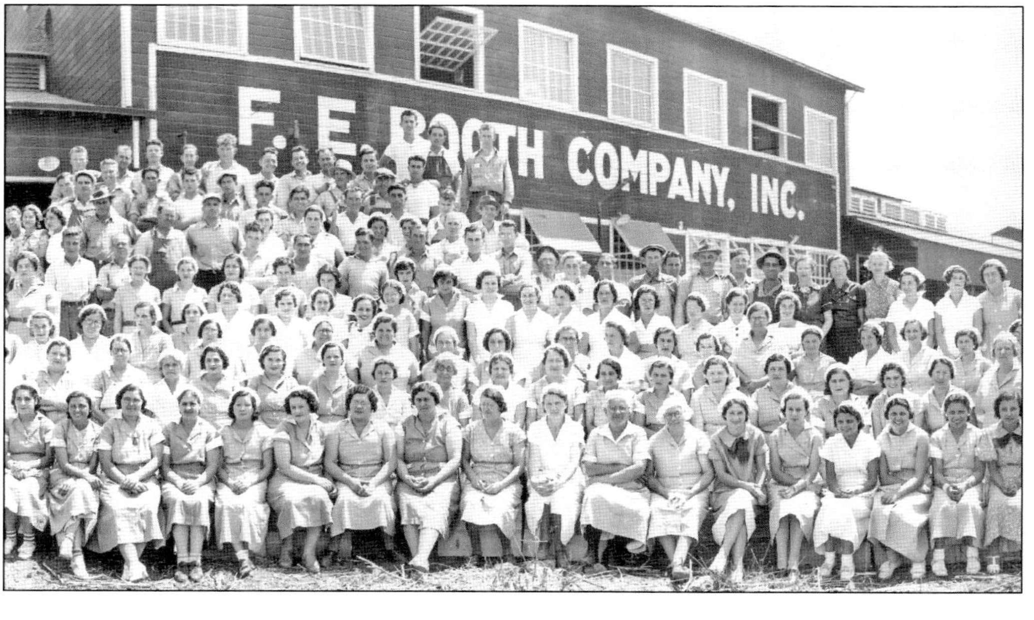

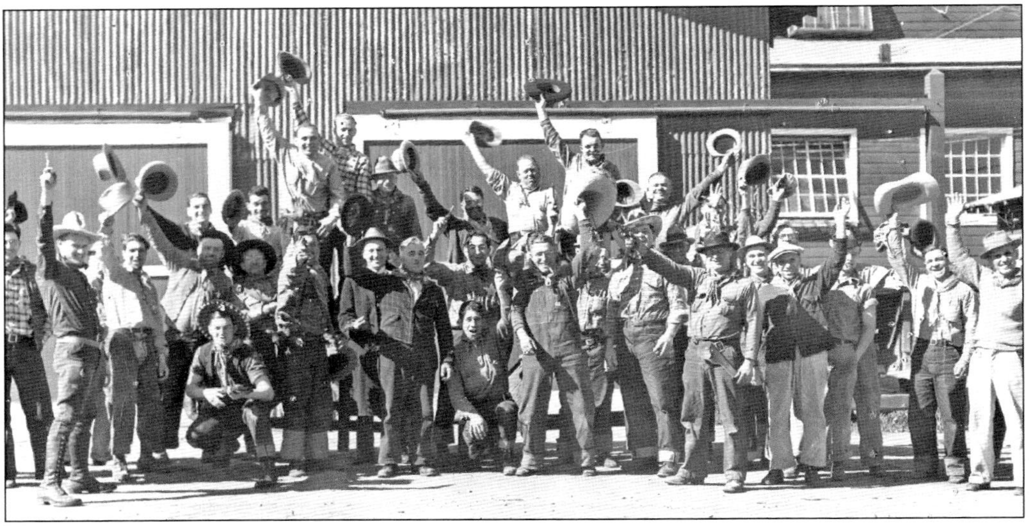

The Golden Gate International Exhibition (GGIE) of 1939 was masterminded by Charles Strub, former promoter for the San Francisco Seals baseball team. In addition to national promotion, Strub encouraged locals to make the most of the fair by having theme days. Booth Cannery participated in the Wild West Days event with workers dressing up in cowboy gear before heading off to the fair. The president of the GGIE was Leland Cutler, formerly of Centerville High School's 1898 football team. Treasure Island was built in San Francisco Bay to provide a site for the GGIE and for later aviation use.

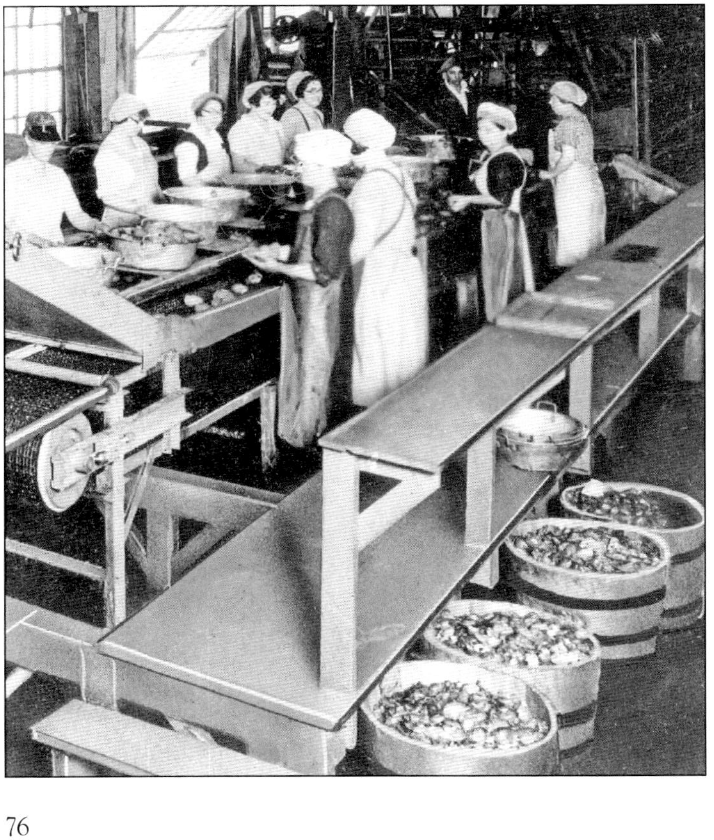

In 1933, Booth Cannery No. 3 at Centerville was automated with a partial assembly line, but it still allowed for groups of workers to enjoy each other's company while peeling, slicing, pitting, and cutting fruit by hand. Workers were paid by the piece—the more a worker processed, the more he or she was paid.

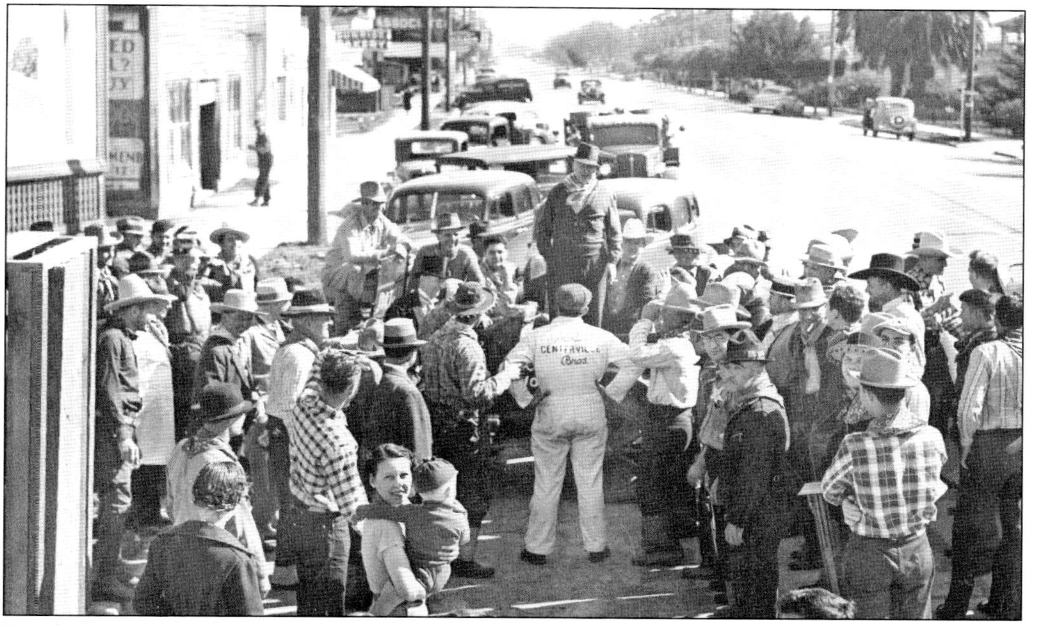

Booth Cannery workers conduct a kangaroo court on Centerville's Main Street as part of the Wild West Days that were sponsored by the Golden Gate International Exhibition. The Treasure Island site for the Golden Gate International Exhibition was planned as an international airport for Clippers flying to Asia, with facilities already contracted to Pan American Airways. With its modern vision, Treasure Island set the stage for the modernizing of the San Francisco Bay Area.

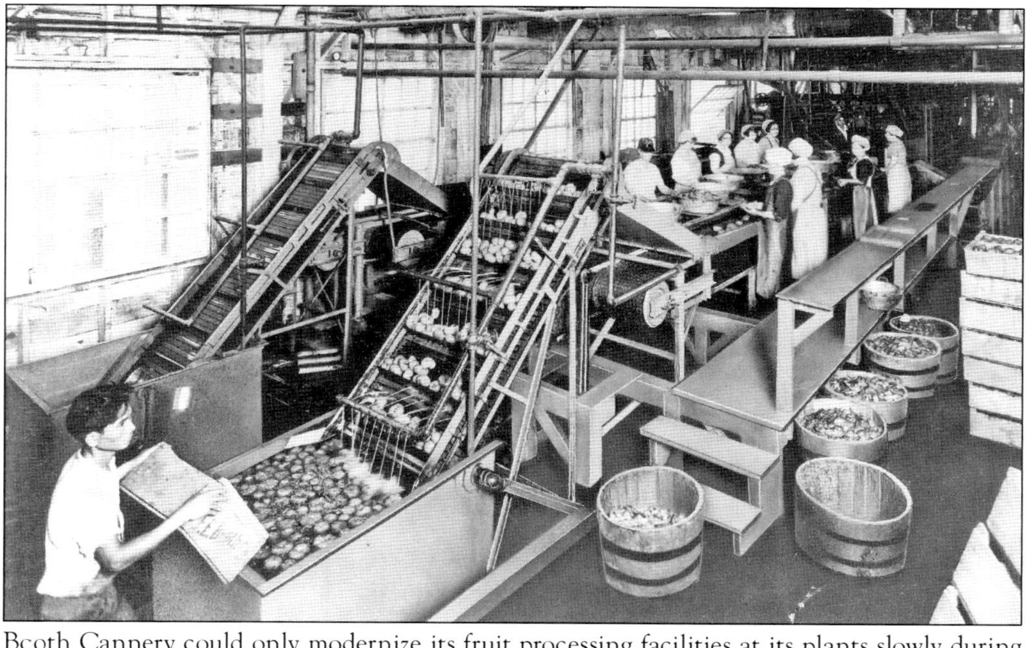

Booth Cannery could only modernize its fruit processing facilities at its plants slowly during the off-season. Maintenance of equipment was a major project for employees and for the nearby machinist businesses, such as the Centerville Machine Shop, owned by Frank Madruga and Herman Mau.

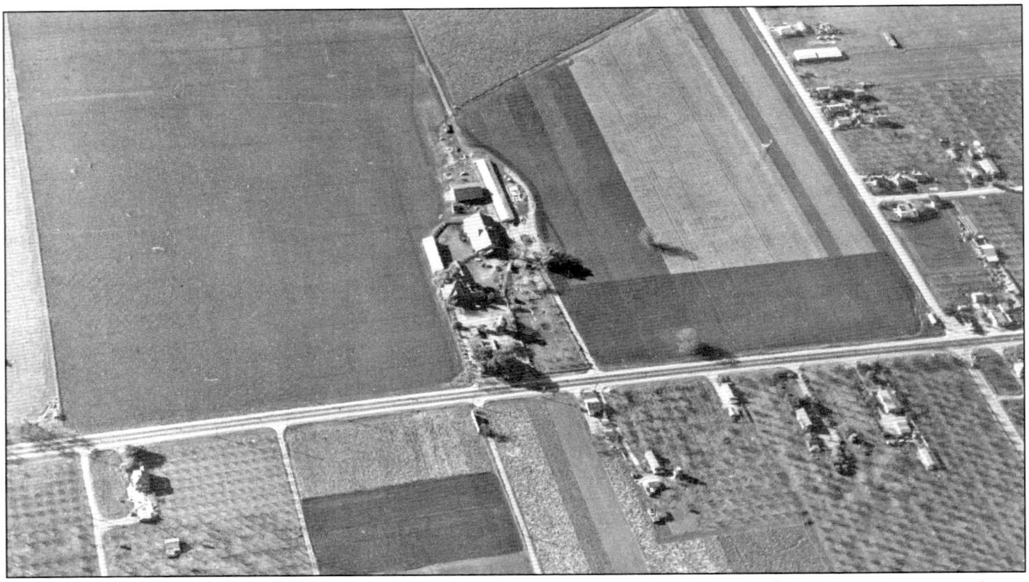

The Williams brothers, Leland, Myron, Burdette, and Irving, began shipping tomatoes from Centerville in 1924. They expanded to peas and by 1928 had arrangements with the Southern Pacific Railroad to use warehouse and packing sheds across from the Centerville train station. On February 19, 1942, Federal Executive Order 9066, forcing the evacuation of Japanese Americans from the West Coast, was passed, which meant citizens and legal residents of Japanese ancestry within 50 to 60 miles of the West Coast of the United States were ordered to assembly centers and internment camps inland. For Centerville, this meant hundreds of citizens and their families registered at the Japanese School, located near the Williams operations, where many Japanese Americans worked in the fruit and vegetable packing business, shown at work behind the Williams brothers below.

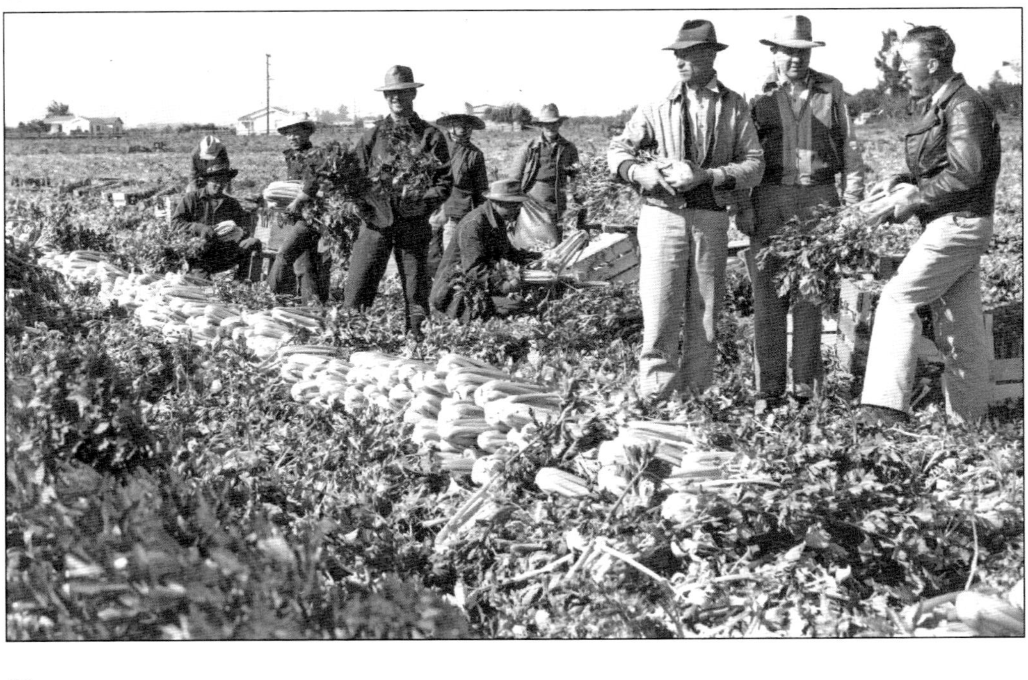

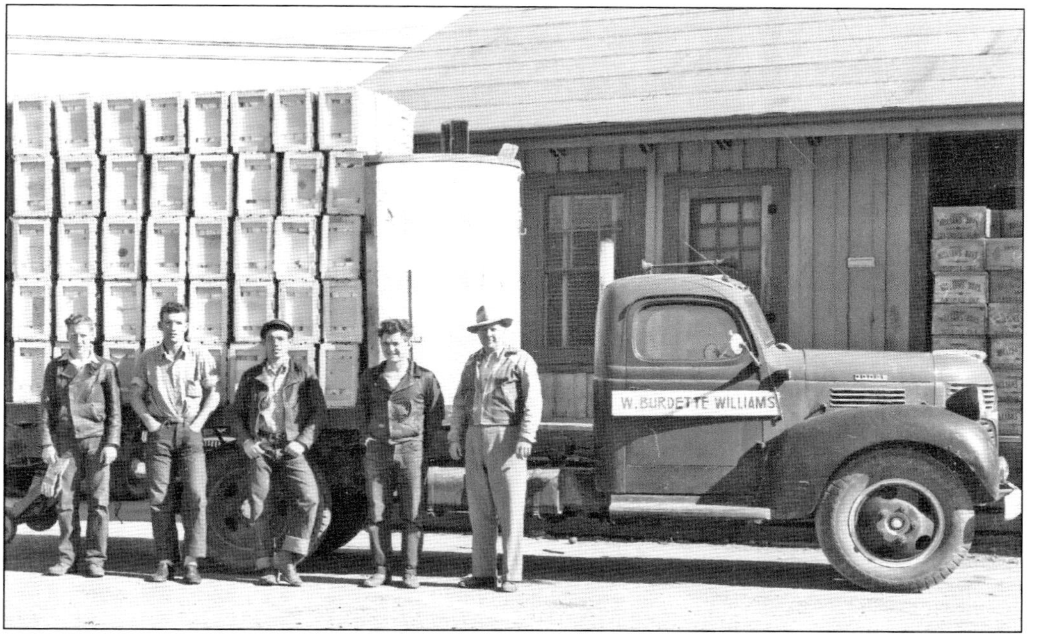

Many War Relocation Authority photographs by Dorothea Lange were taken in Centerville around the Japanese School and in nearby fields and the Williams brothers' warehouse (shown here). In early May 1942, Japanese American children were marched out of class after the February executive order was read. School buses were loaded with Japanese American families and their suitcases, and they were taken to the assembly facility at the Tanforan Racetrack south of San Francisco. The classrooms of Washington Township lost 10 to 20 percent of their students that day. The photographs may be viewed online in the Japanese American Relocation Digital Archives (JARDA) at the Calisphere Web site of the University of California.

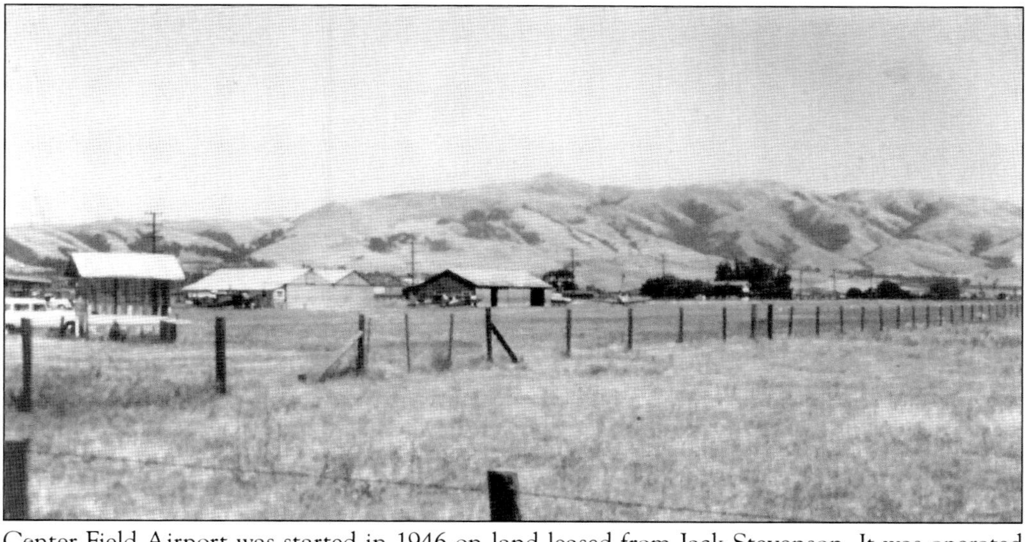

Center Field Airport was started in 1946 on land leased from Jack Stevenson. It was operated by a board of directors and an airport manager. Activities eventually included a flight training school with a ground school, flying lessons, and lights for night flying. It was later called Fremont Airport and was located on Mowry Avenue and Blacow Road.

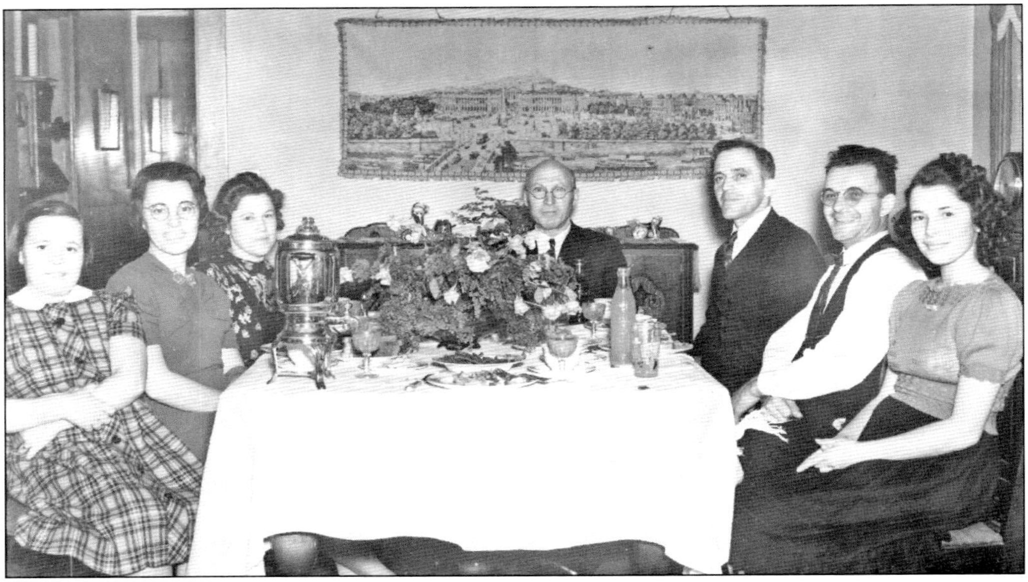

Jack DeLuce (rear, center) and his family celebrate Thanksgiving dinner. Jack was the leader of the Woodmen of the World (WOW) softball team and drill team. In 1946, the Washington Township Softball Association put together a season of games, and the WOW fielded a team, playing 18 games against the likes of Kleine's, Westvaco, Mission San Jose Firemen, Native Sons, Kraftile, Wedgewood, and Central Chevrolet. The latter baseball program advertisement reads: "For a long RUN or a short STOP, You Can Rely on a Chevrolet."

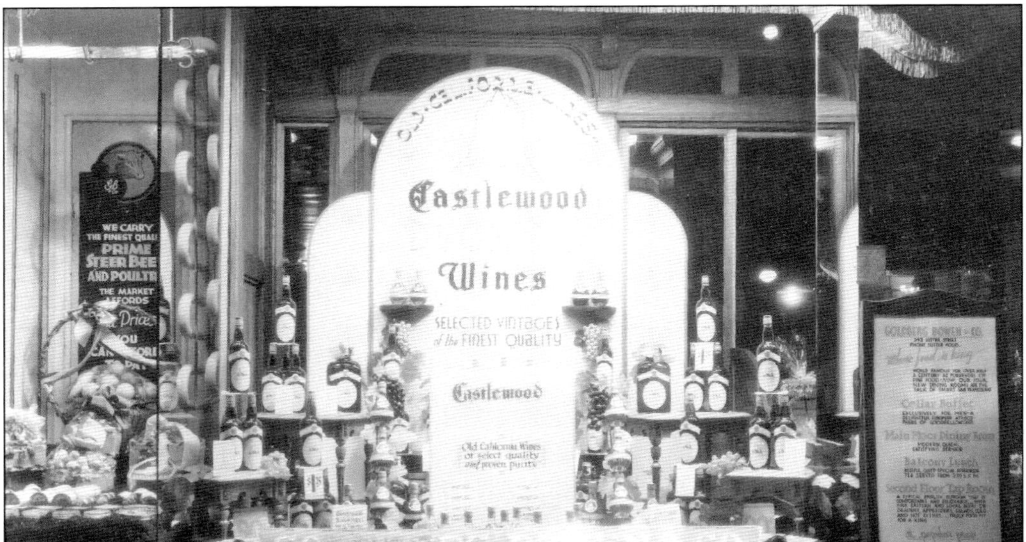

After Prohibition ended in 1933, the Williams brothers expanded operations to include Castlewood Wine Cellars, named after philanthropist Phoebe Hearst's estate at Pleasanton. The wine was bottled in a distinct shape and was referred to as "duckpin wines of selected vintages of the finest quality," displayed here in a show window of Goldberg, Bowen, and Company in San Francisco. The Williams brothers also produced wines from 1918 to 1932, including tokays, sherries, muscatels, and ports that met Volstead Act criteria.

William "Bill" Bauhofer Sr. sometimes rode his horse on the Chadbourne Ranch while the family operated the Innes-Cloverdale dairy. In 1938, Joe Bauhofer Sr., Joe Bauhofer Jr., and Bill Bauhofer moved the business to open the new Cloverdale Creamery pictured below. (BF.)

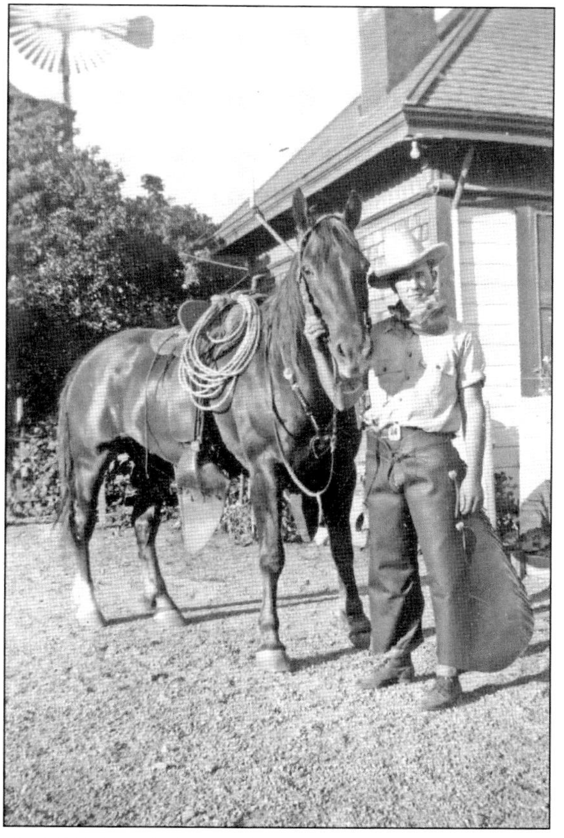

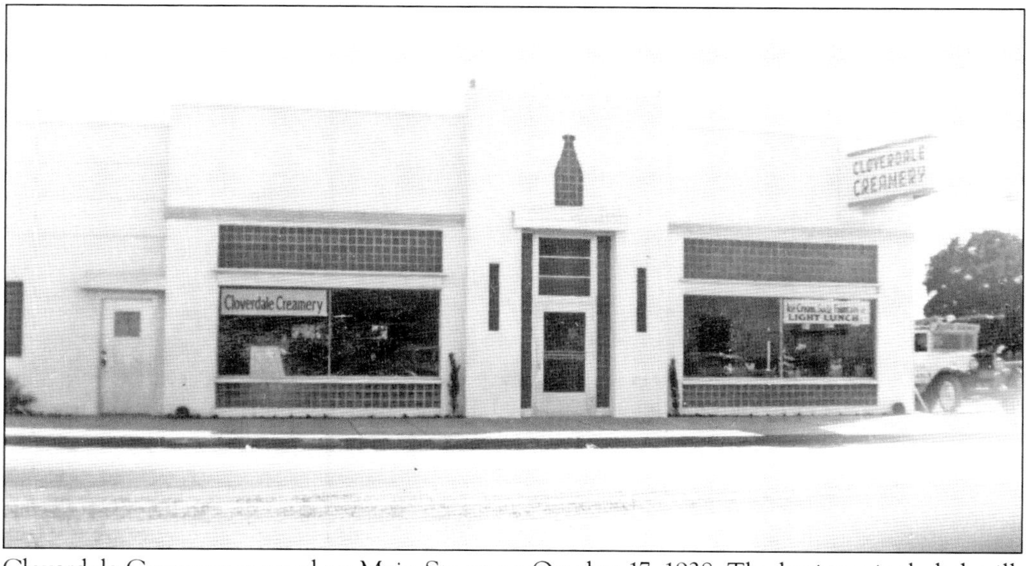

Cloverdale Creamery opened on Main Street on October 17, 1938. The business included milk production and bottling, delivery service, and fountain service. The family continued to run the business and serve the Washington Township community for 63 years. They closed their doors for the last time in March 2001. (BF.)

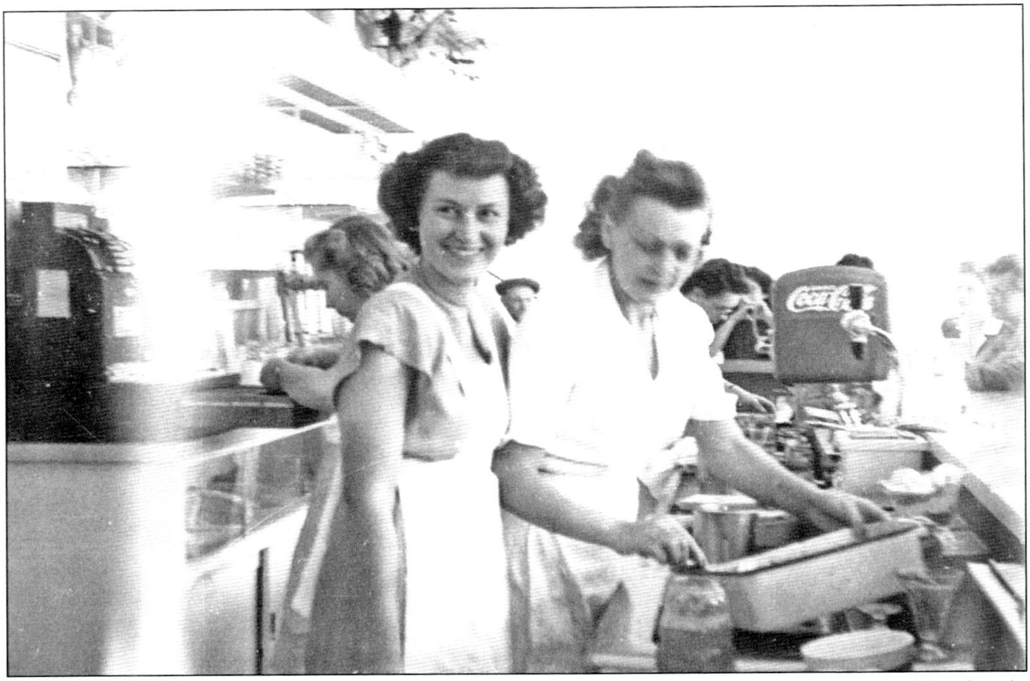

Lily "Lil" Bauhofer Wipfli (left) undertakes a trial run at Fenton's Creamery in Oakland. Lily worked in the Cloverdale Creamery fountain and as bookkeeper for the business for 40 years before retiring with husband John "Johnny" Wipfli to Nevada. (BF.)

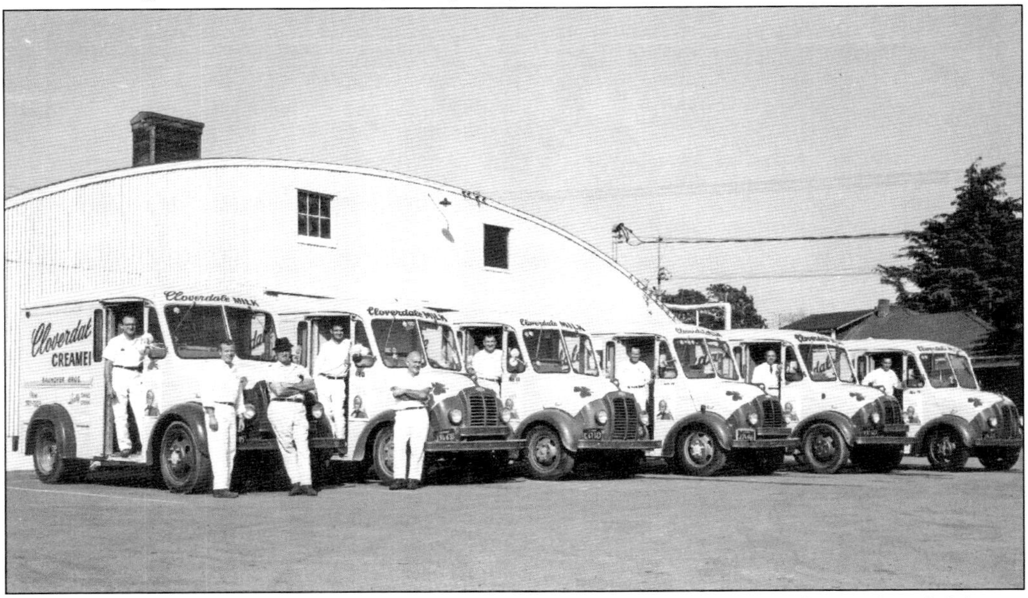

The milk drivers for the Cloverdale Creamery are lined up with their yellow-colored delivery trucks behind the creamery building in 1967. Since 1938, the Bauhofer family had been in the milk delivery business, also running an ice cream plant and diner-fountain restaurant. The days of managing herds of dairy cows and their pasture were long behind them. By 1967, dairies had left Washington Township forever. (BF.)

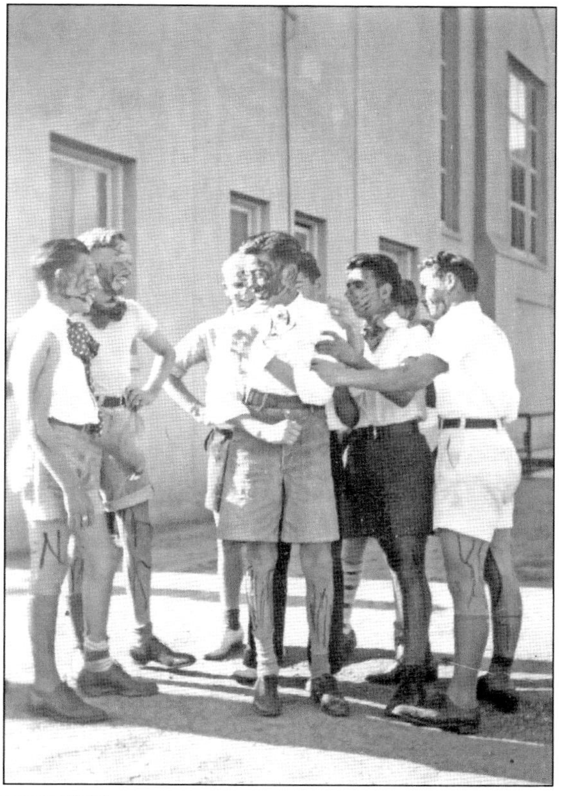

Freshmen in rolled-up dungarees plan nefarious deeds for Spirit Week at Washington High School in 1938. As part of Scrub Day, a campus-wide cleanup took place, along with good-natured pranks, such as those seen below. The principal and custodian are being driven around campus on a piece of grounds equipment. Scrub Day as a name has its American origins with the various camp institutions at the beginning of the 20th century and the required weekly shower and camp-wide clean-up. Scrub Day evolved to become one of the spirit days in high schools across the country by the 1930s.

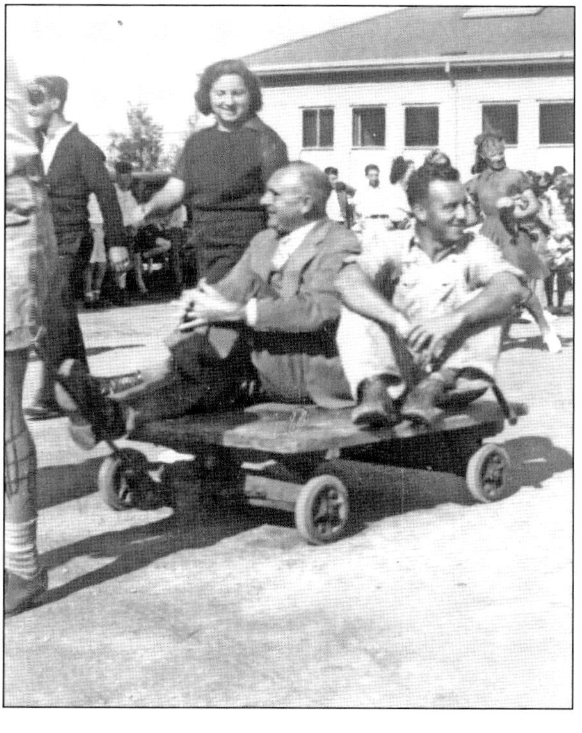

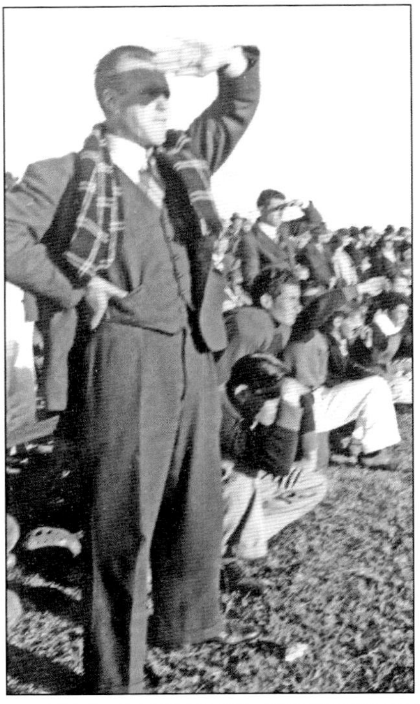

Judson "Jud" Taylor, the football coach at Washington Union High School in 1939, became the principal at James Logan High School in Union City when it opened in 1959. The football field and stadium there were named for him. American football in the 1930s was strongly influenced by coach Amos Alonzo Stagg, famous for developing the lateral pass. While in his 70s, Stagg coached at the University of the Pacific from 1932 to 1946.

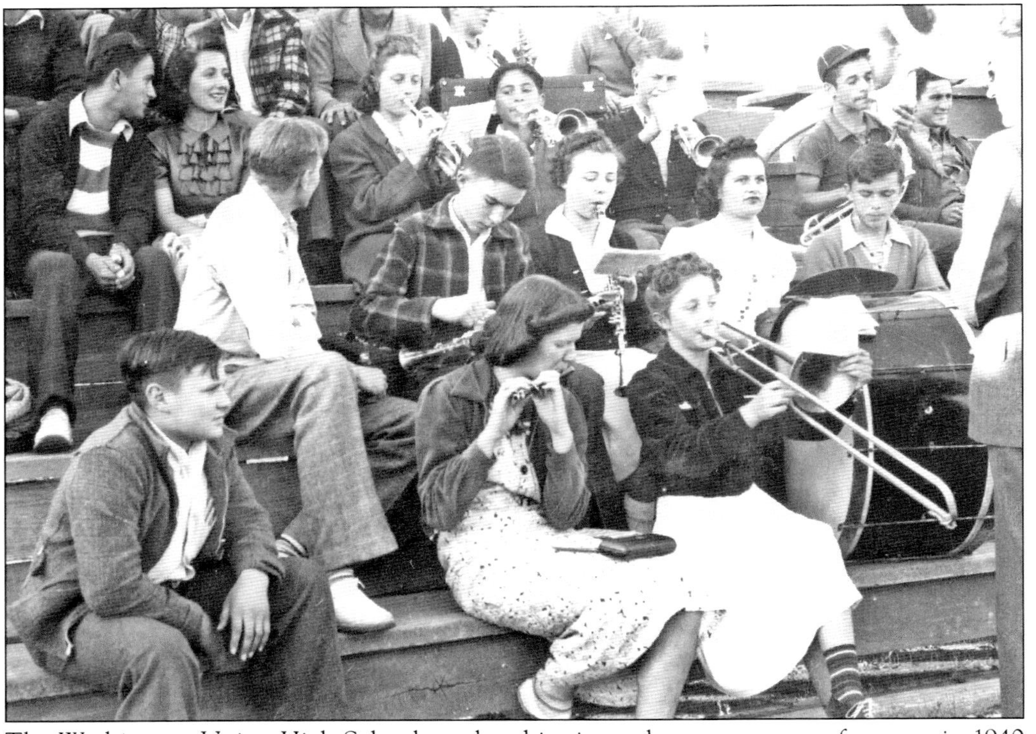

The Washington Union High School pep band is pictured on an autumn afternoon in 1940 playing at a Huskies football game before such things as night games and lighting were thought feasible for any level of sport.

Five

Fruits of the Earth 1940–1959

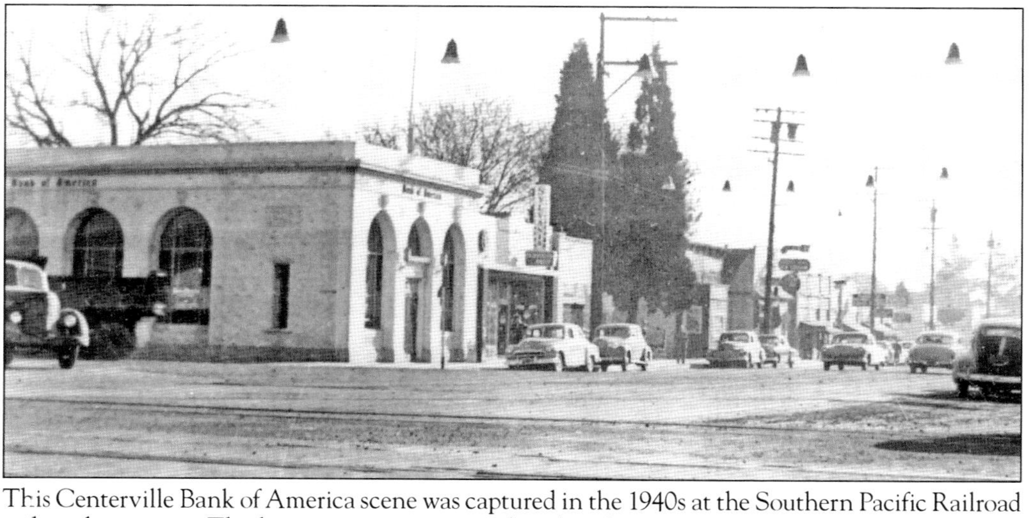

This Centerville Bank of America scene was captured in the 1940s at the Southern Pacific Railroad rail grade crossing. The last passenger train in that decade ran on March 29, 1940, and the next passenger train did not run until June 4, 1993, by which time the Bank of America had long outgrown its Centerville Main Street home and relocated at the Fremont Hub Shopping Center.

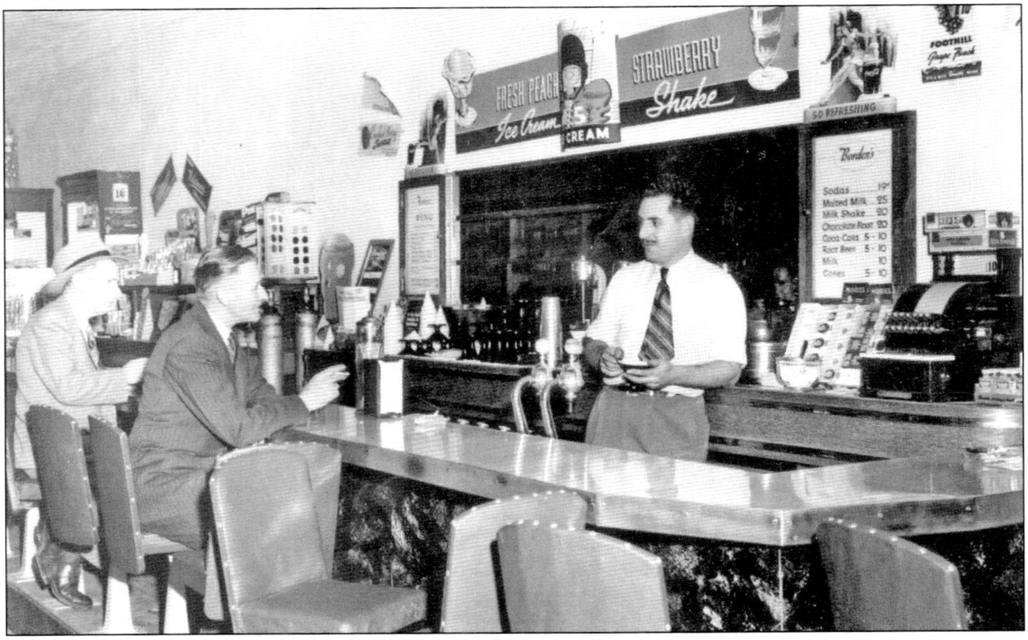

Syd's Pharmacy in 1942 served standard fountain offerings, such as chocolate soda for 15¢. It was made by drizzling chocolate syrup into a tall fountain glass, parking two scoops of chocolate ice cream on top, and pouring carbonated water flavored with syrup all over. Some whipped cream and cherry on top was extra special.

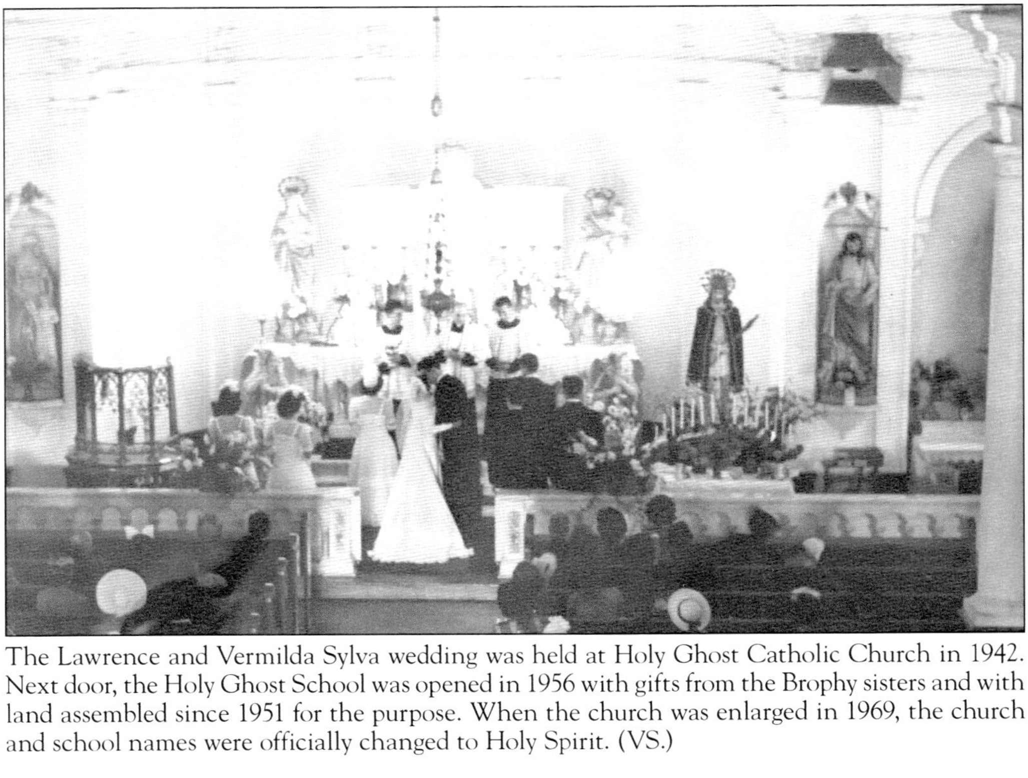

The Lawrence and Vermilda Sylva wedding was held at Holy Ghost Catholic Church in 1942. Next door, the Holy Ghost School was opened in 1956 with gifts from the Brophy sisters and with land assembled since 1951 for the purpose. When the church was enlarged in 1969, the church and school names were officially changed to Holy Spirit. (VS.)

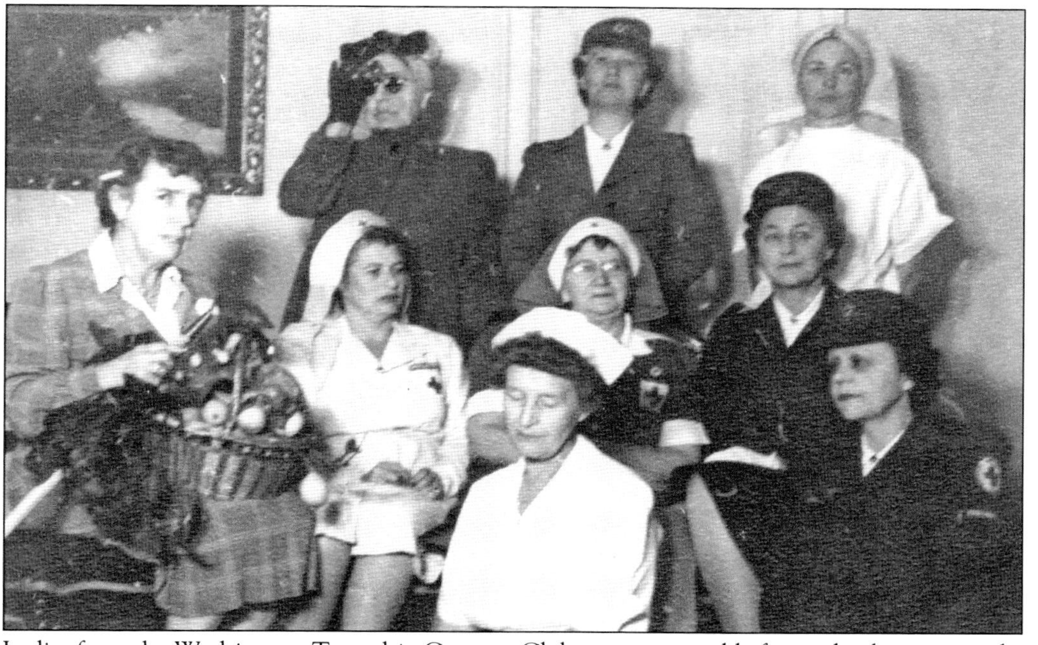

Ladies from the Washington Township Country Club were responsible for medical support tasks in the county during World War II. Pictured, from left to right, are Edna Overacker, Ida Holman, Dora Hudson, Dorothy Robinson, Lillian Goold, Estelle Hirsch, Patricia Bailey, Estelle Williams, and Sally McWhirter.

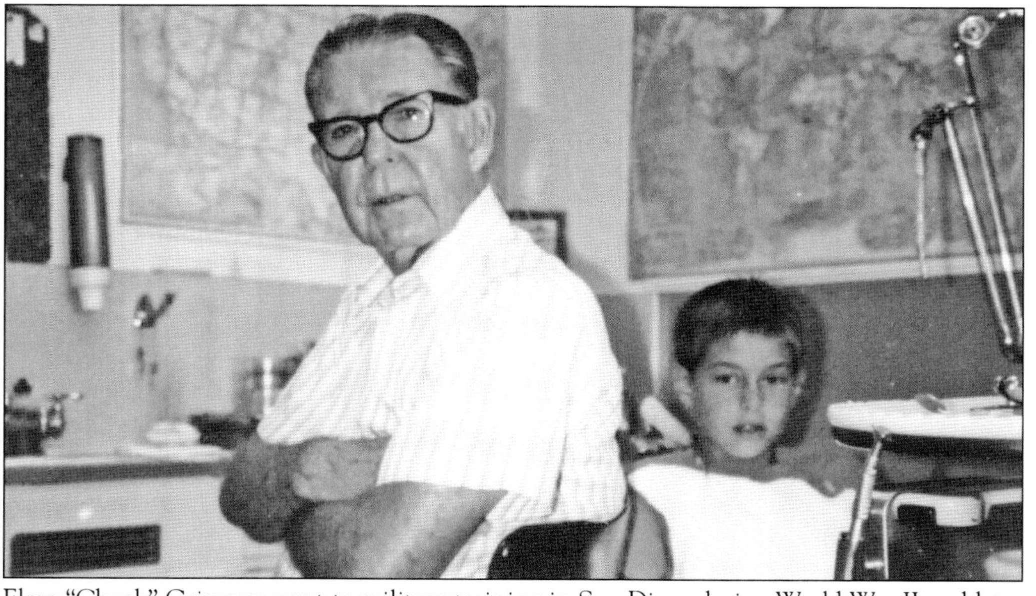

Elmo "Chuck" Grimmer went to military training in San Diego during World War II and later opened a dental practice in Centerville. In 1950, Irvington, Niles, and Centerville squabbled over a new county building. The board of supervisors finally accepted Grimmer's offer for 3 acres on Fremont Avenue, now named Peralta Boulevard, for the building. The side street was named Martha Avenue for a Grimmer family member. The first man assigned to the county sheriff substation built on Martha Avenue was detective Lowell Creighton. (CG.)

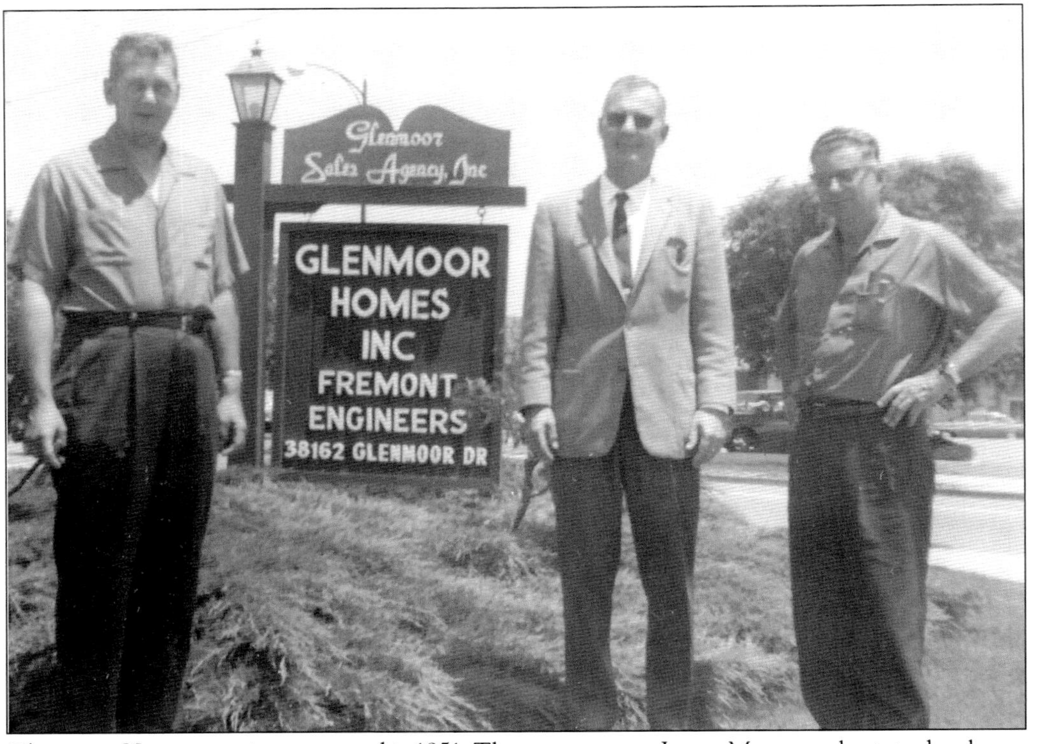

Glenmoor Homes was incorporated in1951. The owners were James Meyer, real estate developer, president; Ralph Cotter, civil engineer, secretary; and James Reeder, general contractor, treasurer, Robert Reeder was a general contractor and served as superintendent. The vision of the developers—a family-oriented community—has materialized with three schools, two community parks and pools and a homeowners association which sponsors many activities throughout the year. (JR.)

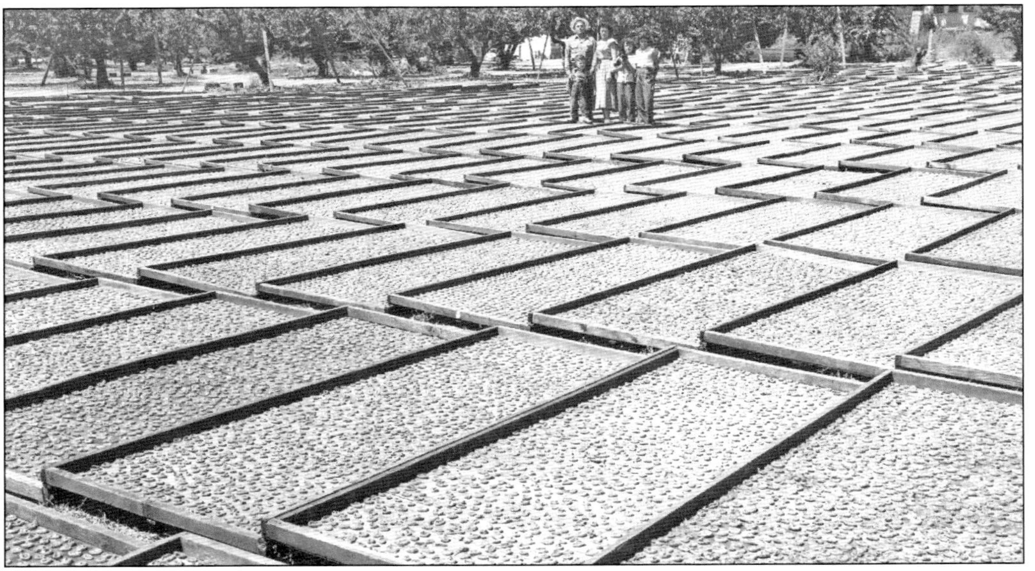

The photograph above shows trays of "cots" at an apricot drying yard at the Freitas ranch in 1953. (SB.)

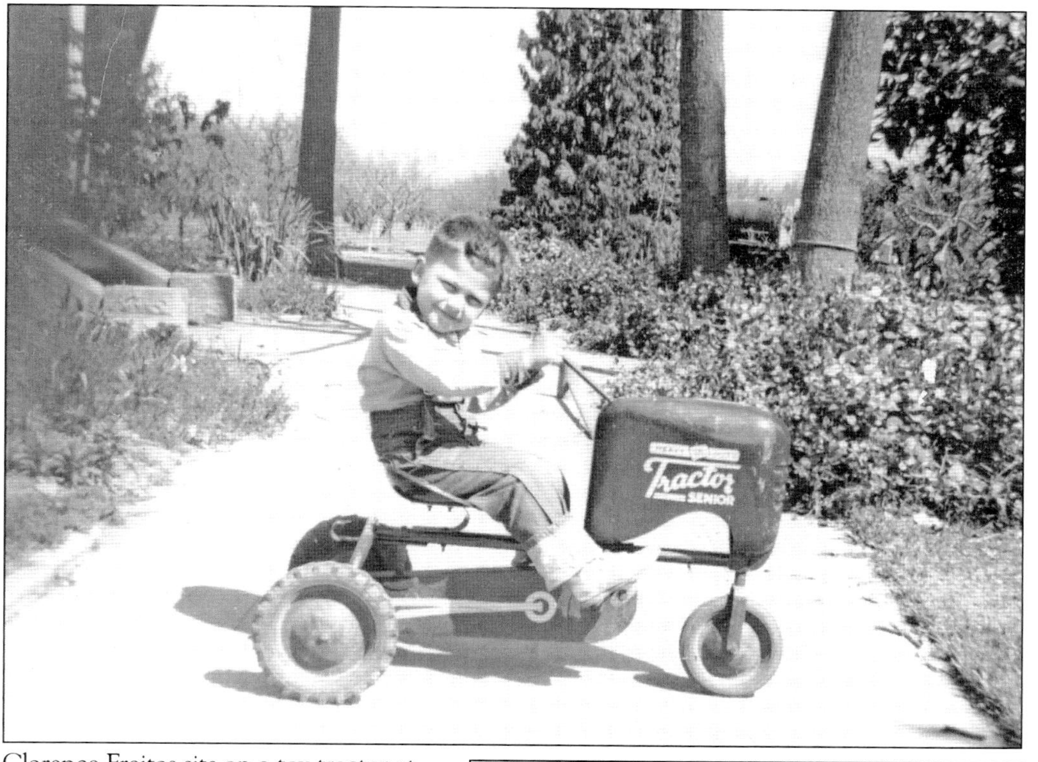

Clarence Freitas sits on a toy tractor at the Freitas ranch in the 1950s under the palms that were planted in 1900. In Washington Township, "cutting cots" was a classic summer job for students and family members. Apricots would dry best if their sides touched each other across the drying tray. The trays sat overnight in a closed sulfur house that was set up at the end of the day's work. A can of sulfur burned overnight to kill parasites. (SB.)

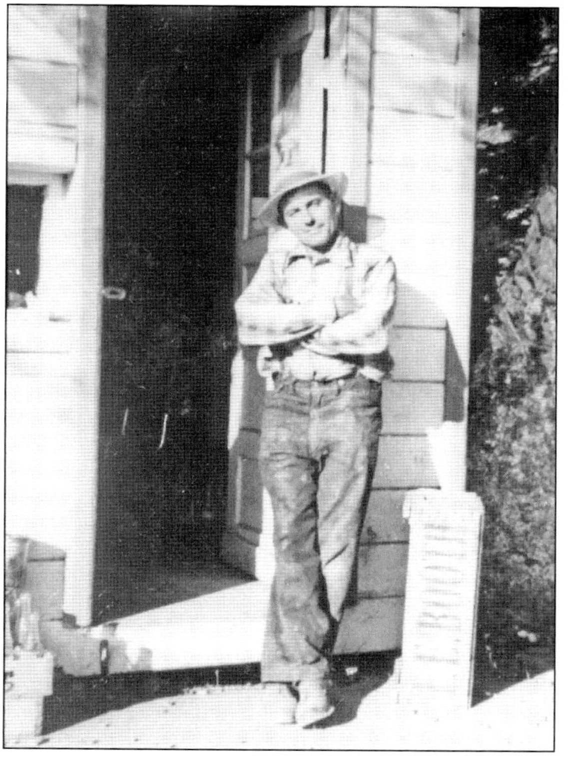

Manuel Freitas and wooden boxes for delivering fresh apricots to Booth Cannery are pictured here. The Freitas apricot orchard was used to meet the contract requirements for the canning of fresh apricots, while dried apricots might go to another wholesaler specializing in dried fruits. The sulfured apricots drying on trays needed about a week to dry under the full summer sun. (SB.)

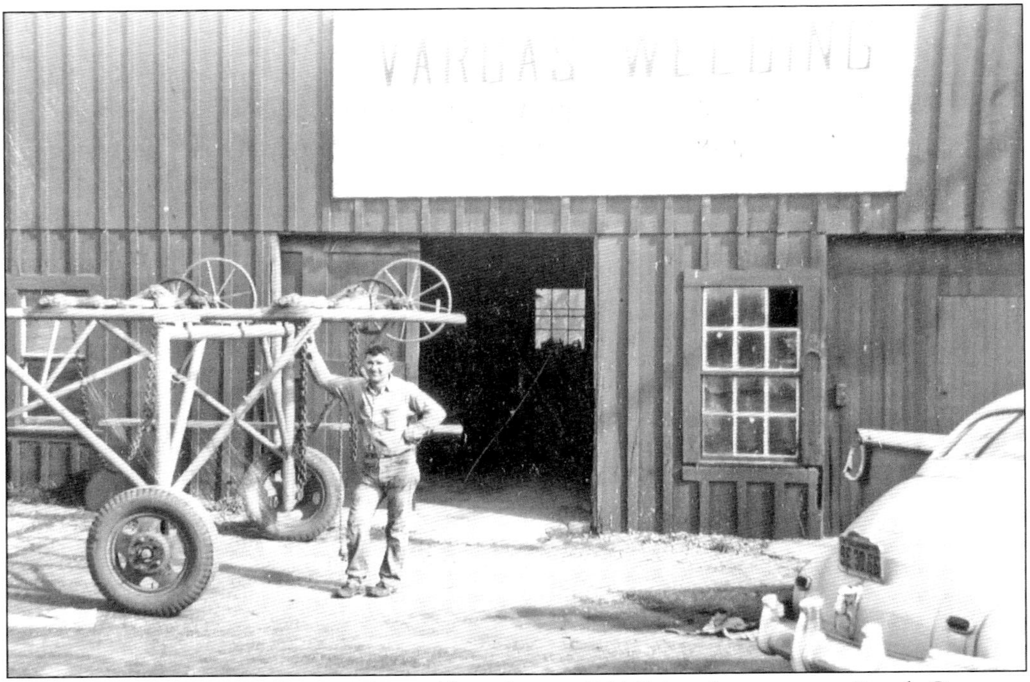

Ernest "Ernie" Vargas is shown at his welding shop at 4114 Baine Avenue, near Booth Cannery. The shop was rented from Joseph "Joe" Jason, who had previously had a well casing shop there. Vargas worked for Jason as a welder prior to World War II and took over the shop until his move to Tracy in 1964. The phone number to the well casing shop was SYcamore 3-0818. (SVM.)

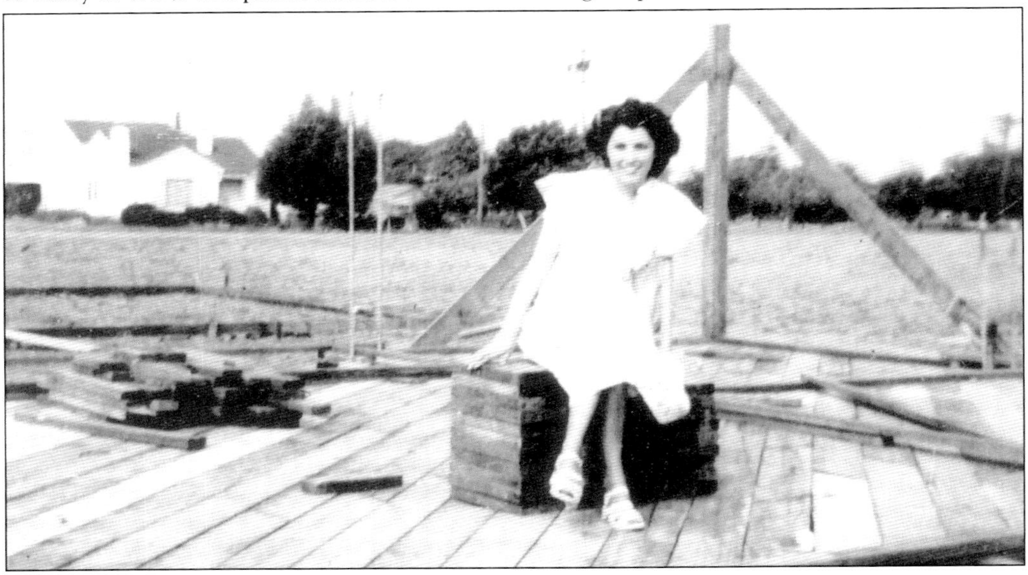

Isabel Maciel Vargas is photographed on the floor of her new house being built at 185 Elm Street (later 37022 Elm Street) in 1948 by Frank Ferreira. Some of the lumber was recycled from barracks at Camp Parks. The back of the Cloverdale Creamery is in the far left. Isabel and Ernie Vargas rented the stable keeper's apartment, which was finished in fine woods, above the empty Bunting stables at the Freitas ranch after Ernie returned from service in occupied Japan in 1946. (SVM.)

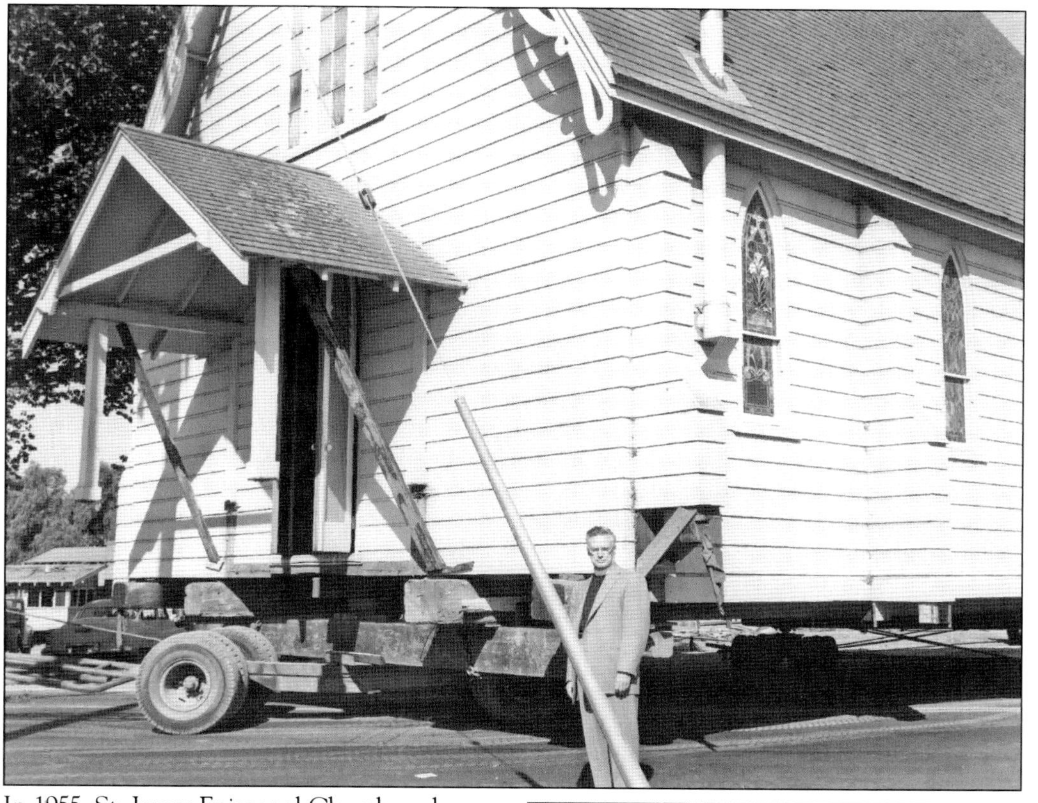

In 1955, St. James Episcopal Church and its guildhall were moved down Thornton Avenue from its 19th-century home at the corner of Thornton and Highway 17, accompanied by Rev. Arthur Freeman, who had achieved parish status for the church in 1948. The procession ended at the new St. James Street off Thornton Avenue.

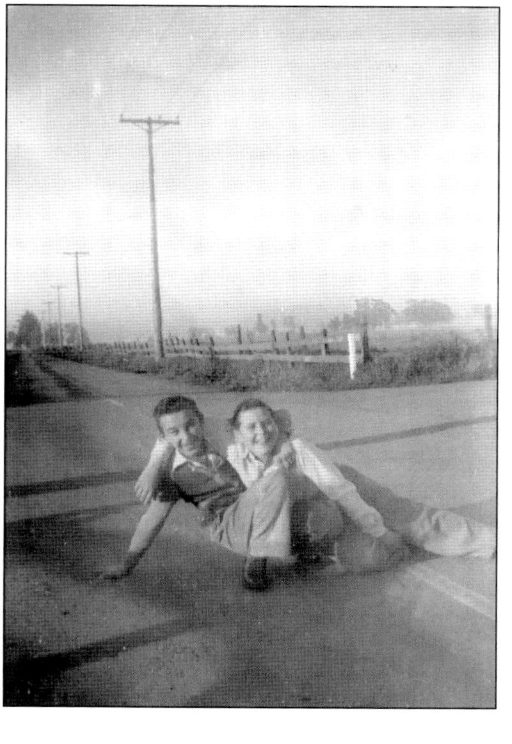

This c. 1937 photograph shows open country and no traffic at the corner of Blacow Road and Mowry Road. Louie Sessa and Ricky Richenbacker did not have to worry much about traffic. (RR.)

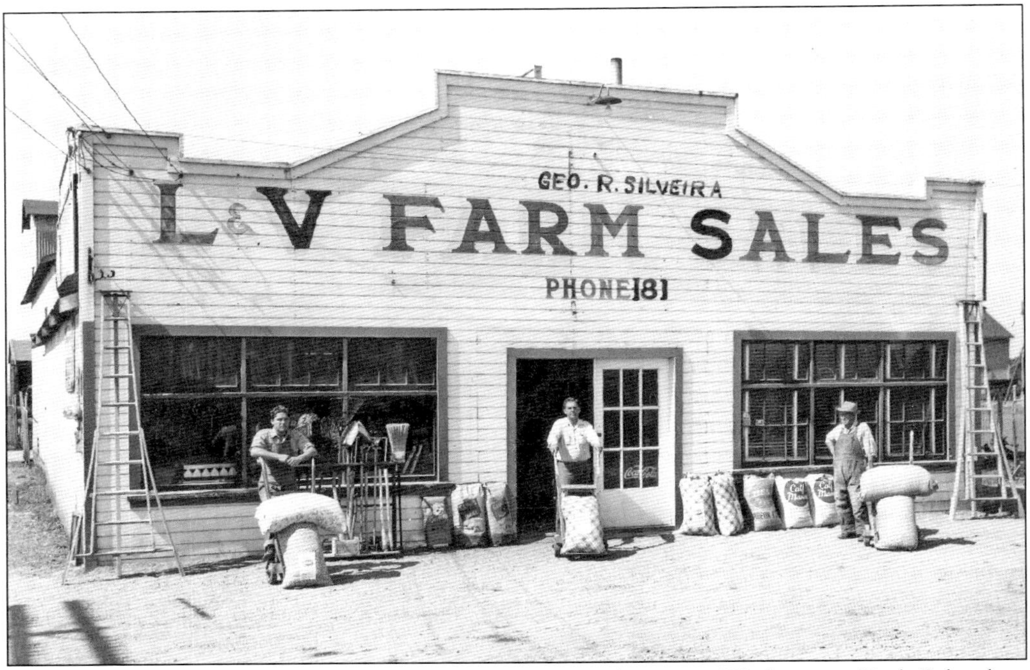

L. V. Farm Sales, operated by George Silveira, was located opposite Washington High School on Highway 17 in the 1940s. A variety of bagged manures, such as calf manure, were in stock, as well as a supply of orchard ladders. Orchard Supply Hardware began in 1931 as a farmers cooperative in Santa Clara, and by the 1950s had expanded into a chain selling general hardware merchandise, with an outlet moving to the location of the Centerville airfield by the 1970s. (AB.)

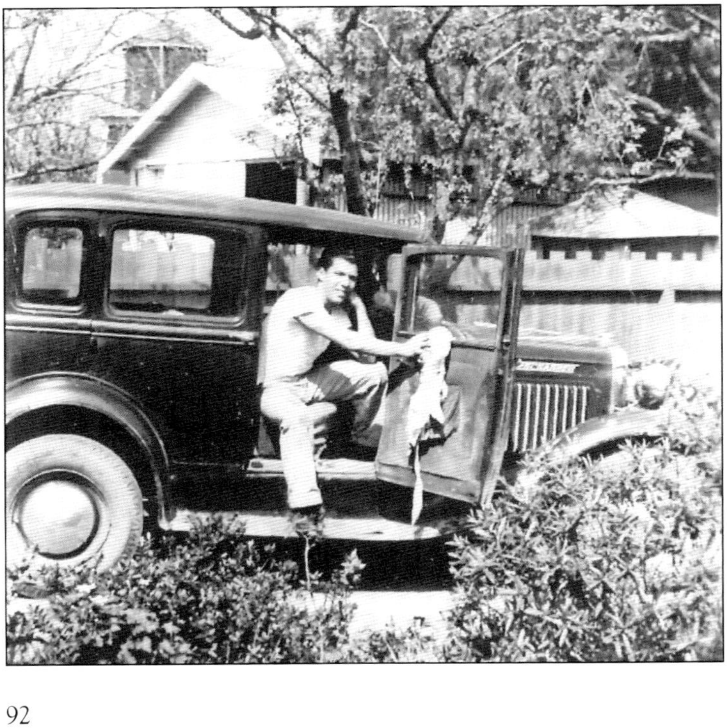

Philip "Phil" Brazil, shown here with his first car, was born in Gustine, California, and moved to Centerville in first grade, eventually graduating from Washington High School. After serving in the U.S. Navy in World War II, he graduated from San Jose State College and returned to teach and coach at Centerville. By 1956, he was the school principal, and after unification, he became superintendant of the Fremont Unified School District in 1973. His leadership and stabilizing presence were greatly admired. (PB.)

Alexander "Alex" Bernard graduated from Washington High School in 1955 as a star athlete on the football team. He worked in carpentry for the expanding Kimber Farms poultry genetics operation on Mission Boulevard while also pursuing his interests in competitive bodybuilding, winning first place in an Alameda County competition. (AB.)

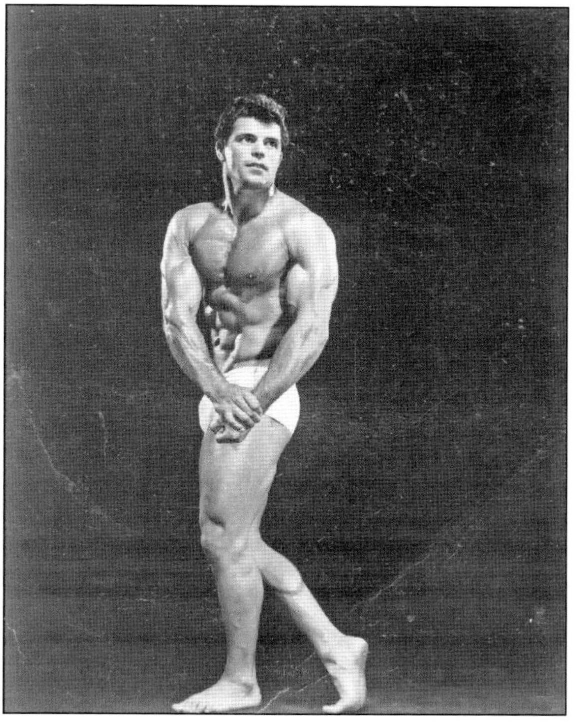

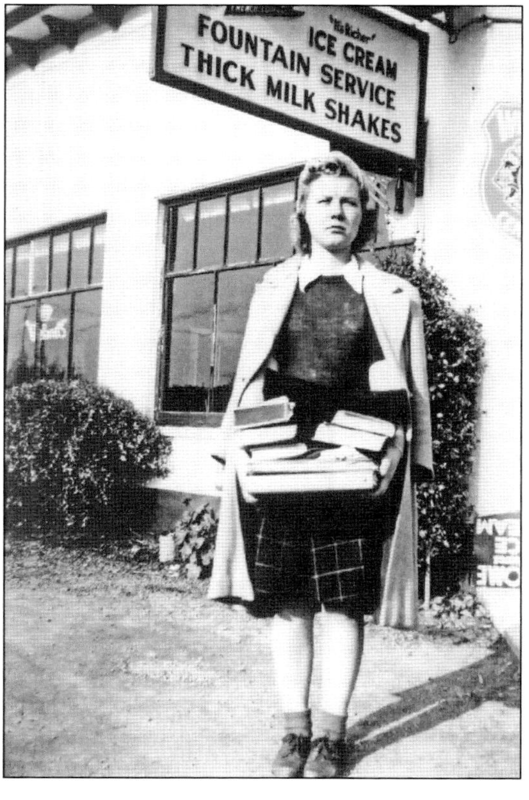

The Snack Shack or the "Black and White" was the place for students to gather at the soda fountain counter just north of the Washington High School campus. The Lions Club was formed and met there in 1931. A full campus cafeteria was planned for 1939 that served hot lunches for several decades. The lunch spot was so popular that the owners returned the favor and hosted a Halloween party one year. It burned down in 1927 but rose quickly from the ashes.

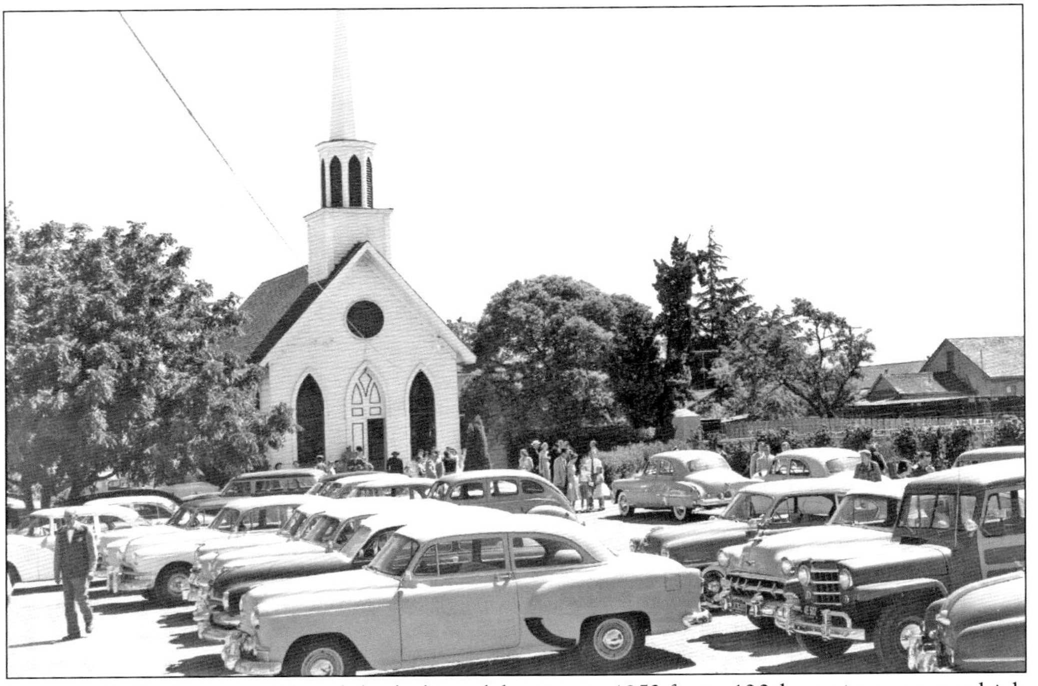

Centerville Presbyterian Church had a big celebration in 1953 for its 100th anniversary, at which time it's membership had greatly increased to 170. Two years later, the church purchased 4 acres on Central Avenue in order to accommodate a fellowship hall and provide for future church expansion. The old white church was burned in an arson fire when it was standing vacant in 1994. The steeple was saved by community leader Dirk Lorenz and stored as a much-loved Centerville landmark.

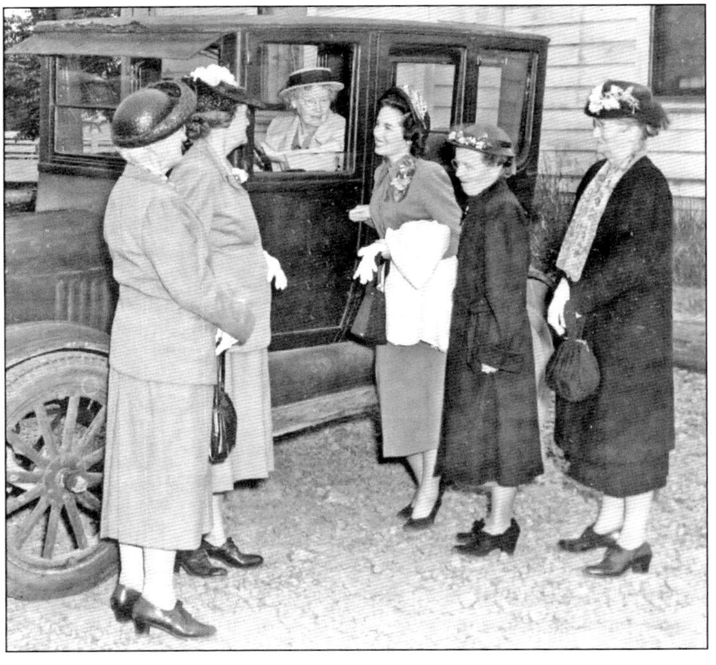

Film actress Colleen Townsend visits with churchwomen at Centerville Presbyterian Church in 1953. In 1948, she was on the cover of *Life* magazine, which profiled her as an example of how the movie industry developed the movie star as a product. Her biggest film was *When Willie Comes Marching Home*. She left the movie star life in 1950, studied theology in San Francisco, raised a family, wrote books, and undertook humanitarian projects.

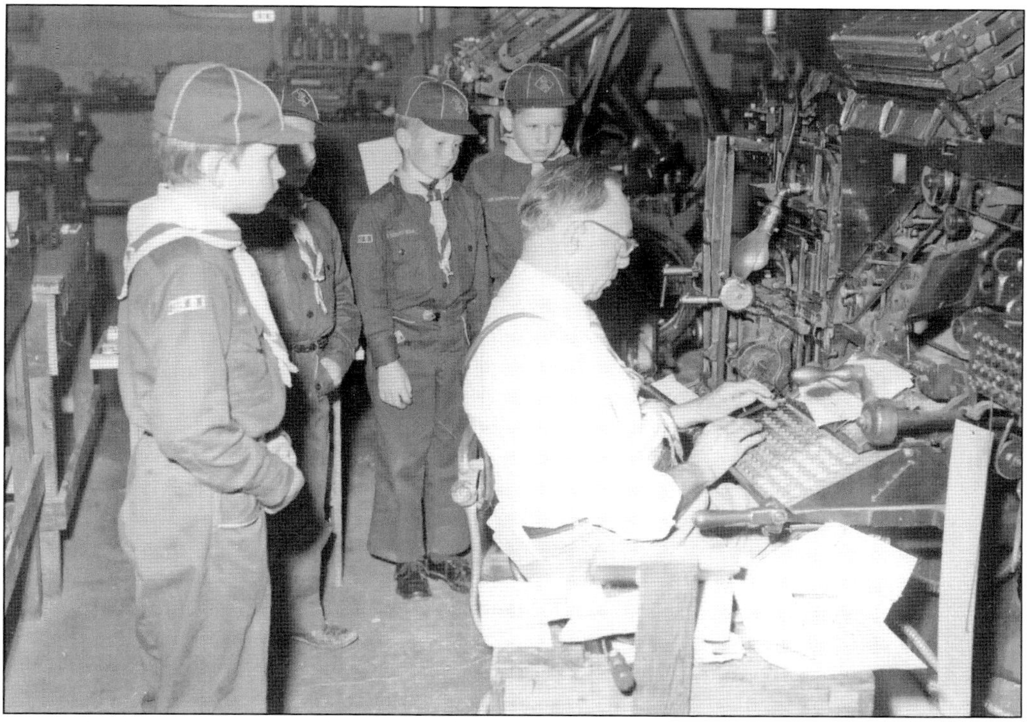

George P. Oakes of the *Township Register* demonstrates typesetting to Cub Scouts in the 1950s. Oakes grew up in the newspaper business in Alvarado. The *Centerville News*, which began in 1917, combined with Stuart Nixon's *Township Register* in 1954 at 3684 Peralta Boulevard. George Oakes became owner by 1959. A rotary press was installed there in 1962. The *News Register* was sold to the *Argus* on April 29, 1972.

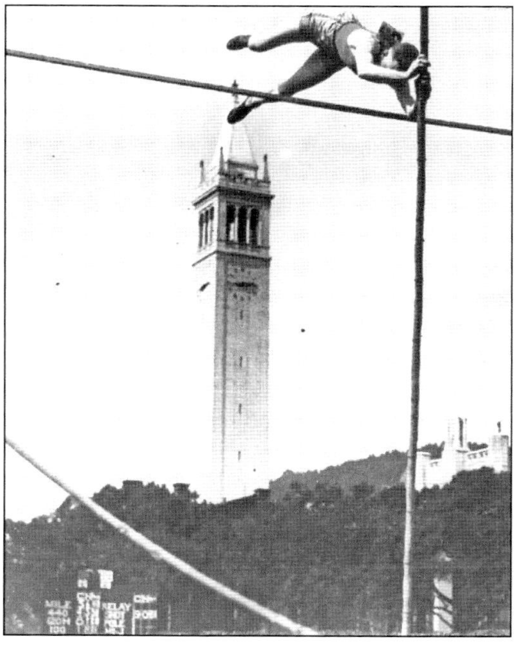

Allen Norris was a champion pole-vaulter at the University of California and was the individual national champion in 1921–1922. He received his law degree in 1925 and served as justice of the Centerville court from 1927 until he was appointed to the Alameda County Superior Court in 1953. He was a leader of many community groups and a perennial speaker and master of ceremonies. He was called "the most popular man in public life in Washington Township" in his 1978 obituary.

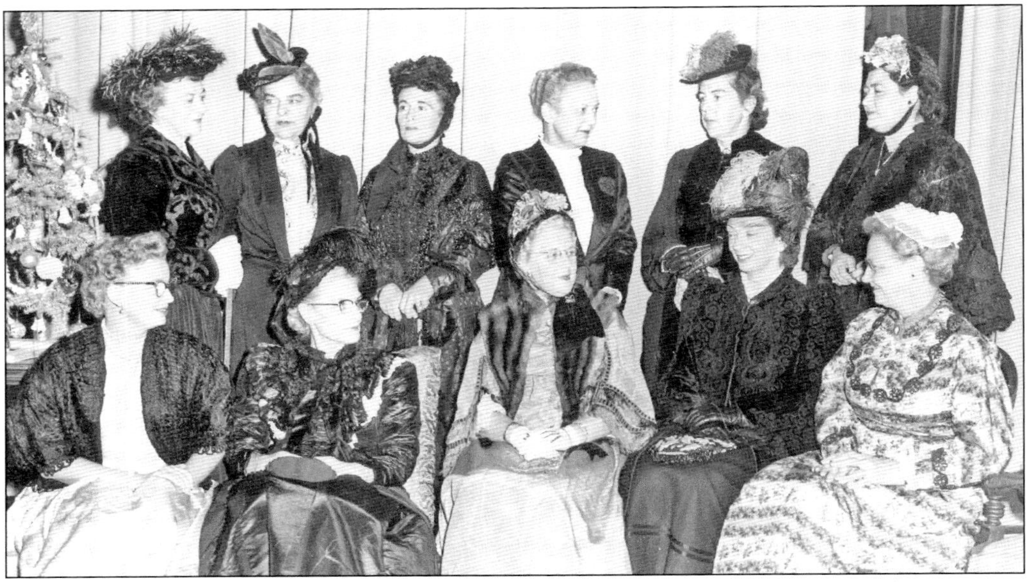

Country club ladies in 1957 celebrate the 61st anniversary of the Washington Township Country Club at the Parish Avenue clubhouse by dressing up as the Country Club of Washington Township founders. Pictured, from left to right, are (first row) Mrs. Vernon Miller, Mrs. Paul Offel, Mrs. Thomas Elliott, Mrs. Elmer Meyer, and Mrs. Samuel Scott; (second row) Mrs. Walter Connolly, Mrs. James E. Shinn Jr., Mrs. Mervin Mento, Mrs. Roy Clark, Mrs. Joseph Svoboda, and Mrs. Ralph Logan.

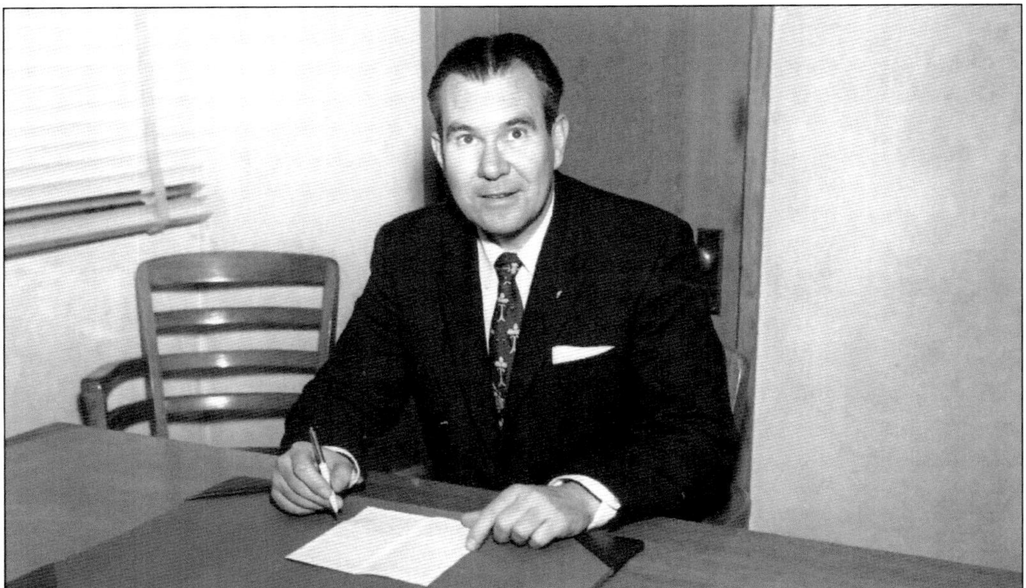

Tom Maloney came to the Centerville School District as a teacher in 1930 and became principal in 1934. He served as district superintendent through the growth years when Centerville expanded from one to eight schools. After unification of the Fremont Unified School District in 1964, he became associate superintendent. He not only served the schools but was a leader of numerous service clubs and community organizations.

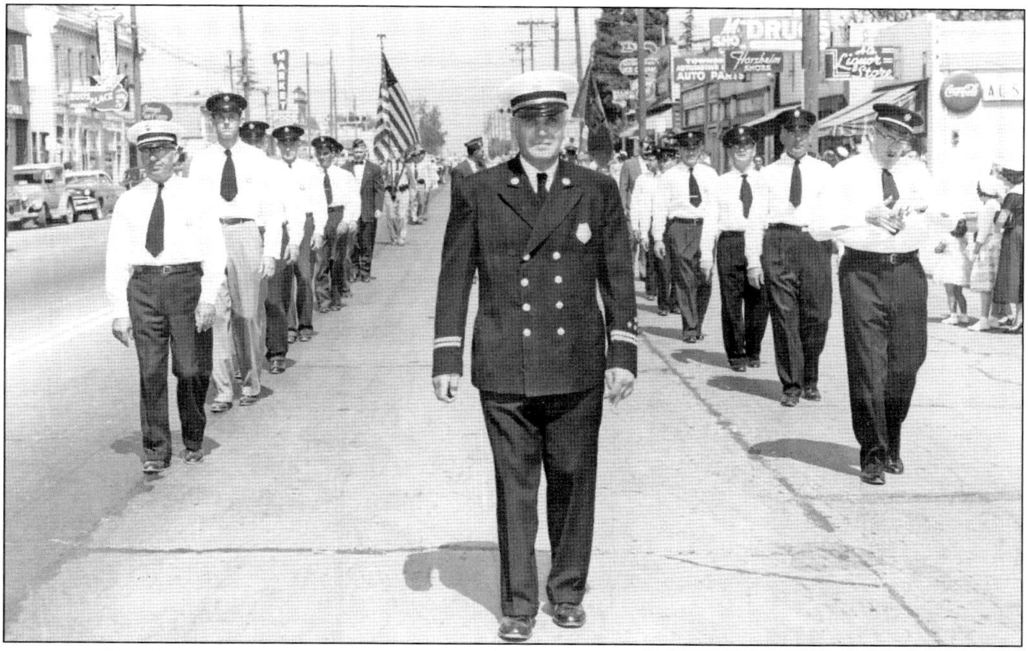

Fire chief Frank Madruga marches in a parade down Centerville's Main Street in 1955. He became Fremont's first fire chief when the city incorporated on January 10, 1956. The present Fremont Fire Station No. 1 was built at the intersection of Mowry Avenue and Argonaut Way in 1963 for the Central Business District. Frank Madruga served as the first Fremont fire chief until 1960. Volunteer firefighters were phased out in 1969.

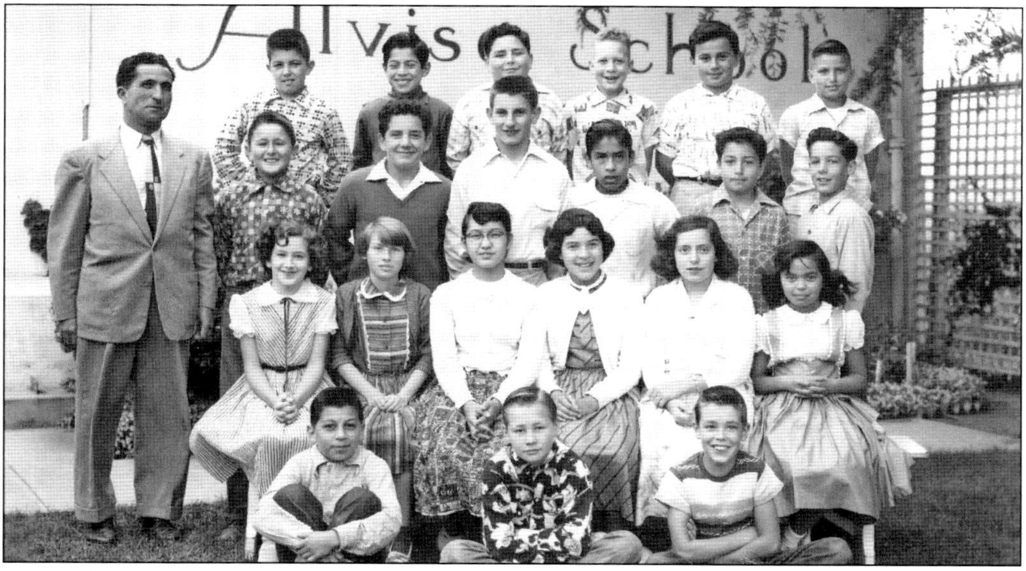

Principal James Nunes poses with fifth- and sixth-graders at Alviso School in 1955. Nunes taught school from 1936 to 1966 mostly at Alviso School. He became principal at Alviso in 1948 and oversaw its transition into the Fremont Unified School District. A new building was erected in 1940, replacing the second school building of 1910. The original school was established in 1856. Alviso School closed in 1978 with the completion of Warwick School. (MN.)

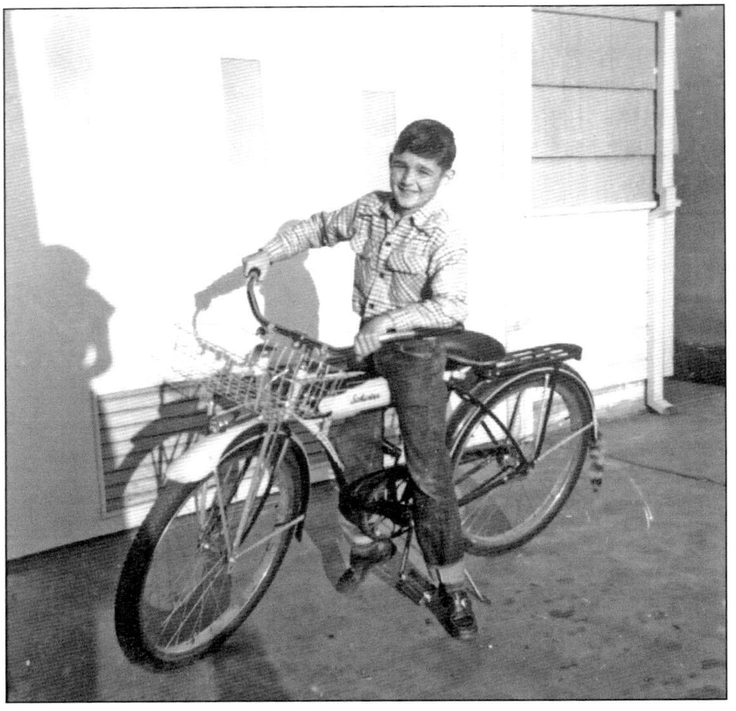

Gene Ramsell Jr., a young Centerville cyclist in 1951, shows off his new three-speed bike from the Oakland Montgomery Ward retail store. Bikes of the day had names like Red Phantom (for its swooping lines) or Air Scout (for its balloon tires)—all suitable for cycling around the streets and sidewalks of the new Hansen subdivision. (RR.)

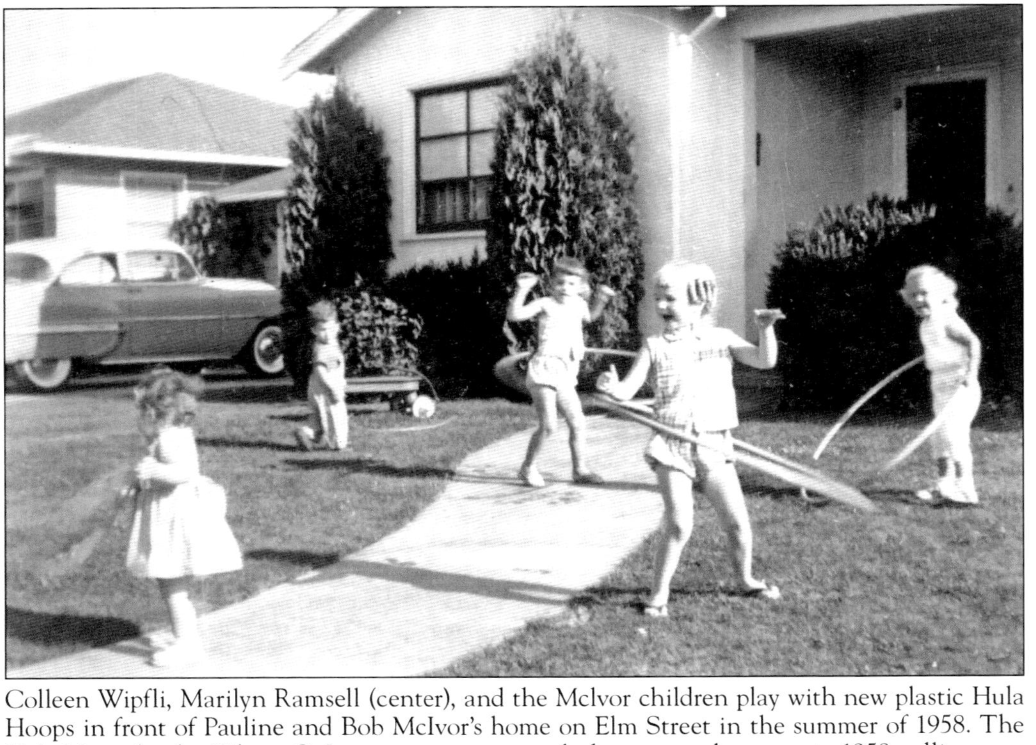

Colleen Wipfli, Marilyn Ramsell (center), and the McIvor children play with new plastic Hula Hoops in front of Pauline and Bob McIvor's home on Elm Street in the summer of 1958. The Hula Hoop, by the Wham-O, Inc., toy company, took the country by storm in 1958, selling over 25 million that summer alone at a price $1.98 each. (RR.)

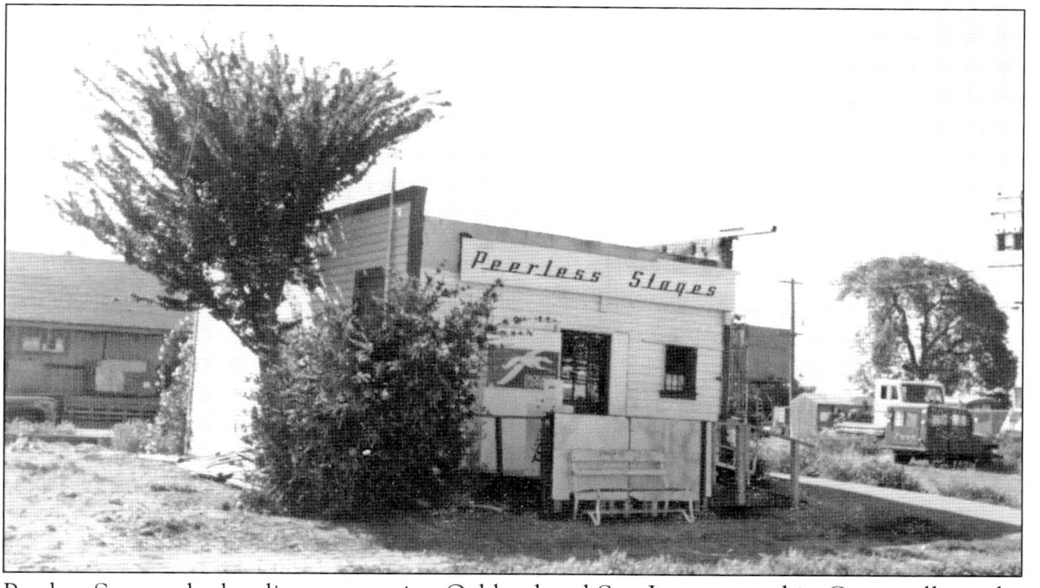

Peerless Stages, the bus line connecting Oakland and San Jose, stopped in Centerville at the former Japanese School building, owned by the Ranoa family, on Bonde Way. Peerless Stages began 1921, derived from a 1914 jitney operation. A Peerless Stage bus made by General Motors in 1955 is part of the "rolling collection" of the Pacific Bus Museum serving the Niles Bus Lines today. The Peerless Station was originally built next to the Williams warehouses as the Japanese School for after school language classes in the 1930s.

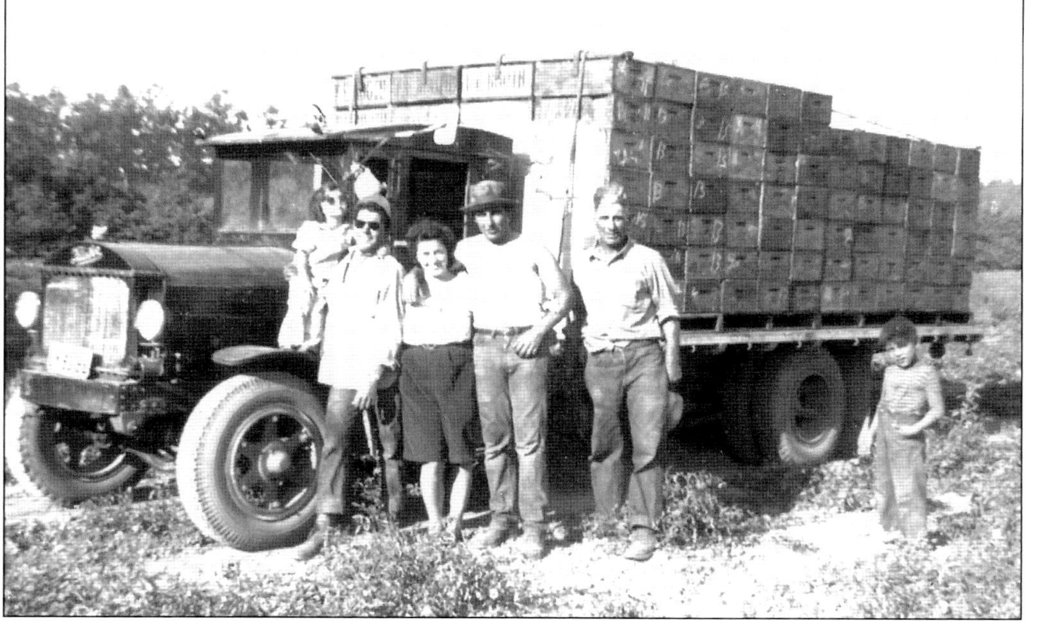

The Maciel family of Warm Springs rented the fine farmland with its Class I alluvial soils at Patterson ranch to grow tomatoes in the 1940s. The family poses here with their successful crated crop. Farmers contracted with Booth Cannery, pre-arranging a delivery contract of the crop at a specific stage of ripeness at a fixed price. (SVM.)

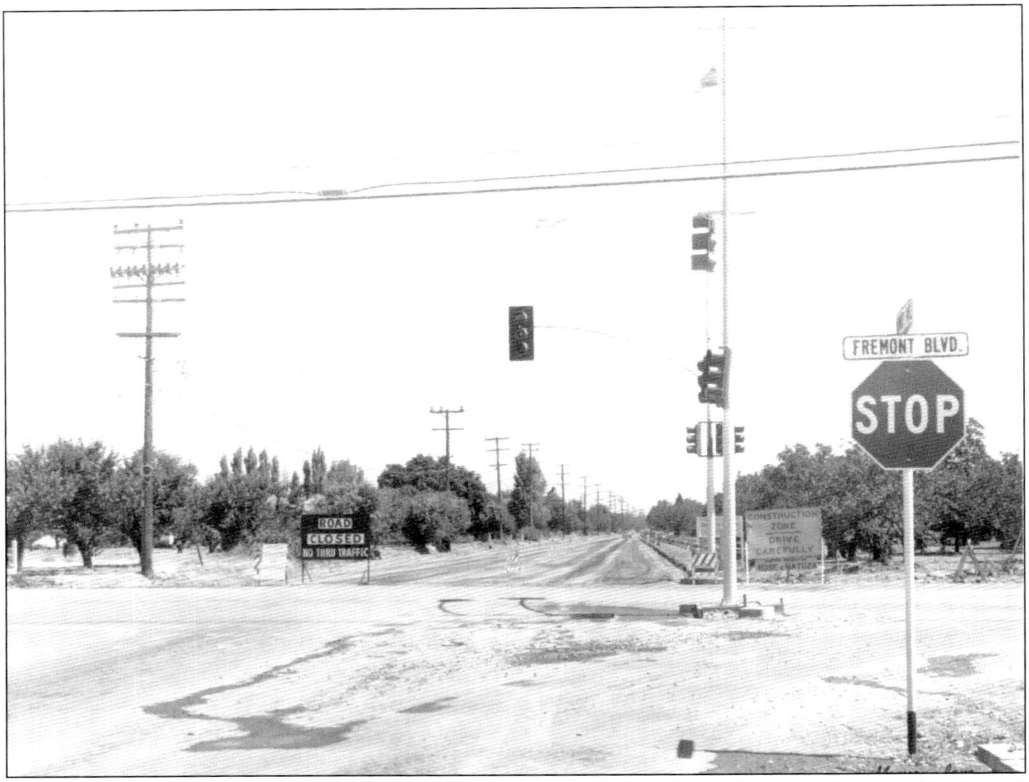

Shortly after Fremont incorporated in 1956, Centerville's Main Street became Fremont Boulevard and Mowry Avenue continued on toward Niles. Washington Hospital, opened in November 1958, was taking shape on Mowry, largely surrounded by orchards and cauliflower fields. This image shows the intersection of Fremont Boulevard and Mowry Avenue as they grew from narrow two-lane streets to four-lane divided thoroughfares. Note the sign on the left: "Traffic permitted to hospital."

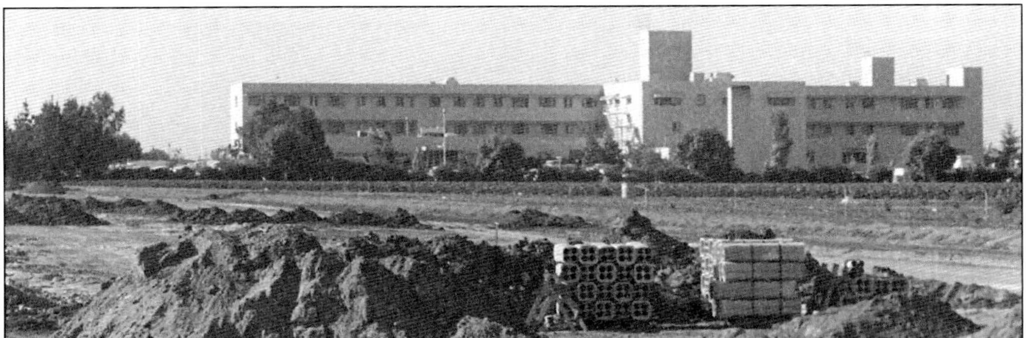

The nearest medical facilities in the 1940s were in San Jose or Oakland. Public meetings regarding the possibilities of securing a local hospital led to the approval of a tax bond and the formation of the Washington Township Hospital District. A future site for the hospital was purchased on Santos Road (now Mowry Avenue) in 1952. Construction was begun in 1956, and the doors opened to the public in 1958. Founding medical staff members were Conrad Anderson, Merle Buehler, Lyle Buehler, Robert Fisher, E. C. Grau, E. M. Grimmer, Frank McMahon, John O'Connor, and Guy Romito.

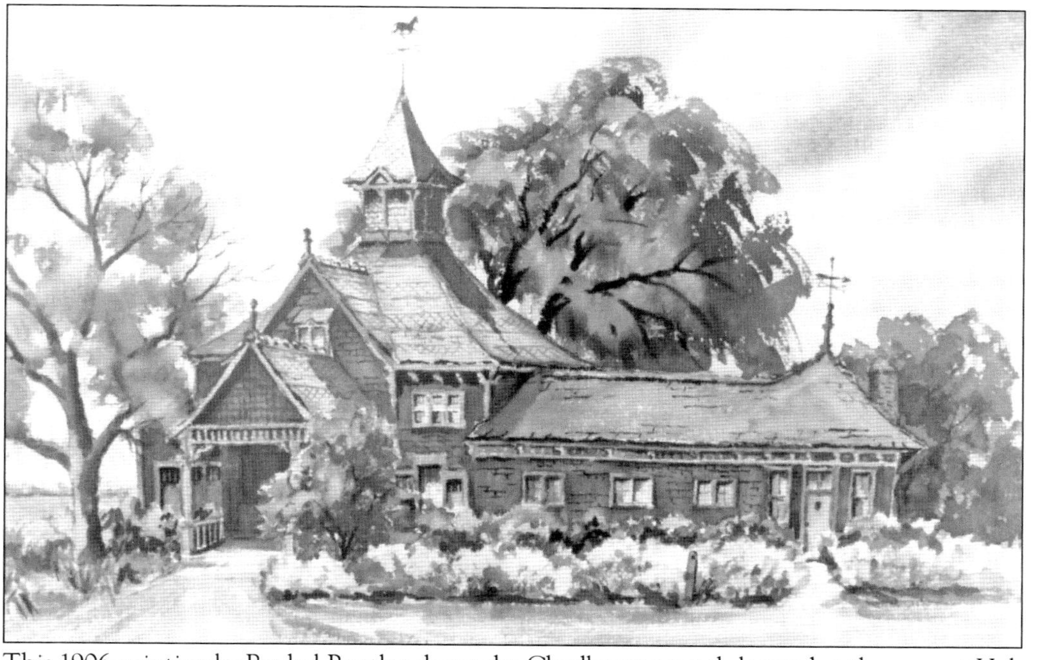

This 1906 painting by Rachel Bentley shows the Chadbourne ranch located at the present Hub shopping center. Joseph Chadbourne purchased 144 acres with an adobe house in 1866. It would stay in the family for 75 years. The Chadbournes built a clapboard house around the 1860s that included two walls of original adobe house. The carriage house dates to 1885. Howard and Mattie Chadbourne inherited it in 1916 and lived there for many years. Howard moved to a new house on Mowry Avenue in 1947 and took the stable wing to that parcel in 1964. The Chilean pepper tree behind the Chadbourne carriage house is from the garden of the original farmhouse.

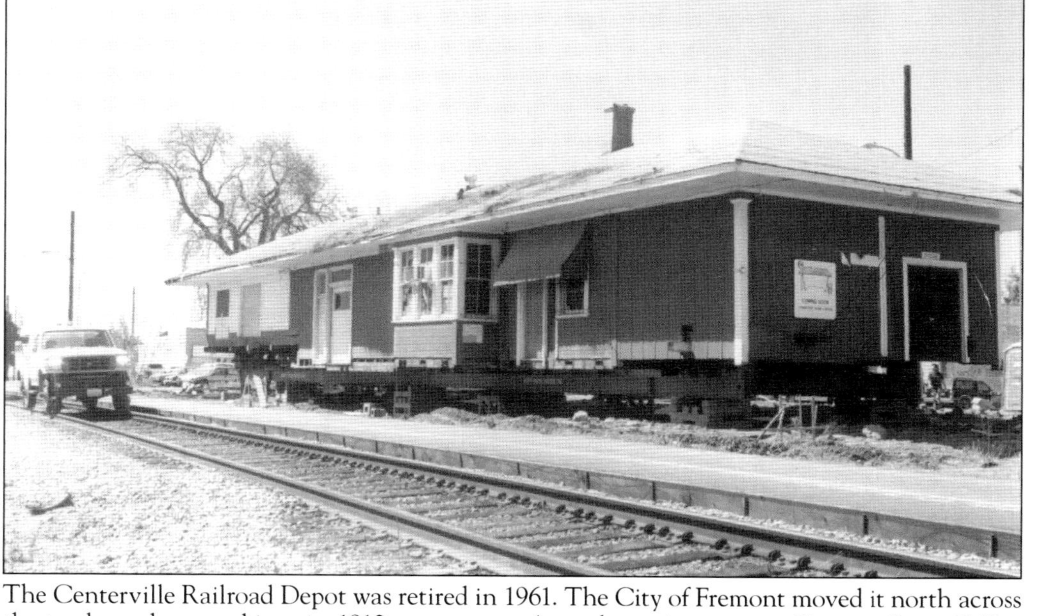

The Centerville Railroad Depot was retired in 1961. The City of Fremont moved it north across the tracks and restored it to its 1910 appearance. Amtrak service came to Centerville in 1993.

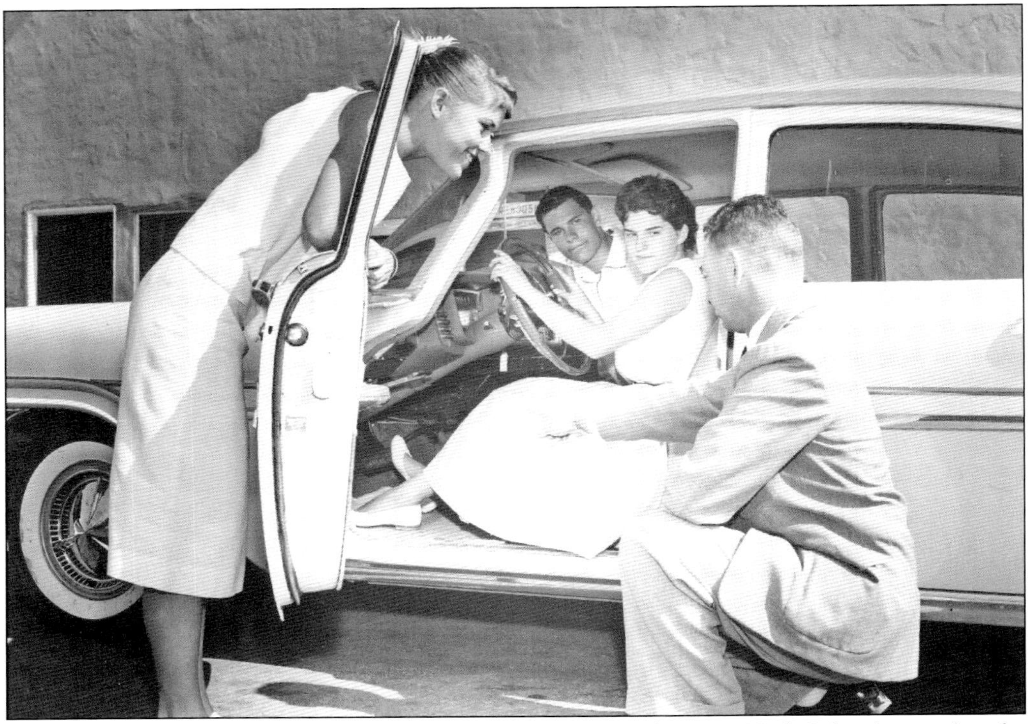

This photograph of the new driver education program at Washington High School was taken for George Oakes of the *News Register*. Pictured, from left to right, are Pat Sorenson, Brad Barham, Joanne Mooney, and instructor Clinton Sparks. In 1967, California required students to receive 30 hours of driver education. In 1998, California passed much greater restrictions on teen driving, but by 2005, the high school had cut back on driver education classes.

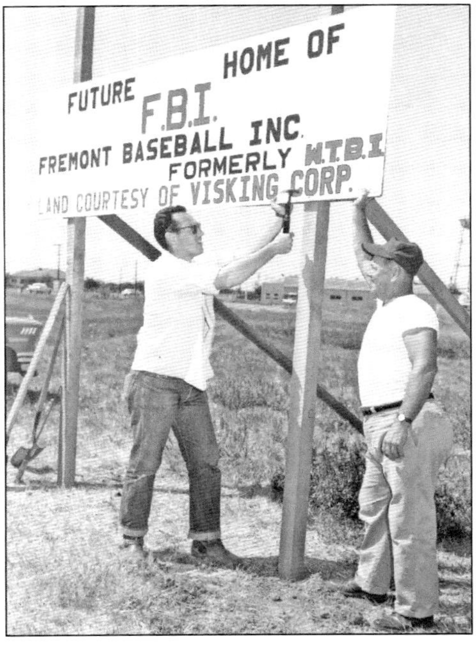

Fremont Baseball, Inc., was founded in 1954 as Washington Township Baseball. In this photograph, its organizers are posting the 1959 start-up at Nordvik Park. Organizers included Carl Nordvik, ? Lamb, and Louis Manuel. The original teams were Glenmoor Homes (Centerville), Passco Steelers (Niles), Our Lady of the Holy Rosary (Decoto), Rick-Mark Shopping Center (Irvington), Mission San Jose, and Fremont Fire Department (Irvington). Later the league was divided into the National League—the original teams—and American League teams, added in 1956 and 1957.

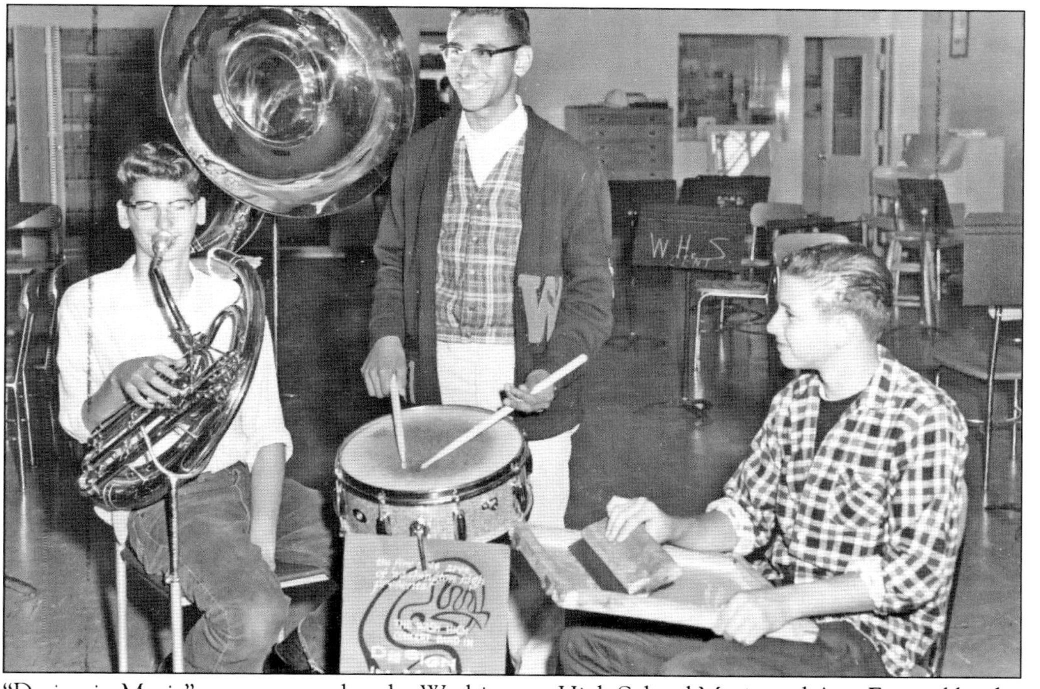

"Design in Music" was presented at the Washington High School Music and Arts Festival by the Washington High Concert Band in the 1950s. Pictured, from left to right, are Dave De George, sousaphone; Robert "Bob" Avila, snare drum; and Ronald "Ron" Pfeiffer, art department squeegee sound effects. The bottom of the silkscreen poster showed the concert price of 75¢.

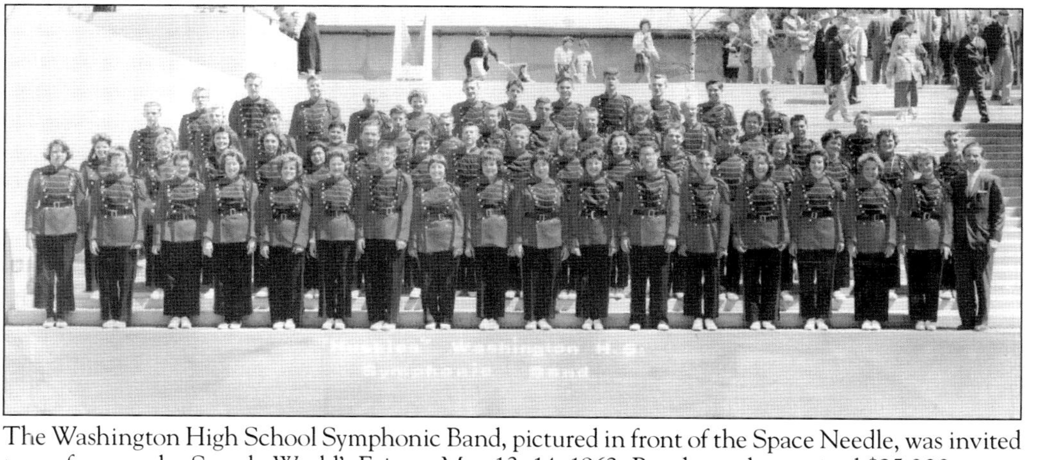

The Washington High School Symphonic Band, pictured in front of the Space Needle, was invited to perform at the Seattle World's Fair on May 13–14, 1962. Band members raised $25,000 to pay for the trip. They held bake sales and car washes, placed collection cans near cash registers at many businesses, and played special concerts. Most money was raised when students went door to door in their uniforms. The director was Orrin C. Cross III. (PB.)

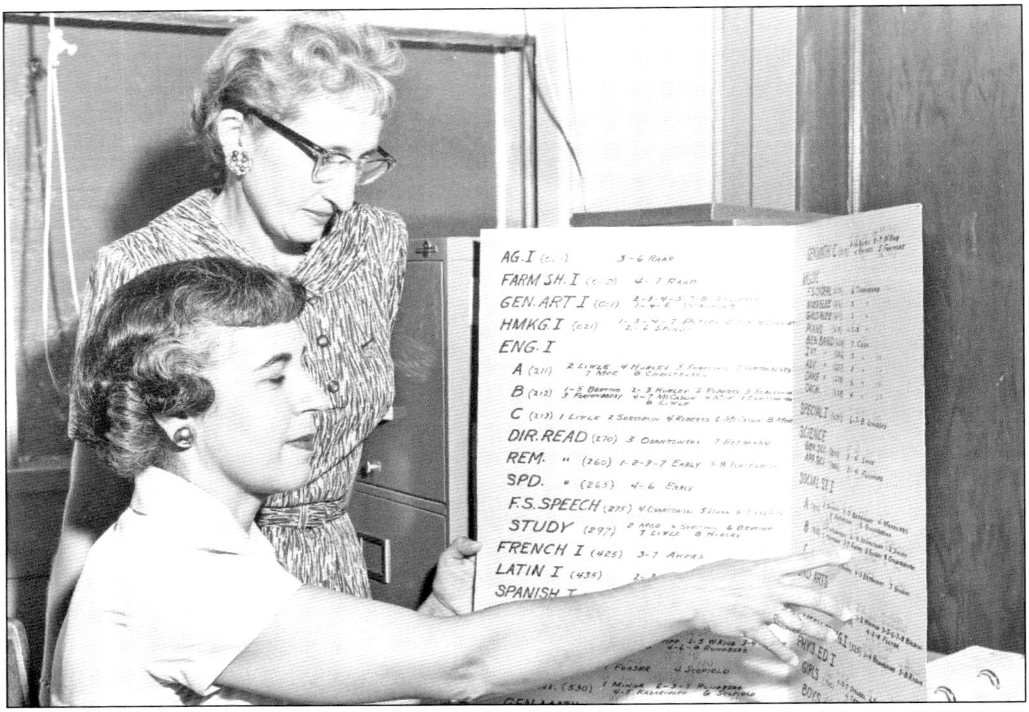

Washington High School teachers show the handwritten final teacher schedules for 1958–1959. Pictured are Doris Van Scoy (sitting) and Georgia Kay. Glee was taught by Dwight Thornburg, and band was taught by Bill Cook. Bill Rapp taught the agricultural courses, and boys physical education was taught by Messrs. Stelle, Walton, Albaugh, King, and Walsh.

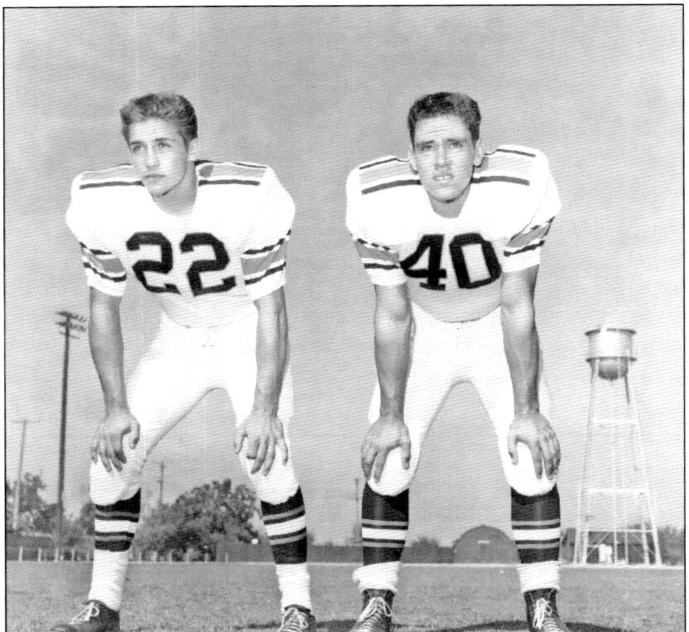

The 1959 Washington High School football players included Charles "Chuck" Wittebort, left, and Kenneth "Ken" Stahl. The October 28, 2009, issue of the *TriCity Voice* reported that at coach Jim Ingram's memorial in 2009, retired U.S. Army Col. Chuck Wittebort (class of 1961) spoke, saying "Success was built around the team, not the individual; there were no prima donnas." Leonard Fudenna, a member of the undefeated 1967 and 1968 Huskies teams, recalled the combative spirit Ingram instilled in his team. "He loved a good fight," said Fudenna, "even if we lost the fight."

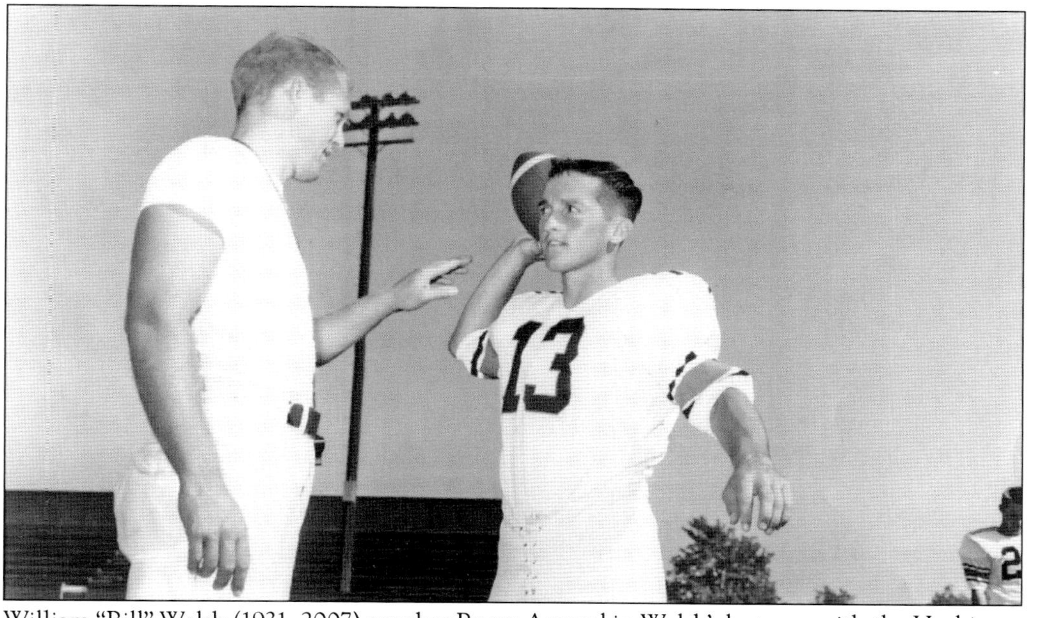

William "Bill" Walsh (1931–2007) coaches Roger Amaral in Walsh's last year with the Huskies at Washington High School. Walsh began in football as a student at Hayward High School. Walsh's master's thesis at San Jose State University was on defending a pro-set formation. His professional football coaching career was from 1966 to 1988 and included seven postseasons and three Super Bowl wins with the 49ers.

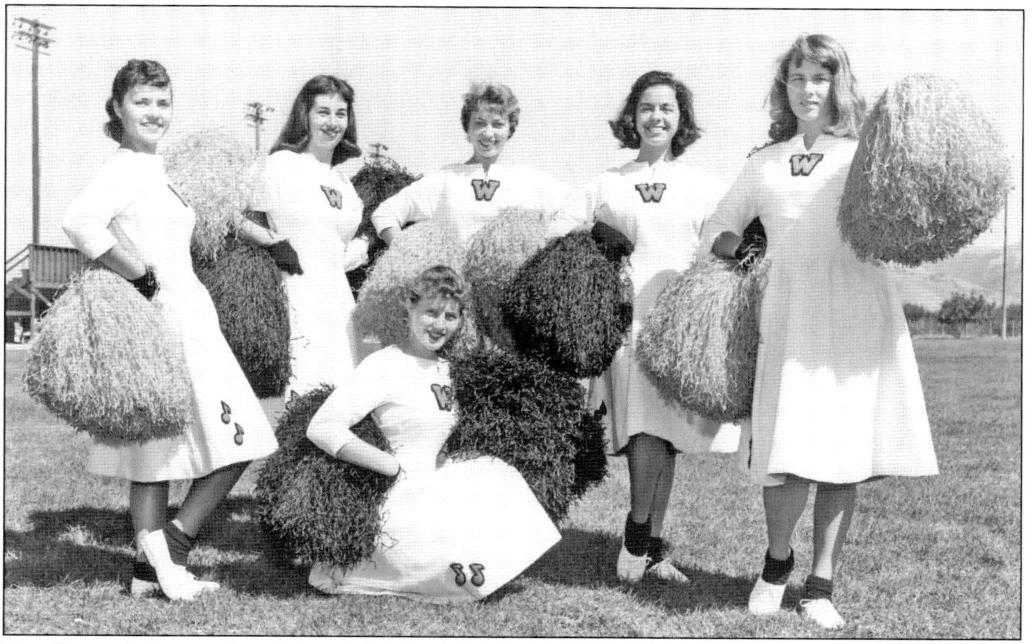

The Song Girls was the name of the Washington High School cheerleading group. Their flared skater-style dresses are set off by black bobby socks and white tennis shoes. Pictured, from left to right, are (first row) Carol Bauhofer; (second row) Patricia Pennington, Adrienne Oliveiria, Judy Winter, Diana Villauer, and Marianne Vochatzer.

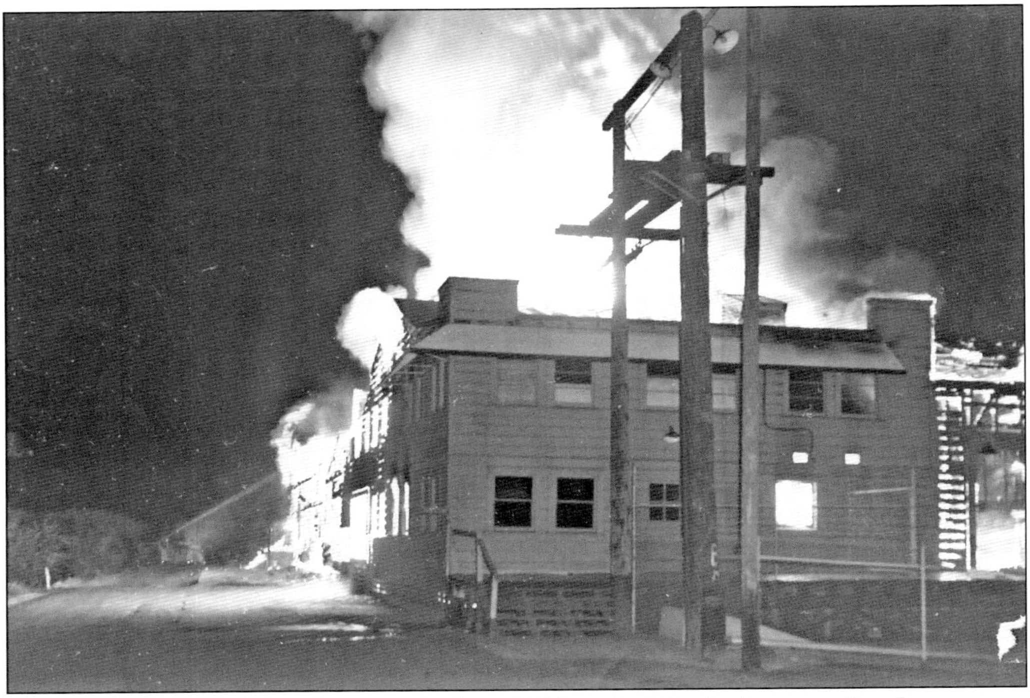

The Booth Cannery burned spectacularly in 1959, and while the Fremont Fire Department contained it from spreading, the cannery facilities were never replaced. Frank Booth began as a fish canner in San Francisco, making his name as a sardine canner in Monterey by 1903 because he mechanized and upgraded the process. Just as the sardine industry collapsed at Monterey in the 1950s, the fields of tomatoes and acres of apricot orchards disappeared in Fremont in the 1950s.

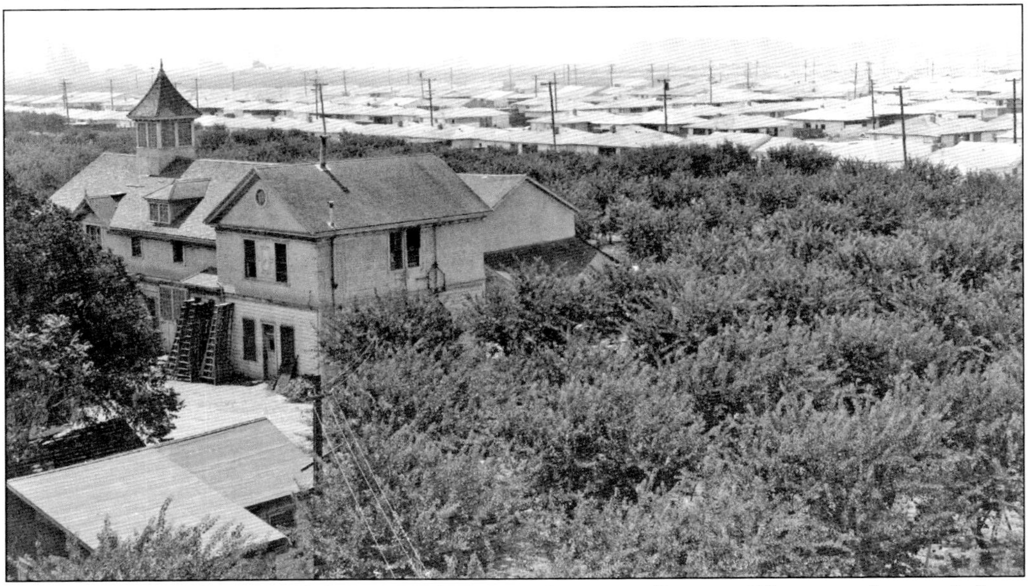

The view toward the new subdivisions adjacent to Sycamore Farm on Thornton Avenue is from the top of the old Bunting tank house around 1960. Most of the old Sycamore Farm buildings burned in 1968 and have been in various states of disrepair for some decades. (SB.)

Six

Fields of Play 1960–2010

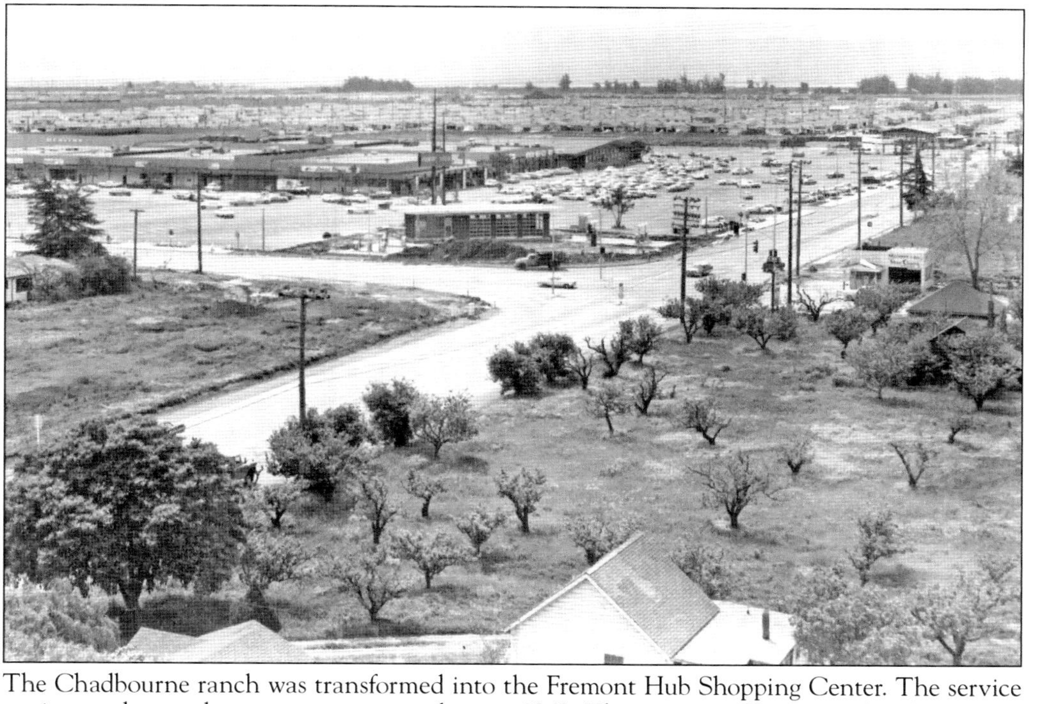

The Chadbourne ranch was transformed into the Fremont Hub Shopping Center. The service station at the northeast corner was in place in 1962. The main road crossing the photograph from lower left to upper right is Mowry Avenue, heading towards the bay. The other street is Fremont Boulevard, also known as Highway 17. Even the cauliflower fields that followed in the Innes-Cloverdale dairy pastures are long gone with the construction of the Fremont Hub Shopping Center.

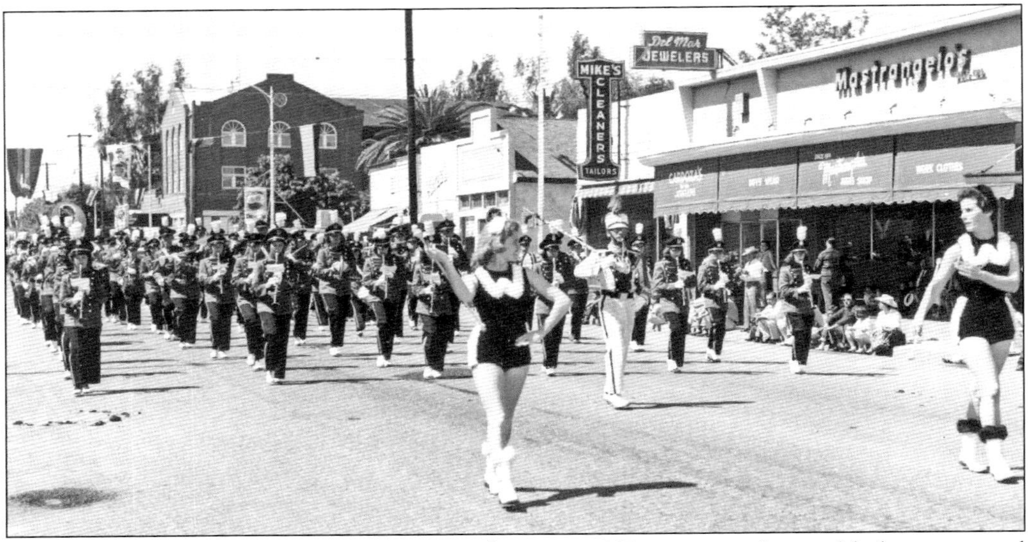

The Washington High School Marching Band poses in 1959 in new uniforms of dark orange wool serge, black pants, and white Dinkles shoes. The parade location in this photograph is unknown but it is likely in Alameda County. The majorettes' costumes cleverly use the same fuzzy trim as their boots to make the letter W on their tops. The old gym floor from the Washington High School with its giant W was rescued after demolition in the 1990s and was cut into pieces for fund-raiser souvenirs.

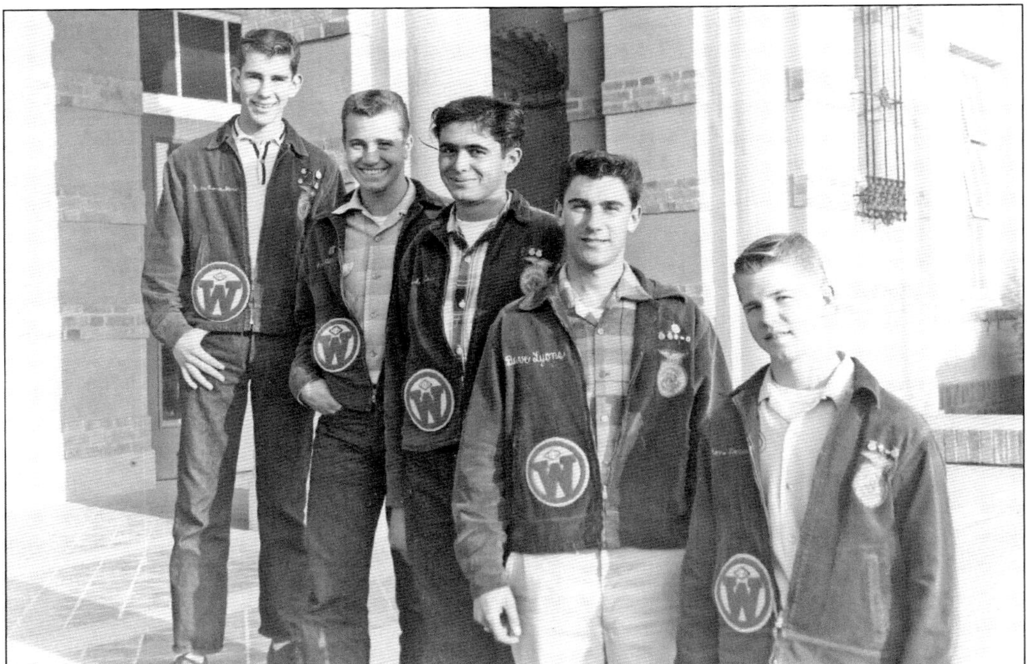

The main entrance arch of Washington High School frames the Future Farmers of America (FFA) leadership team in 1959. The FFA was a widely admired program at Washington High School from 1937 through the 1960s. Pictured from left to right are Michael Overacker Jr., two unidentified, David Lyons, and unidentified.

In this c. 1963 image, Louise, Jim, and Bill Orsetti wait for the bus on Decoto Road to attend Alviso School. The Orsetti family (Italian-born Bruno, Florence, and their three children) lived on the 25-acre farm established by Bruno's father, Giovanni, in 1934. They farmed vegetables, packed and delivered to the Oakland produce market. Bruno's brother Virgil had immigrated to the area before Giovanni. Virgil Orsetti had a very large produce operation and formed a family partnership called. V. Orsetti and Sons and eventually distributed produce at Golden Gate Brokerage in San Francisco. (Courtesy of Bruno Orsetti.)

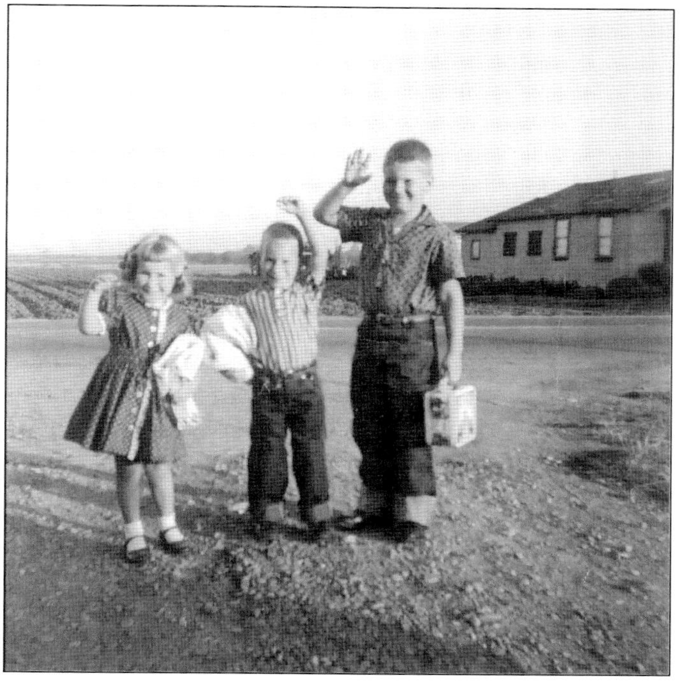

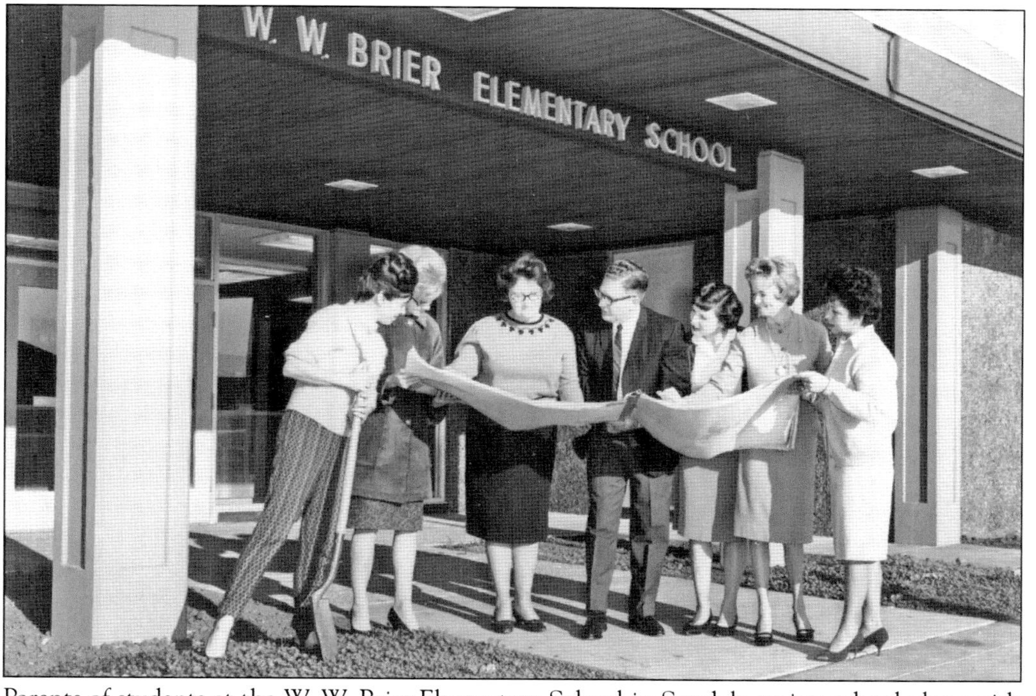

Parents of students at the W. W. Brier Elementary School in Sundale review school plans with principal Dee Clark (center). The school opened in September 1965 after the adjacent 4-acre baseball complex, Brier Park, opened in May 1965 for little league games. Former California governor Ronald Reagan met Fremont Unified School District (FUSD) board members at W. W. Brier Elementary School while electioneering in 1980.

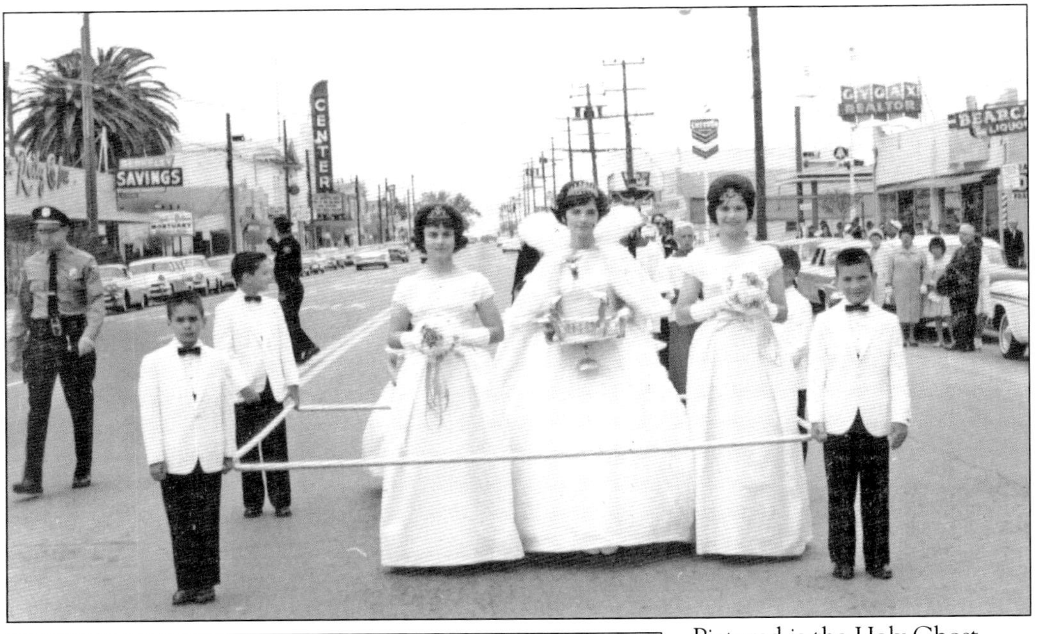

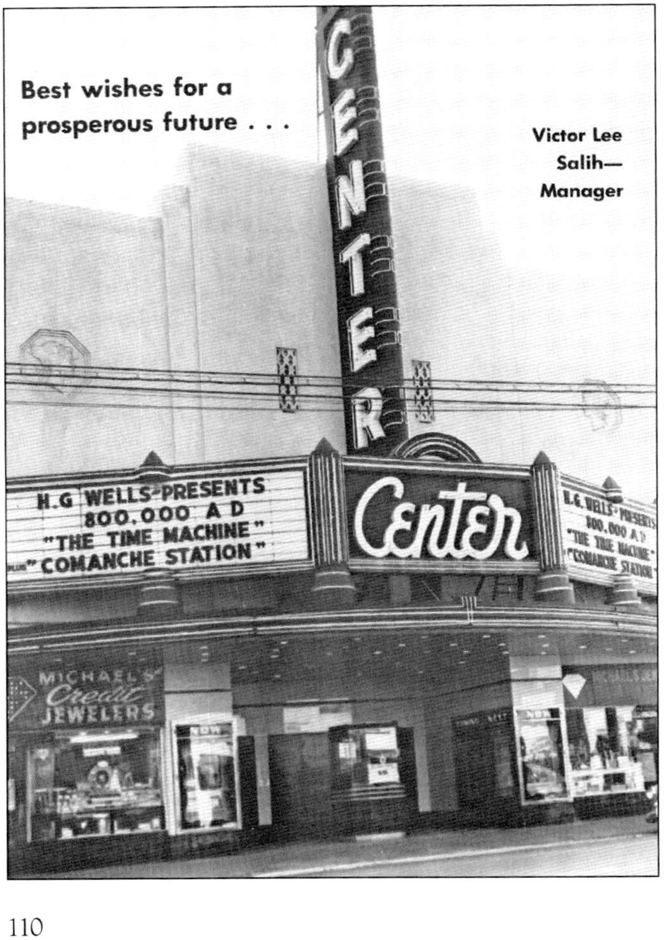

Pictured is the Holy Ghost procession down Centerville's Main Street toward Holy Spirit Catholic Church in 1963. Shown, from left to right, are bar boys Michael and Mark Cordenz, side maid Carol Andrade, queen Susan Vargas, side maid Mary Jane Rivers, and bar boy Emanuel Vargas. The signage behind from left to right includes the Sprouse-Reitz five and dime store, Berkeley Savings, Chapel of the Palms, Center Theater, and Gygax Realtor.

The Center Theater is pictured in 1964. No construction was allowed during World War II. A month after the war ended, the Salih brothers announced their plans for a $150,000 theater to be called the Center. It soon became a mecca for residents who have many fond memories of family movie adventures.

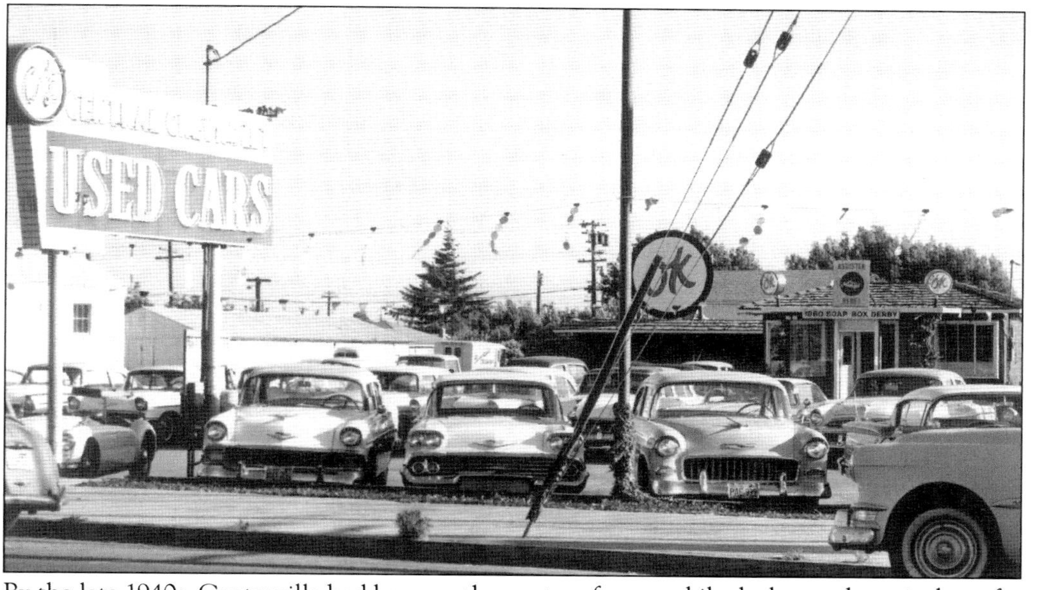

By the late 1940s, Centerville had become the center of automobile dealers and repair shops for Washington Township. A few of the dealerships included the Ford agency operated by Joe Adams; the Central Chevrolet Co., owned by Romeo Brunelli and John Calcagno of the Plymouth and Chrysler agencies owned by the Santos brothers; and the Dodge agency of Paul Hockinson. In the 1990s, most automobile facilities were moved from the Centerville area. Some were relocated to the Fremont Auto Mall.

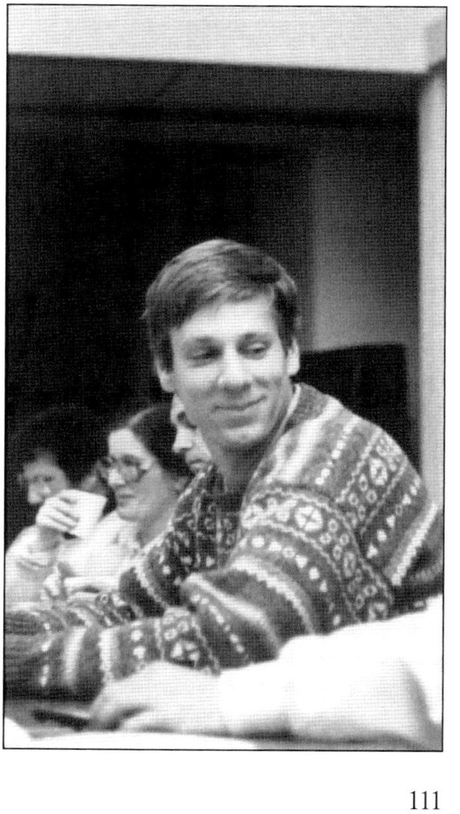

Garth Smith is photographed at a Fremont Telesis Vision committee session in 1989 at the Central Park meeting space. Smith is the owner and manager of Dale Hardware on Post Street in Centerville, a business that his parents began in 1955 in the Center Square Plaza. In 2009, expansion plans were announced to include a garden center and café. Pictured are Jill Singleton (drinking tea) and Garth Smith (right). (JMS.)

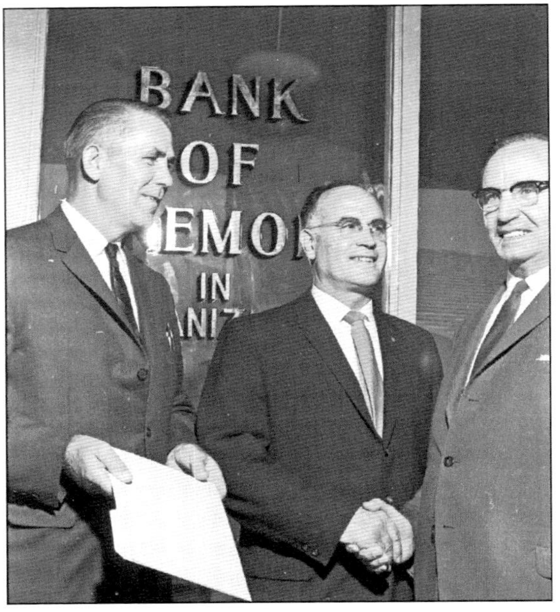

Morris Hyman, center, a Stanford University graduate, was one of the founders of Fremont Bank on September 3, 1964. Fremont Bank opened its first office in the post office building on Post Street in Centerville and the main office near the Fremont Hub Shopping Center in 1968. The following is an excerpt from the *Oakland Tribune* in 2005: "During an era when independent community banks were becoming increasingly rare, Hyman, 84, saw his company grow from six employees working out of a former Centerville post office to a regional bank with 24 branches, 450 employees and $1.6 billion in assets. Fremont Bank pioneered Saturday banking in the country in 1969."

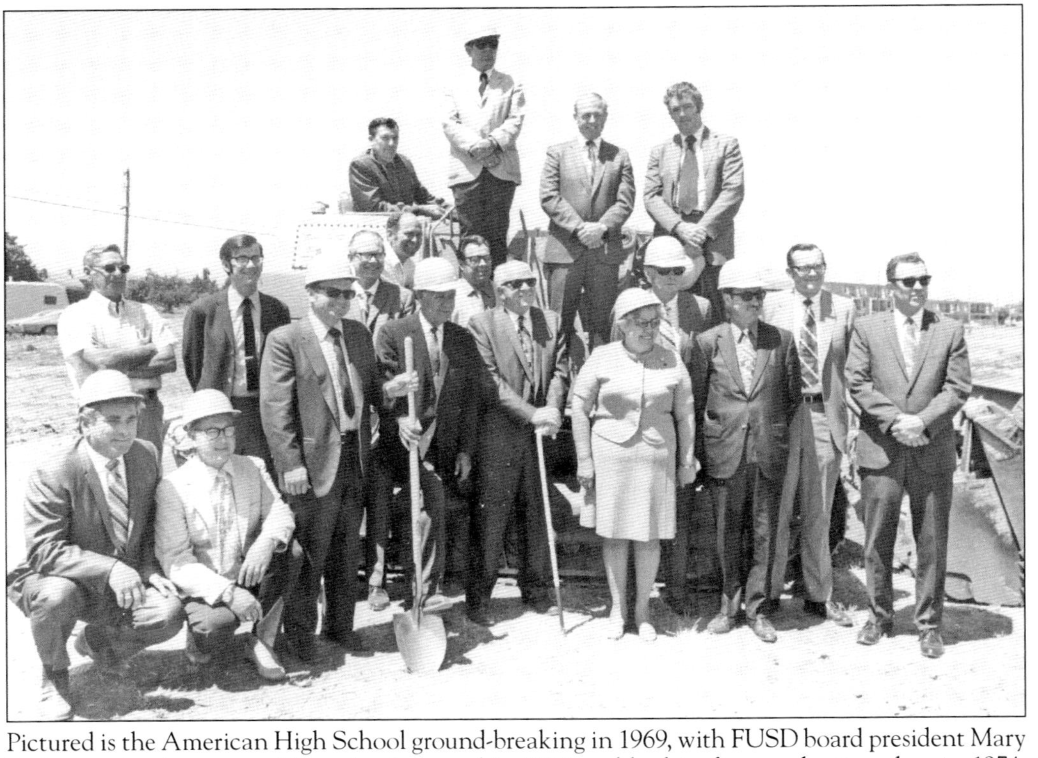

Pictured is the American High School ground-breaking in 1969, with FUSD board president Mary Rodrigues in the center. The school opened in 1972 and had its first graduating class in 1974. Mary Rodrigues, a 1958 Washington High School alumna, was the vision behind the Center Square Plaza, located opposite of the Cloverdale Creamery. The plaza was home to small retail and a local grocery store by 1955. The City of Fremont Redevelopment Agency acquired and cleared the plaza in 2003, with plans for another plaza.

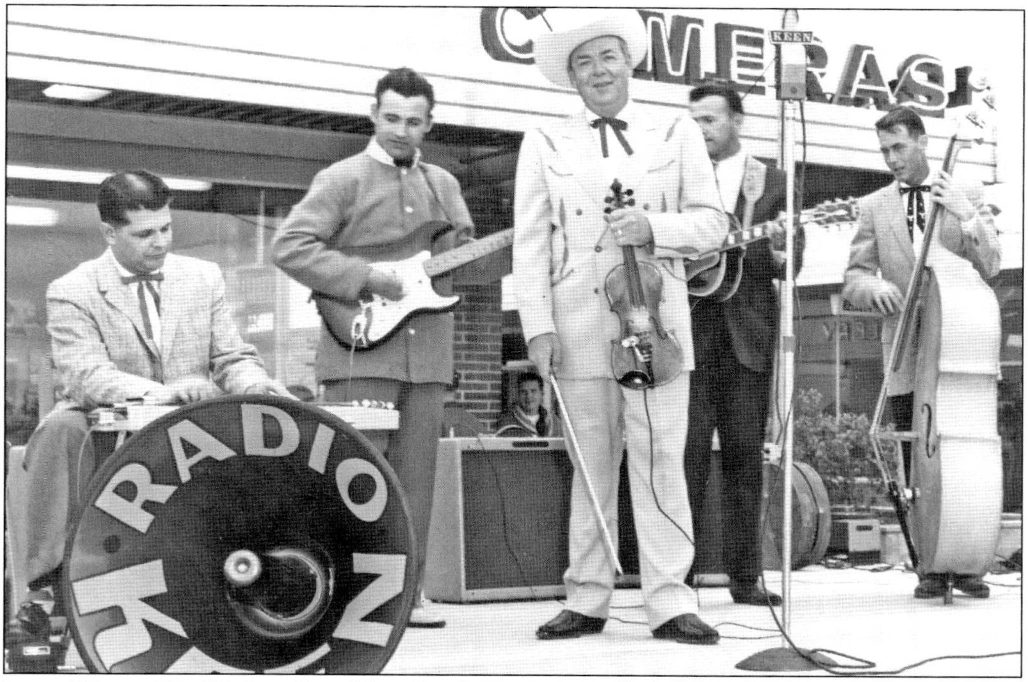

Joyce Wayne "Red" Murrell and his Ozark Playboys, called some of the best Western swing performers in California, play at the new Glenmoor Mall in the early 1960s. In 1954, Murrell began a career as a disk jockey with KEEN radio, an AM station in San Jose. He also played with the Pals of the Pecos and country greats such as Merle Travis and Porky Freeman. Murrell made 12 *The Durango Kid* western movies with Travis between 1940 and 1952.

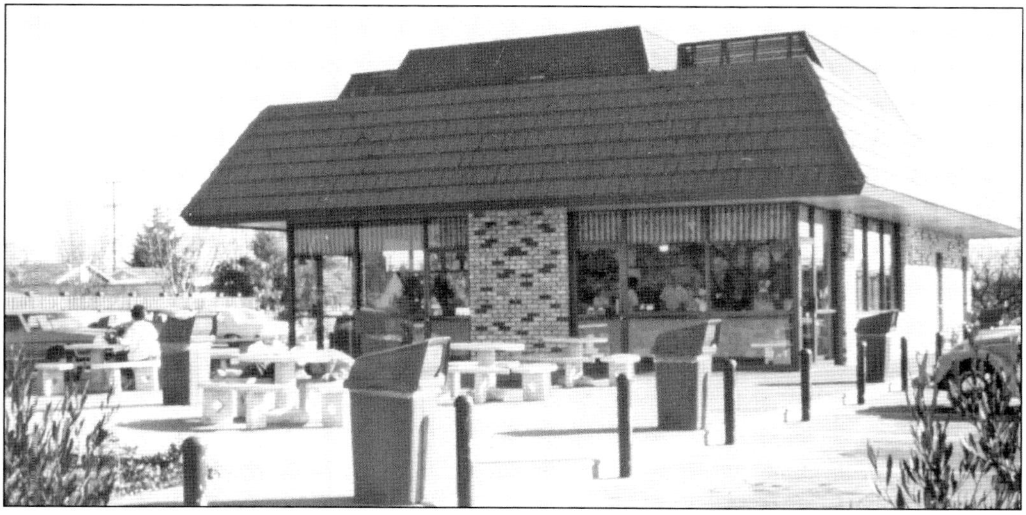

McDonald's opened at 4318 Thornton Avenue in 1969 under the visionary ownership of Al Bernardin. In February 1971, he pioneered a "New Adult Hamburger" for 75¢, now called the Quarter Pounder. An original *Argus* advertisement proclaimed "Today Fremont, Tomorrow the World. . . . We asked you, the people of Fremont, to taste our new quarter-pound, 100% pure beef, hot, pink and juicy star. So tell us: Are we Broadway material? . . . After all, Broadway isn't as nearly as friendly as Fremont." (Courtesy of the Bernardin family.)

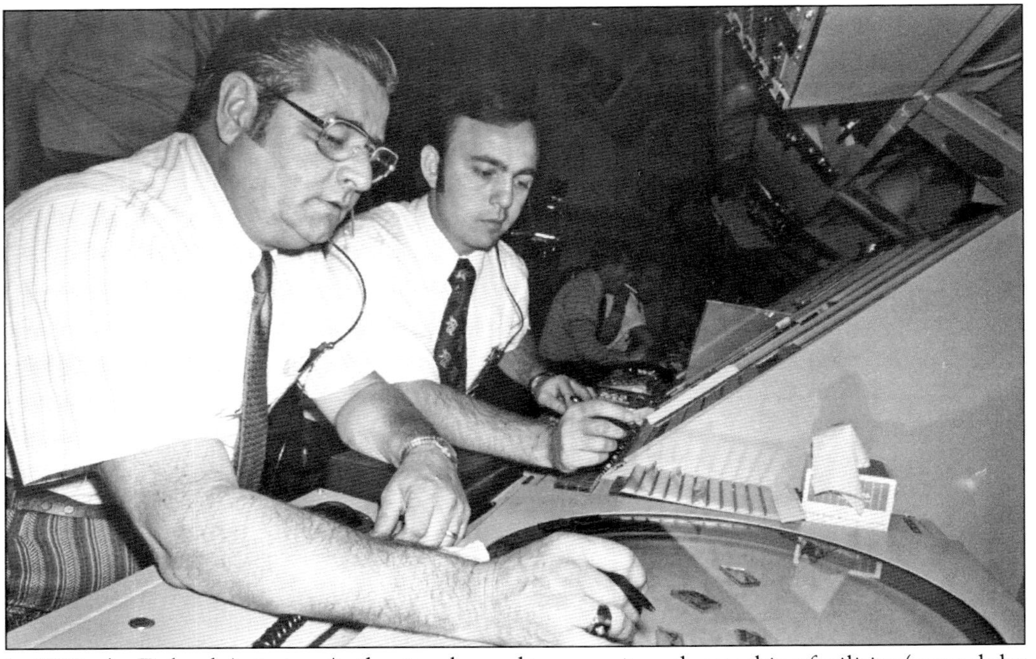

In 1950, the Federal Aviation Authority planned to move its radar tracking facilities (named the Oakland Center) to 5125 Central Avenue near Centerville, not far from the Nike missile base at Coyote Hills, in order to serve the Pacific air traffic control operations to Hawaii. Fremont's three-letter Area Control Center (ACC) code name is ZOA. By the time the ACC move took place, it was to the City of Fremont. The ACC still retains the official name of Oakland Center to the present day.

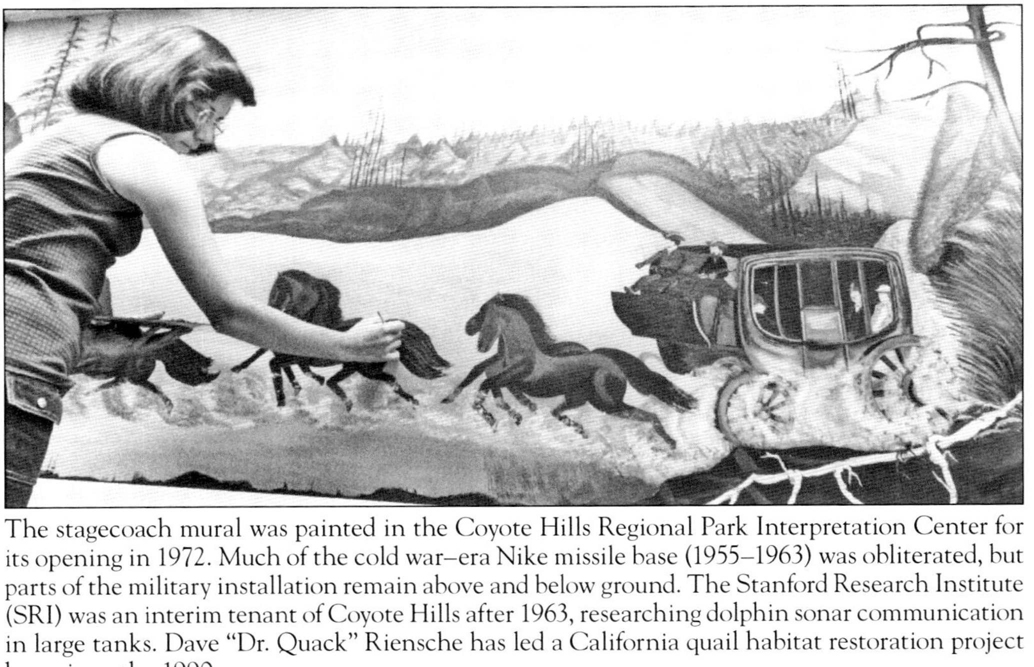

The stagecoach mural was painted in the Coyote Hills Regional Park Interpretation Center for its opening in 1972. Much of the cold war–era Nike missile base (1955–1963) was obliterated, but parts of the military installation remain above and below ground. The Stanford Research Institute (SRI) was an interim tenant of Coyote Hills after 1963, researching dolphin sonar communication in large tanks. Dave "Dr. Quack" Riensche has led a California quail habitat restoration project here since the 1990s.

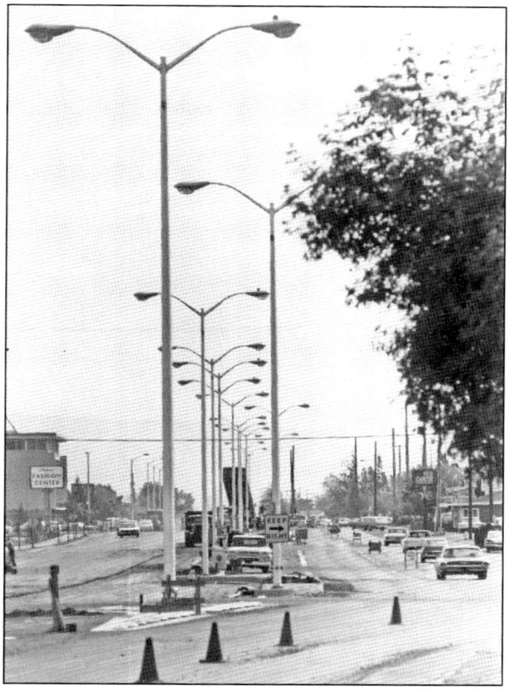

The Fremont Fashion Center opened in 1968 with anchor tenant Capwells of Oakland. Now called the Gateway Plaza, it was the sixth mall-type center in Alameda County. On September 11, 1972, it became one of the first malls in the country to be accessed by a rapid transit station. Highway 238 was initially planned to access the new central business district in Fremont; it now ends at Mission Pass. Farrell's Ice Cream Parlor and See's Candies were popular stops in the open-air mall.

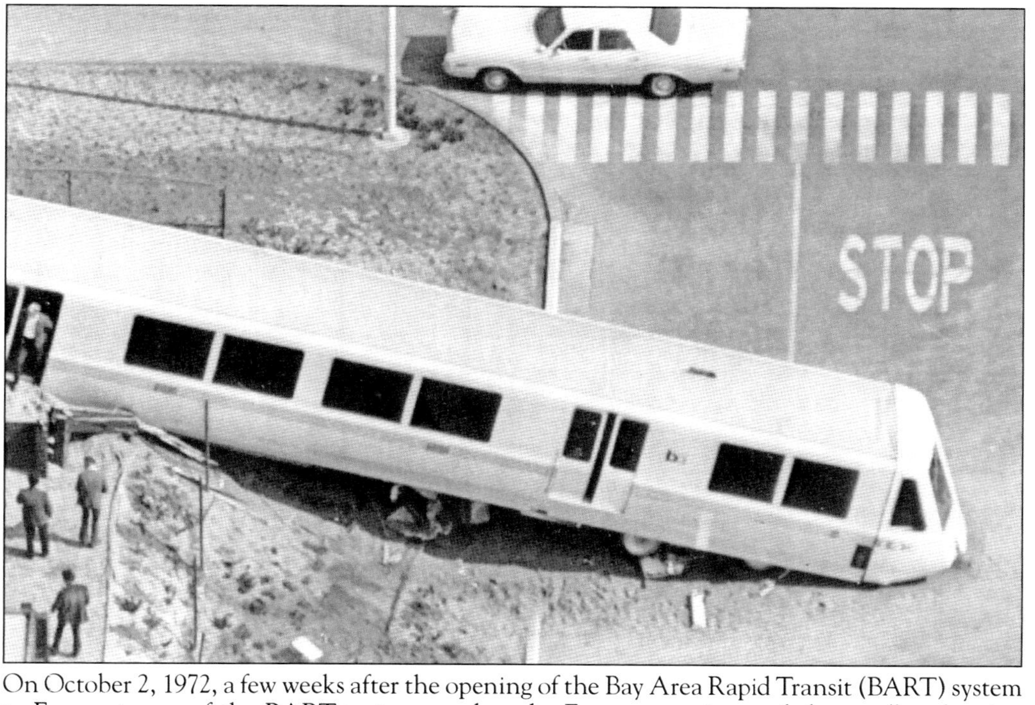

On October 2, 1972, a few weeks after the opening of the Bay Area Rapid Transit (BART) system to Fremont, one of the BART trains overshot the Fremont station and the sandbox barrier. Apparently four passengers and the train's attendant Eli Palmer were treated for minor or internal injuries. The *Oakland Tribune* referred to it as the "Fremont Flyer." The lead train car is 75 feet long and seats 72 passengers.

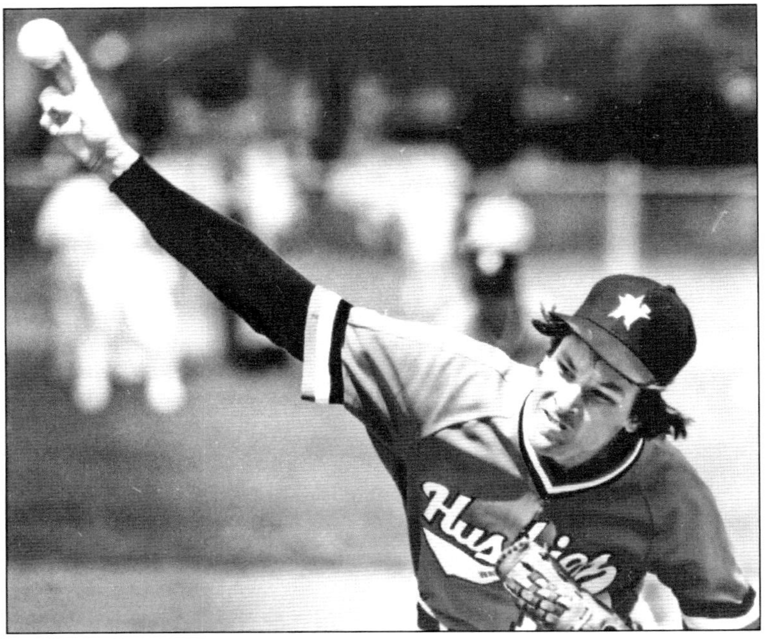

Dennis Eckersley made the honor roll at Patterson School in 1965, receiving the award from Donald Glankler. A May 16, 1970, article in the *Argus* reporting on a Washington win over Irvington stated, "it was the Huskies' Dennis Eckersley that came through when the chips were down." Dennis Eckersley entered the National Baseball Hall of Fame in 2004, and in 2006 Dennis Eckersley Field was dedicated at Washington High School.

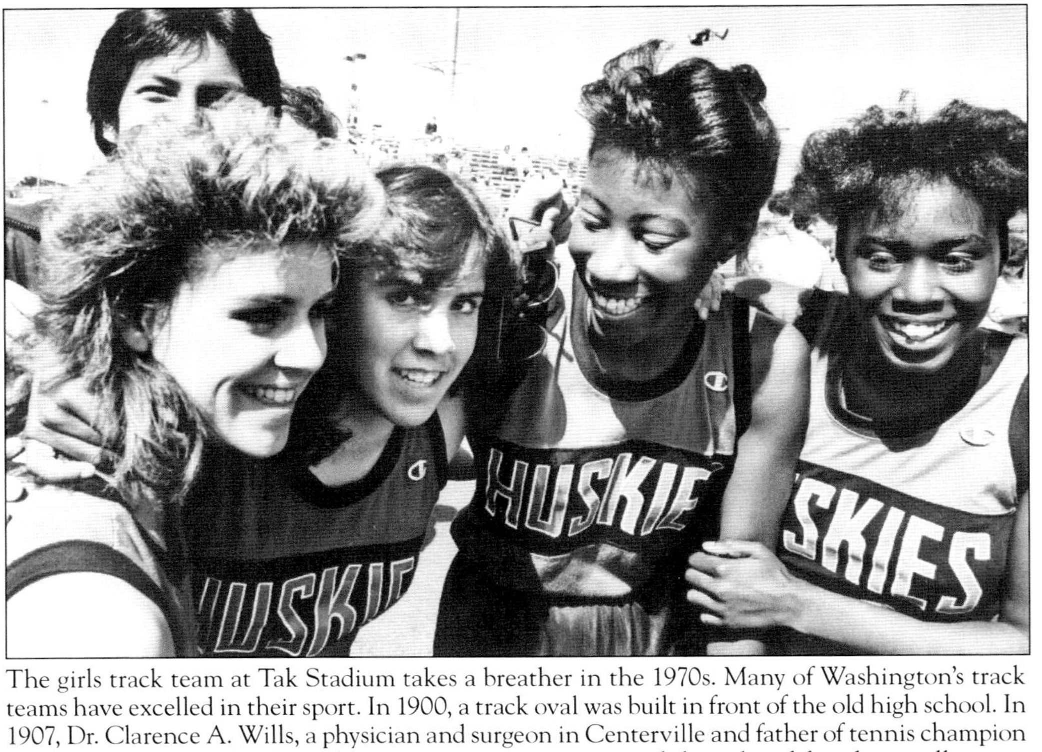

The girls track team at Tak Stadium takes a breather in the 1970s. Many of Washington's track teams have excelled in their sport. In 1900, a track oval was built in front of the old high school. In 1907, Dr. Clarence A. Wills, a physician and surgeon in Centerville and father of tennis champion Helen Wills, coached 42 boys during a cross-country run, and they placed fourth overall.

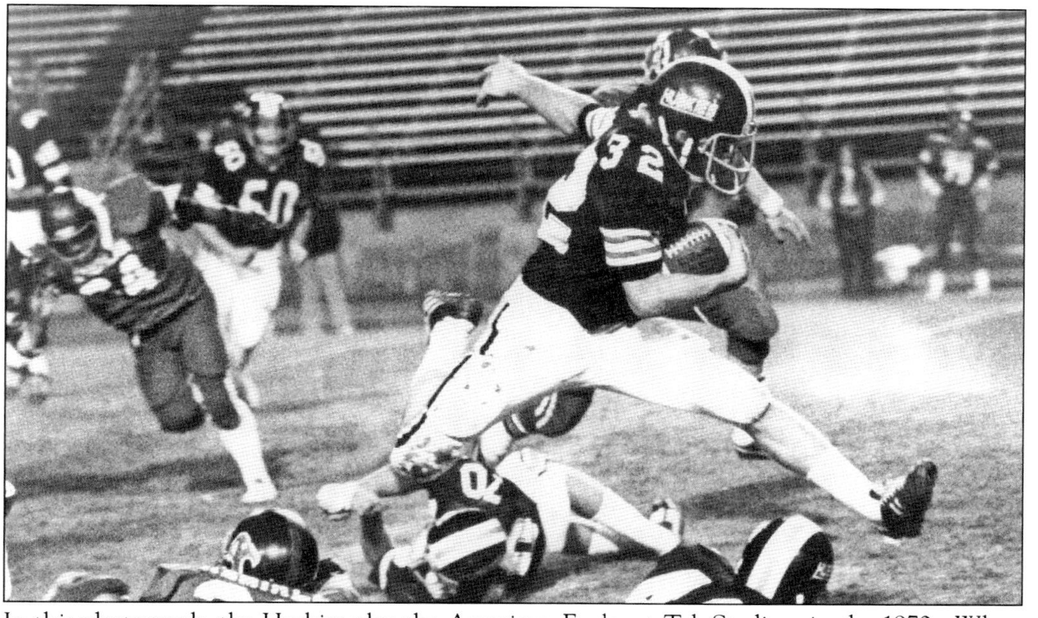

In this photograph, the Huskies play the American Eagles at Tak Stadium in the 1970s. When the stadium was reconstructed and opened in 2005, a plaque was also dedicated in memory of Rob Vares, Mission Valley Athletic League commissioner and former vice principal of Centerville Junior High.

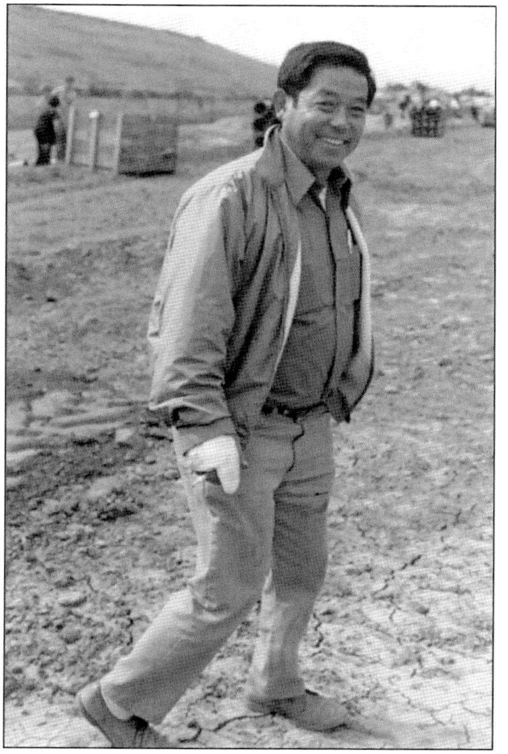

Takeo Fudenna (pictured) graduated in 1939 from Washington High School, where he developed a love for sports. A member of the prominent Fudenna family, he gathered a number of friends, all local businessmen, and proposed the building of an outstanding athletic facility. Each contributed equipment, materials, and labor to build the stadium at Washington High School and donated it to the community. Sadly, he was killed shortly before its completion. It was dedicated as the Tak Fundenna Memorial Stadium in October 1972. (Courtesy Fudenna family.)

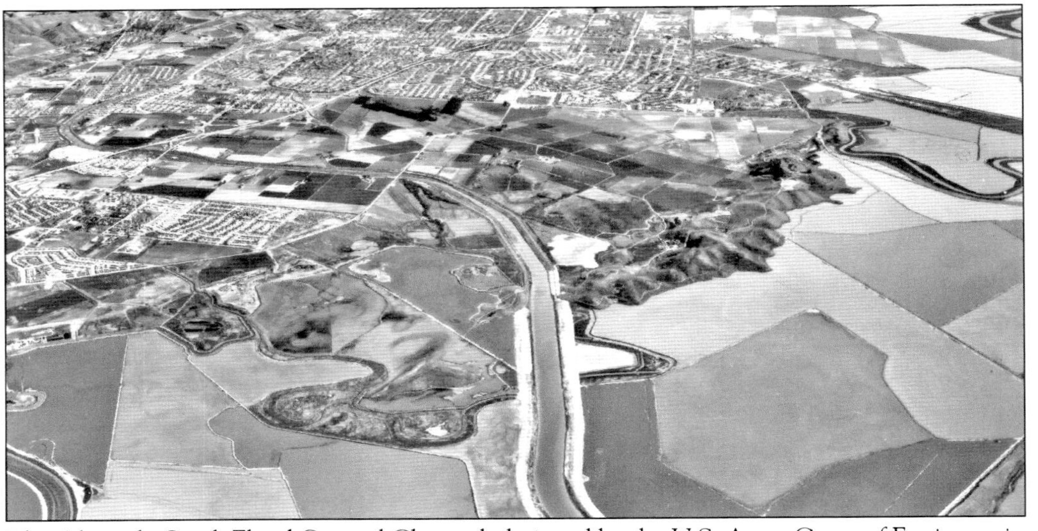

The Alameda Creek Flood Control Channel, designed by the U.S. Army Corps of Engineers in 1972, snakes toward Coyote Hills in this aerial photograph. Before World War II, the marshes were better known as a duck-hunting club. The salt marshes are still home to the endangered salt marsh harvest mouse. Logitech, founded in Fremont with its corporate home between Coyote Hills and Ardenwood, pioneered production of the handheld computer mouse, which was invented by Douglas Engelbart of Fremont and patented by SRI in 1970.

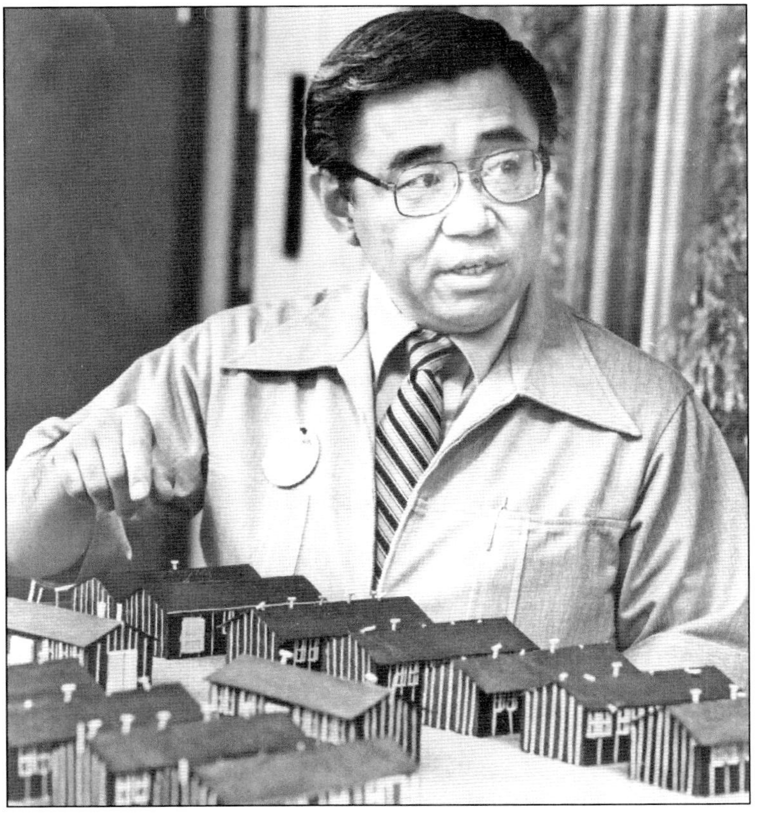

Dr. Walter Hashimoto describes life in the Japanese internment camps from 1942 to 1945 in an interview around 1980. The Hashimoto dental office is still on Martha Avenue, where Dr. Elmo Grimmer also opened his dental office after his military service. The Martha Avenue business center also housed a courthouse for Alameda County at one time before becoming the New Horizons School in 1988.

Huskies basketball was led by coach Guin Boggs in the 1980s and 1990s, and he is enshrined in the Washington High School Basketball Hall of Fame. Boggs led Washington High School's varsity boys basketball team to the 1991 state championship game and was the Mission Valley Athletic League Coach of the Year seven times. A Huskies player competes here against the Pittsburg Pirates in the 1980s.

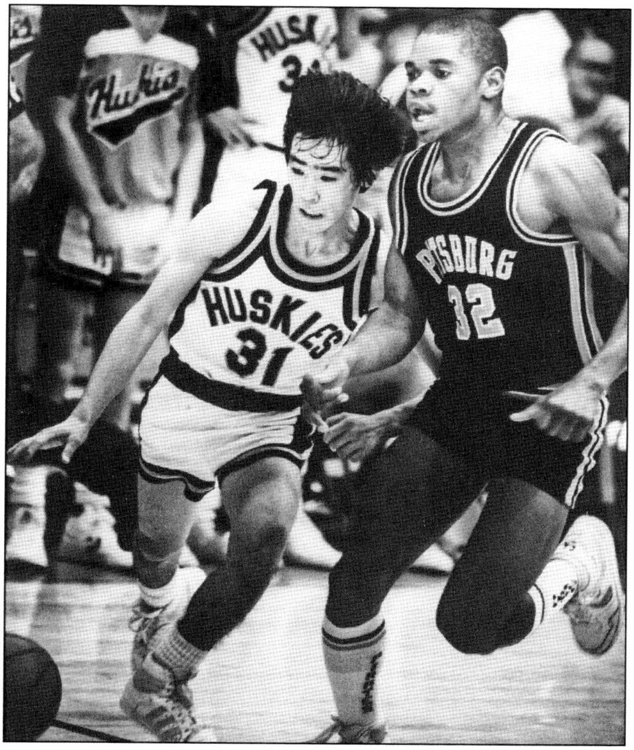

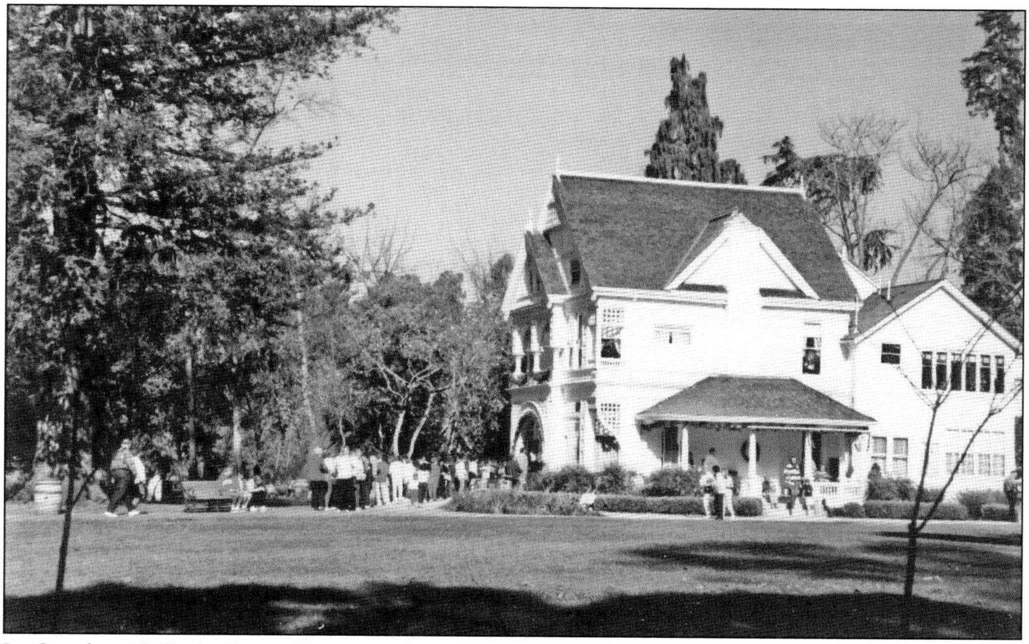

In October 1989, the Loma Prieta earthquake damaged the chimney of the Patterson house. Out on the Fremont Baylands, the KGO radio transmission towers that were built on bay mud in a salt evaporation pond were also impacted, causing the conical wire-frame towers to flop over in the middle. (JMS.)

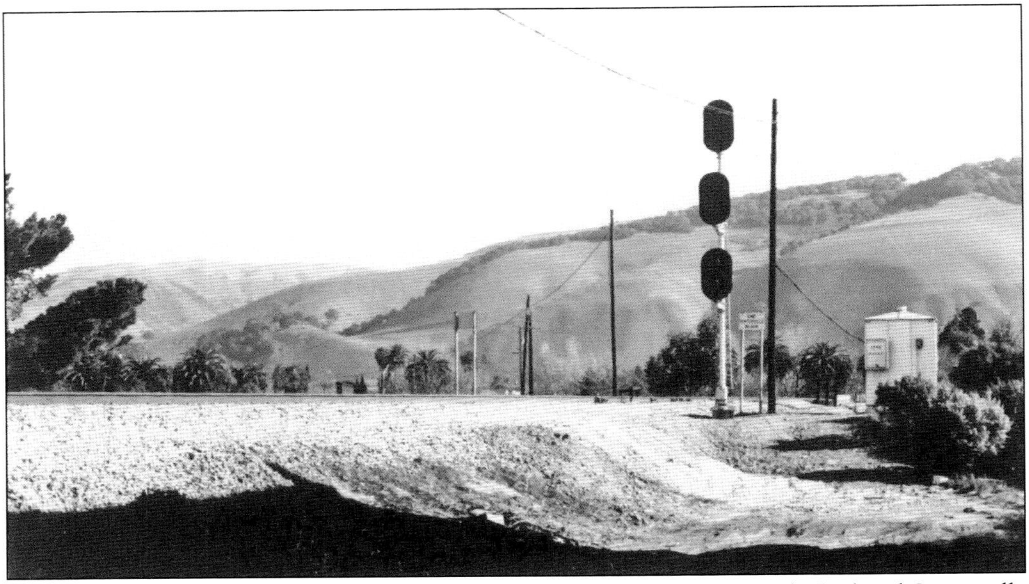

Photographed in 1991 with Niles Canyon in the background, the Union Pacific Railroad Centerville block now serves several pass-through freight trains: the Amtrak Capitol Corridor 14 times daily, the Altamont Commuter express on weekdays, and the Coast Starlight daily to Seattle. The railroad right-of-way here parallels the old Spring Valley Water Company's 36-inch pipeline that connected the Niles Cone Groundwater Basin and the Sunol Water Temple to the San Francisco Water Department facilities on the peninsula. Work on the water line project began in 1887.

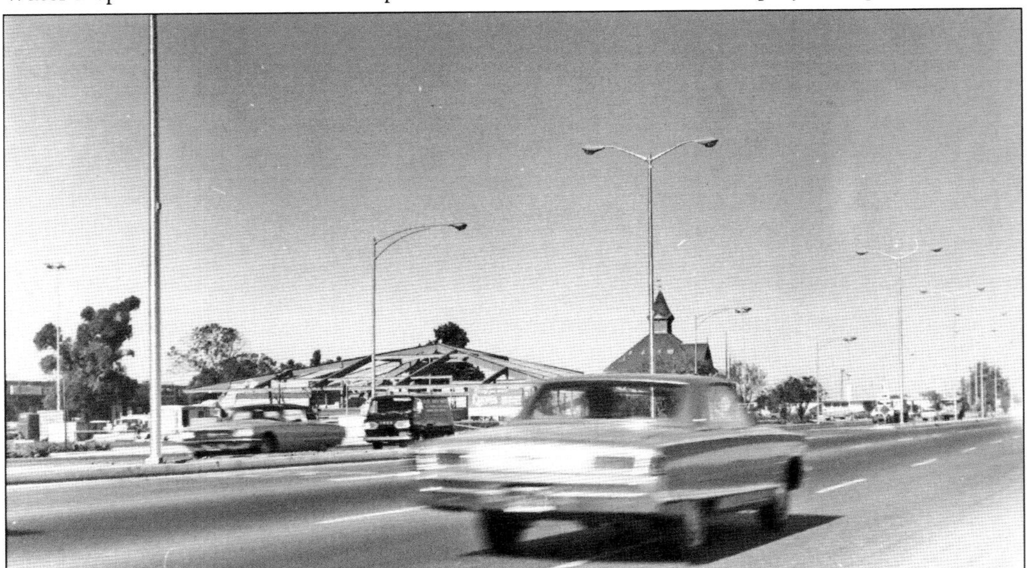

Lyon's, located at the Fremont Hub Shopping Center, is recorded as being constructed around 1960. Lyon's of California was founded in Sacramento in 1952 as a chain of diner-style restaurants. Around the time of Lyon's bankruptcy in 1998, the Fremont restaurant closed to be remodeled as one of the first Elephant Bar franchises in California, opening in the fall of 1999. The massive date palms that had originally faced Highway 17 were relocated to shade an outdoor patio to the south.

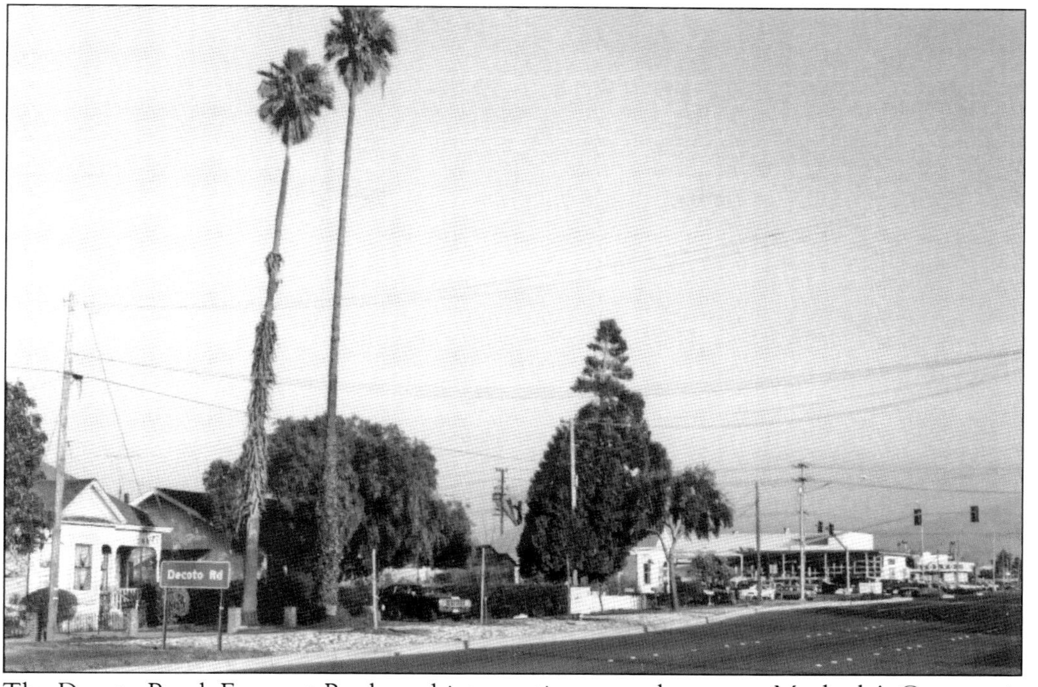

The Decoto Road–Fremont Boulevard intersection, once known as Machado's Corners, is photographed in 1991. The Victorian cottage was known to all as the "party house," thanks to graffiti painted on the roof that persisted for years. This corner was the original holding of Rev. William Brier, subdivided and sold by his daughter Elizabeth in 1897 to members of the Machado family. In 2010, the corner is home to the Bank of Fremont. (JMS.)

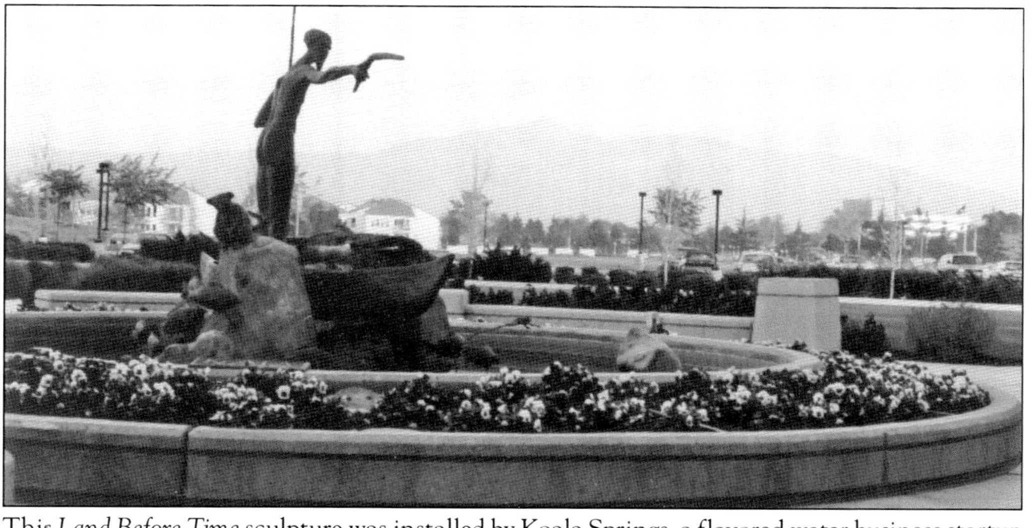

This *Land Before Time* sculpture was installed by Koala Springs, a flavored water business startup located at the southeast corner of Walnut Avenue and Civic Center Drive. This photograph of the sculpture was taken in 1990. Based in Fremont, Koala Springs was acquired by Nestlé in 1996. Across the street in the former Fashion Center, space was rented for the rapid growth of the Worlds of Wonder startup toy company, which created the Teddy Ruxpin teddy bear phenomenon in 1985. (JMS.)

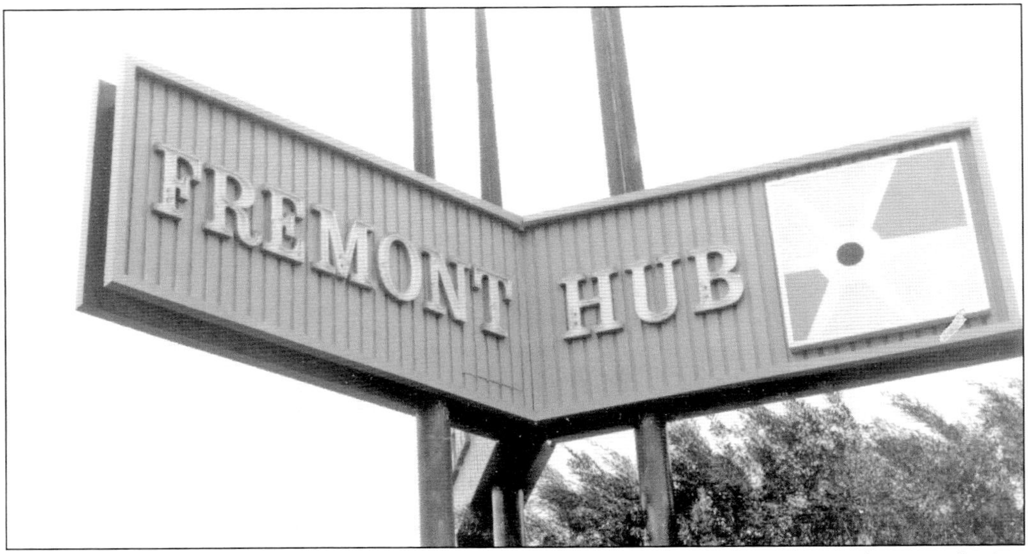

This is the original Sputnik-style Fremont Hub Shopping Center sign from 1962, photographed in 1991. Maurice "Hap" Smith partnered with Frederick Nicholson in 1956 and formed the Hapsmith Company to develop the Hub, a community shopping center in the new City of Fremont. It was the second shopping center that Mervyns and Sears agreed to co-anchor. Smith and Nicholson went on to develop numerous shopping centers, including the Tanforan Park Shopping Center at San Bruno in 1973. (JMS.)

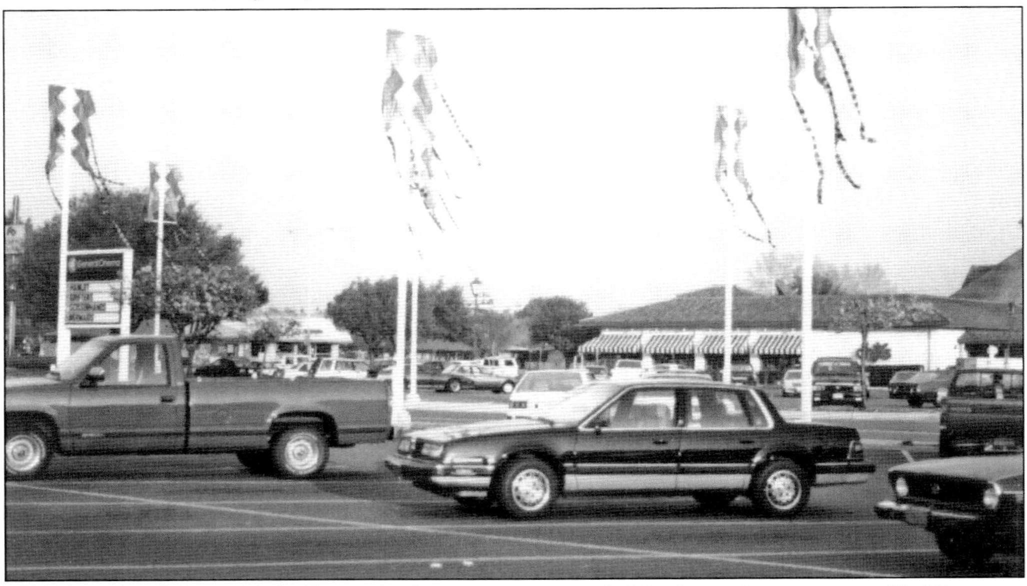

Shown is the Fremont Hub Shopping Center revamp in 1990, where the entrance off of Fremont Boulevard was brought to life with banners with lively striped tails. Behind, from left to right, are signs for Fremont Bank, General Cinema (playing *Hamlet*, *Drifters*, *Edward Scissorhands*, and *Mermaids*), a printing shop, Hobee's, Chili's, and the distinctive roofline of the Chadbourne carriage house. This part of the Hub parking lot was the first location for the Fremont Wine and Art Festival from 1983 to 1986. Now the Fremont Festival of the Arts, it is the largest free street arts festival west of the Mississippi, held the last weekend of July. (JMS.)

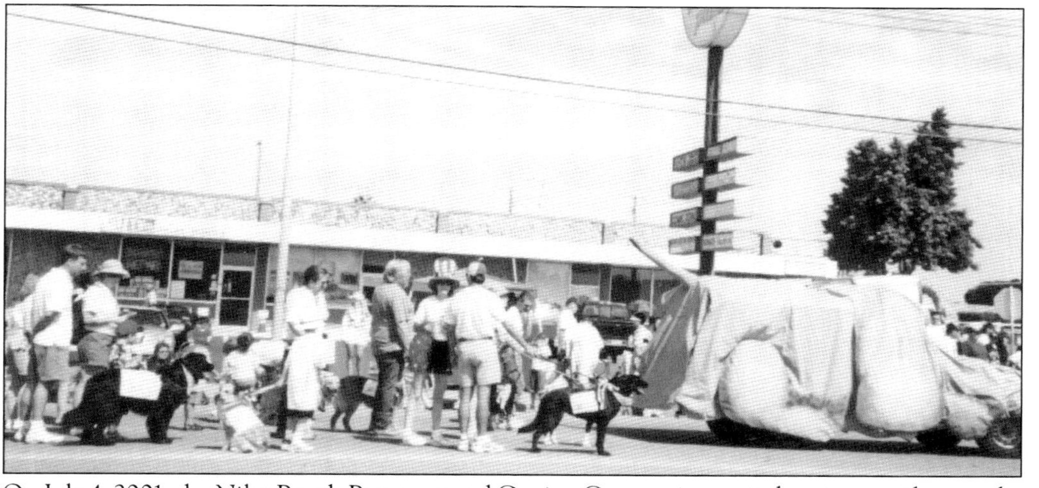

On July 4, 2001, the Niles Pooch Pow-wow and Canine Convention wait their turn in the parade. The congregating zone was on Peralta Boulevard east of the relocated Haller's Pharmacy to the east, and between Peralta Plaza and the Flamingo Palace to the south. People involved in the convention included Natalie Munn, Nancy Haylock, Donald Dewey, and numerous others. Ann Keeler sewed the dog costume for the compact car as the group's signature parade entry. (JMS.)

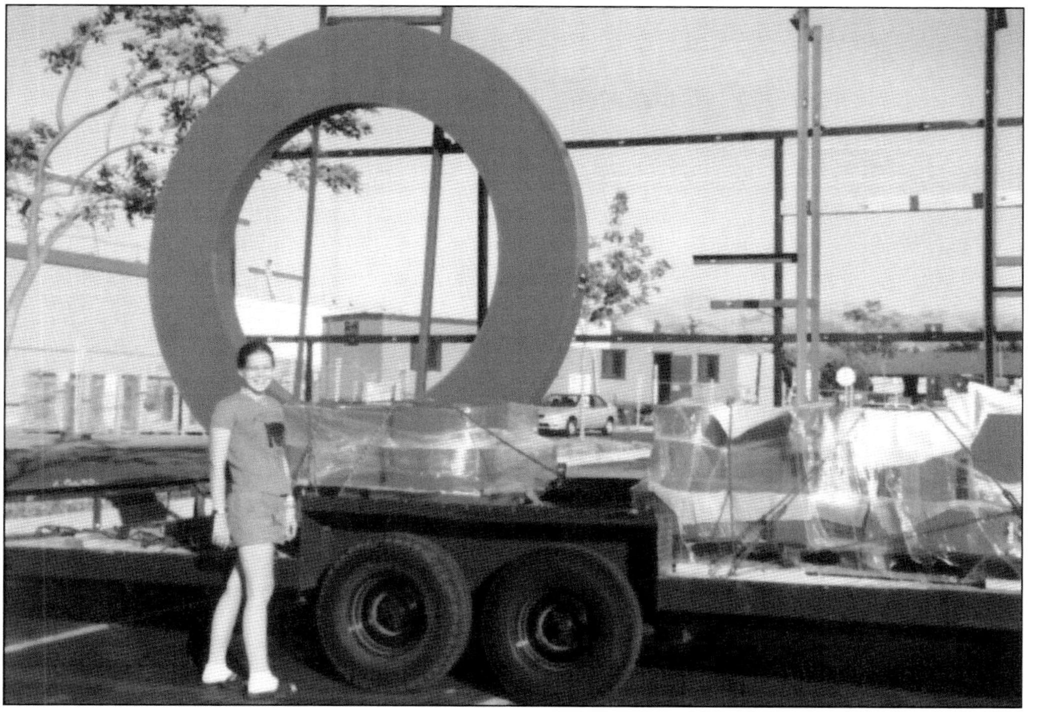

Target opened at the Fremont Hub Shopping Center on September 13, 2002, in the remodeled Montgomery Ward space. The big O in the Target symbol was photographed in the parking lot in August 2002 between the garden center and the General Cinema (later Naz 8 Cinema). While stores such as Tower Records and Home Express were a recent memory in 2002, and others like Mervyns and Woolworths are long gone, a few businesses such as Radio Shack, H. Salt Fish and Chips, and Safeway continue to weather the years. (JMS.)

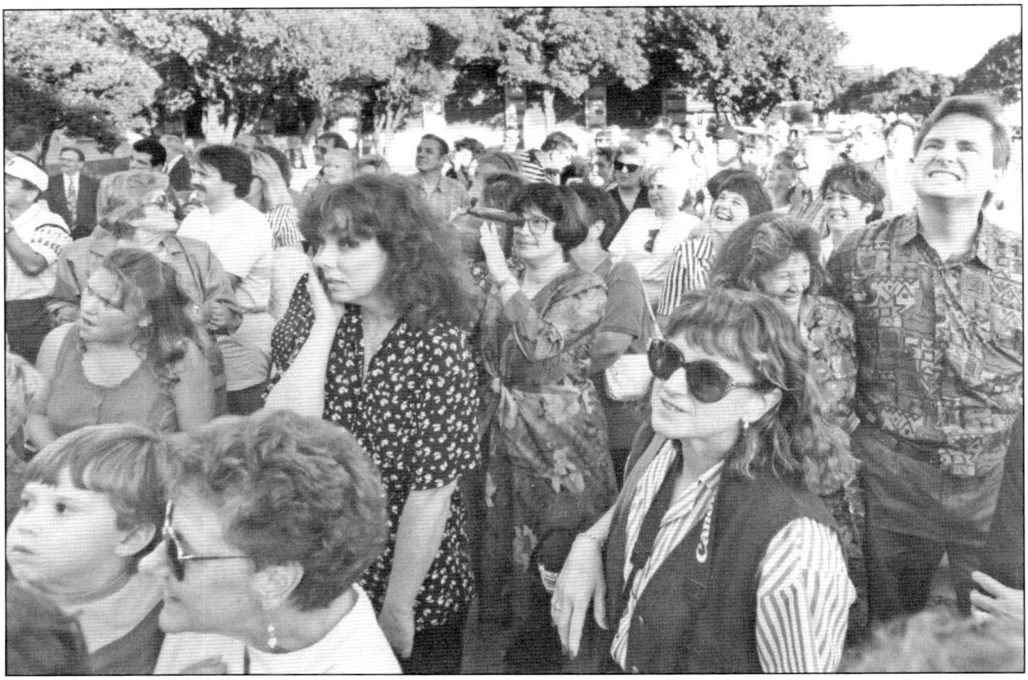

The oldest parts of Washington High School were briefly closed in 1933 after the Long Beach Earthquake, permanently closed in 1972, and demolished on October 26, 1990, with many alumni watching, as shown in this photograph. After the Loma Prieta earthquake in 1989, serious plans were made to address the need to expand for the incoming demographic bulge as the children of baby boomers reached high school age. The Henry Meyers–designed arched doorway of 1924 was retained with alumni support, new classrooms were erected, and the main school reopened in December 1997. The worn-out portables disappeared from campus without fanfare. The gymnasium was also replaced, designed by Bunton Clifford Associates of Fremont. The spring 2003 photograph below shows the bands of the Washington High School attendance area in the new gym, with conductors Duane Mitchell, Kurt Kellersberger, and Michael Toschak. (JMS.)

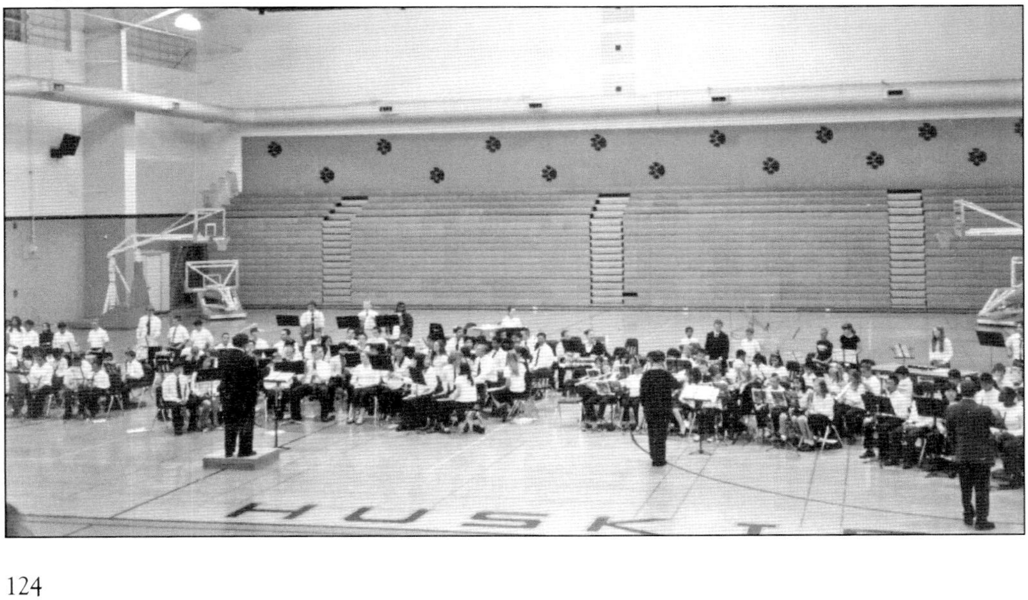

Fencing students Ramiro Orosco (left) and Nicola Stathers duel in the fall of 2002 in the new gymnasium designed by Bunton Clifford at Centerville Junior High School. Alumnus Matthew "Mat" Goebel and others provided highly disciplined tutoring. Fencing has a long history of intramural and interscholastic competition at Centerville. The Mustang school symbol graces the proscenium over the stage. The sunny day in June when the yearbook is released has happily been known as Round-Up Day since the 1950s.

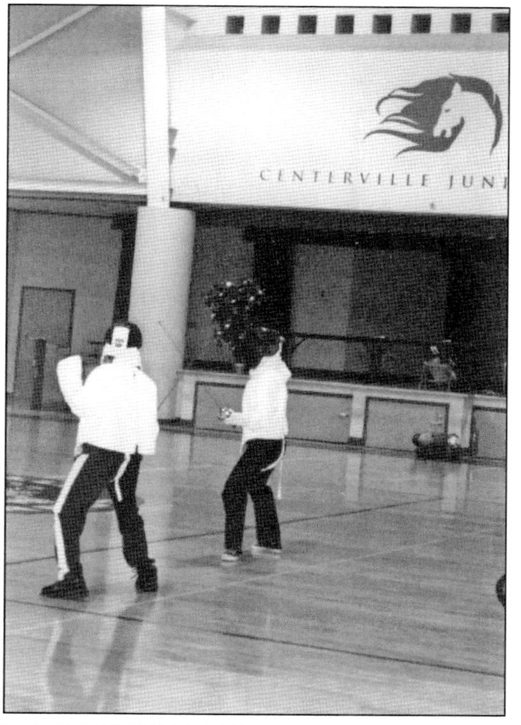

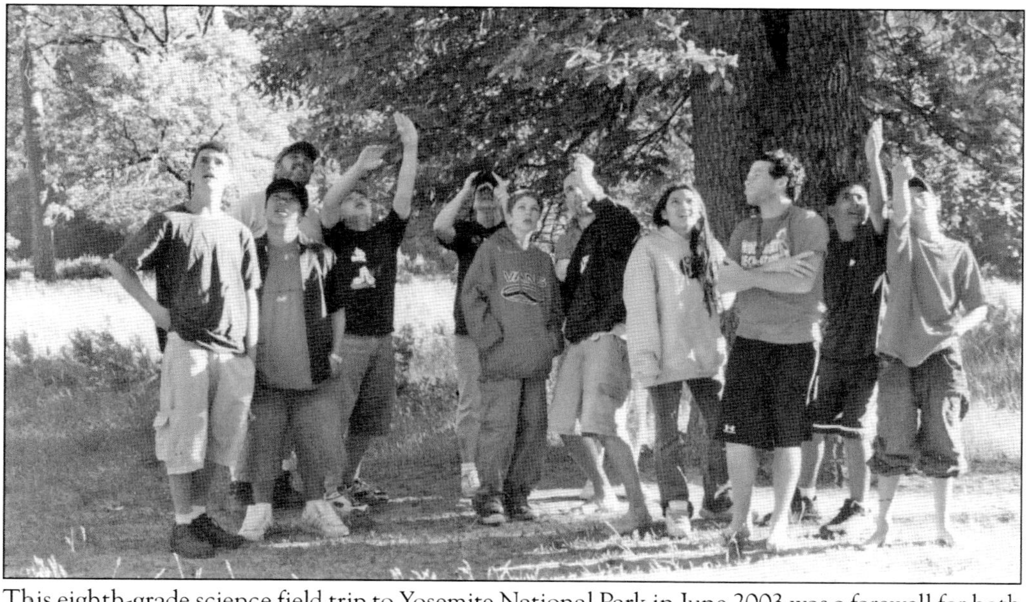

This eighth-grade science field trip to Yosemite National Park in June 2003 was a farewell for both students and teachers, some of whom had worked together on the play *Once Upon a Mattress.* Pictured, from left to right, are David Lyons, James Kim, Mr. Salet, Daniel Salet, Lauren Carpaccio, Conor Hanrahan, Elizabeth Tyler, Douglas Cembellin, Jessica ?, Samuel Almquist, Tanveer ?, and Anthony Koch. Almquist, who left for military medical school (dermatology), would famously return to give the "Wear Sunscreen Speech" (by Mary Schmich) to the Centerville Junior High School graduating class of 2003. (Courtesy Nicola Stathers)

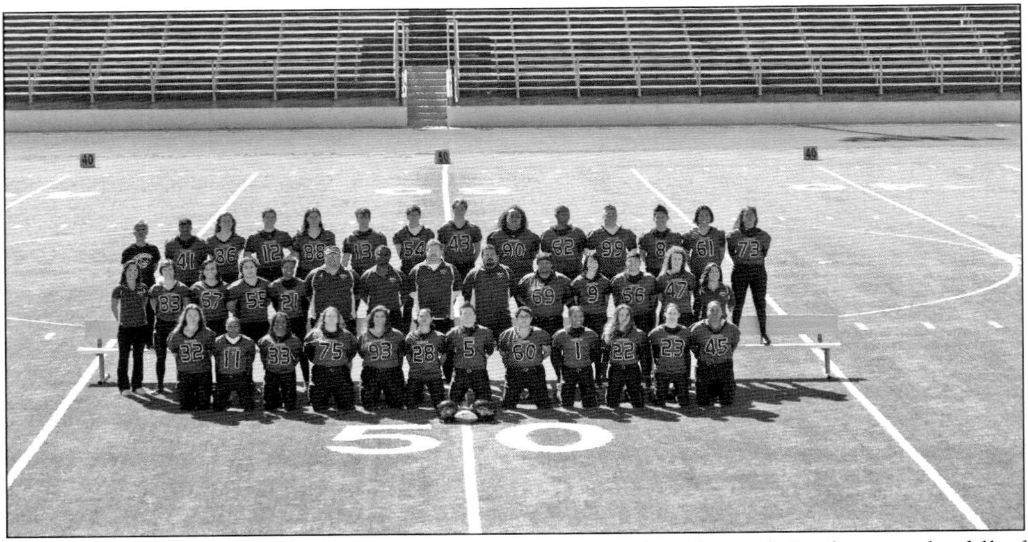

The Bay Area Bandits, a women's tackle football team, debuted at Tak Stadium in the fall of 2009 and won the International Women's Football League regional championship in July 2010. Pictured, from left to right, are (first row) April Paraiso, Kim Mosley, Jenae Beverly, Jenell Summers, Julia Jalalat, Sharon Santos, Rachel Darrow, Cecilia Barba, Dakura Smith, Kara Kimmel, Dana Cordell, and LaStar Brown; (second row) Neda Mohammadi (alumna), Esmi Mendoza, Syretta Watkins, Valu Muti, Cori Evans, Johnnie Hamm, Tony Macon, Jim Goulden, Jose Zavala, Jasmine Davis, Farris Pine, Lanecia Strom, Rosaria Del Cuore, and Michelle Herrera; (third row) Dr. Maria Manabog, Latrice Johnson, Sarah Henry, Lou Vitellaro, Meghan Thompson, Jennifer Romanini, Anne Kendall, Danielle Golay, Loisi Takapu, Jackie Taylor, Sam Brinkerhoff, Sandra Hernandez, Monica Gudiel, and Shalom Kimbel. Below, Dorothy Rodrigues, No. 13, receives a pass as Marianne Vochatzer, No. 20, moves in for a tackle at Washington High School in 1959. (Above, courtesy Neda Mohammedi.)

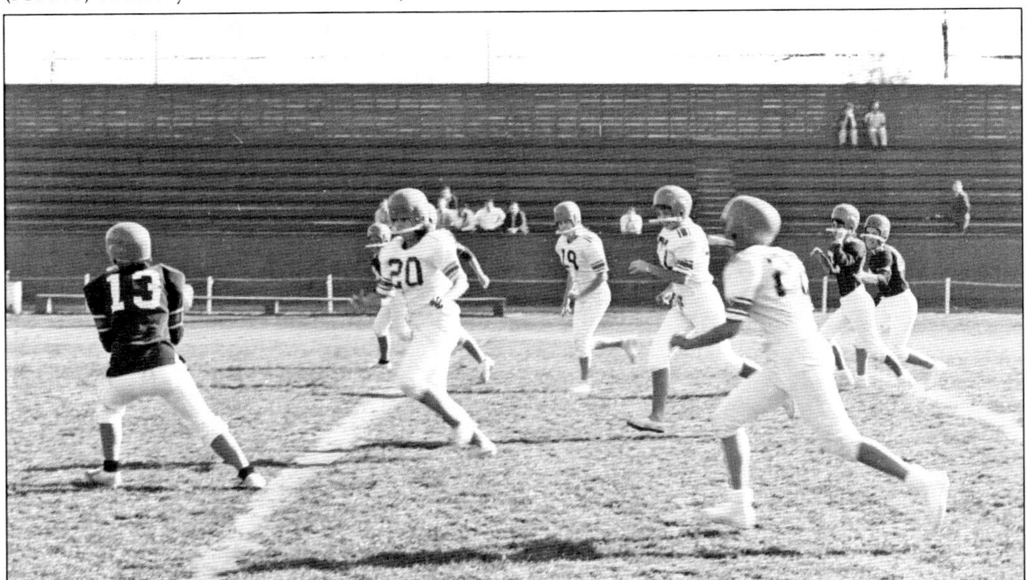

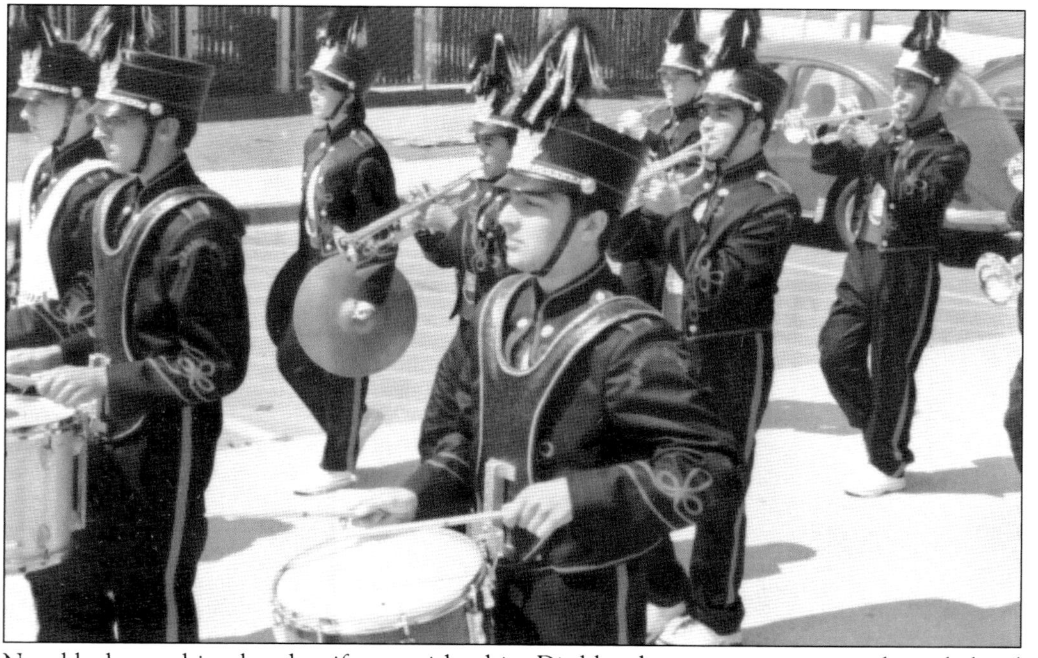

New black marching band uniforms with white Dinkles shoes were given a trial run behind Washington High School in September 2002, the week before the sweltering hot Newark Days Parade. The band had not had real uniforms for more than a decade. Pictured from left to right are Brian Perry, Brian Phillips, Kimberley Stathers, unidentified, Matthew Goebel, Amberlee Mitchel, Kyle Brazelton, and unidentified. Ikhlas Haleem (not visible), in the white uniform of the drum major, led the marching band to practice in Tak Fudenna stadium (JMS.)

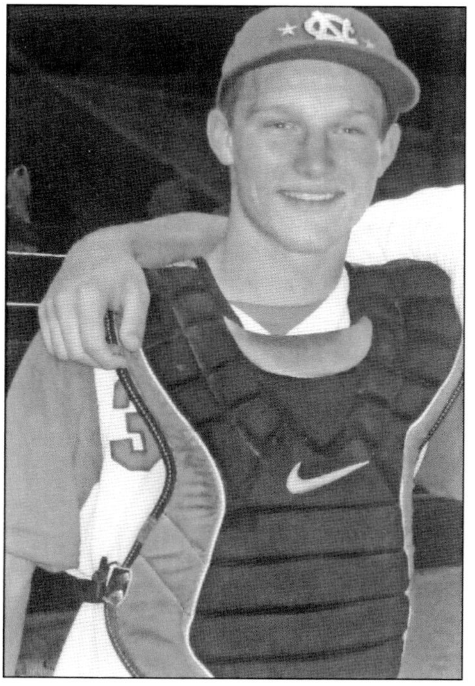

Casey Jennings was the catcher of the Niles-Centerville Little League's senior division team that won the California championship at Ray Littleton Field in Ontario in September 2009. The backdrop was ivy, and the locker rooms were the ones built for the movie *A League of Their Own*. The Niles-Centerville team went on to be in final contention at the 2009 National Little League Championship in Bangor, Maine. (Courtesy Jennings family.)

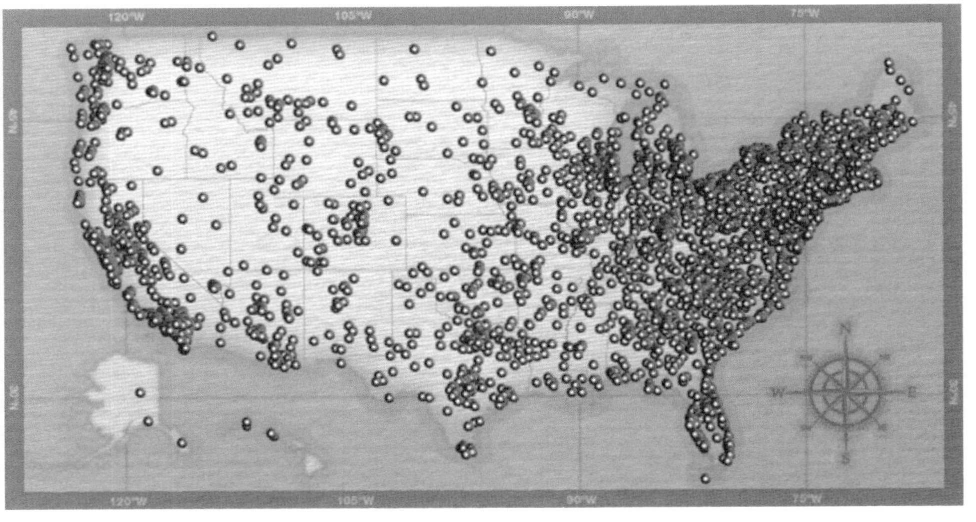